Culture, Identity, and Politics

Culture, Identity, and Politics

Ernest Gellner

William Wyse Professor of Social Anthropology
University of Cambridge

CAMBRIDGE
UNIVERSITY PRESS

Published by the Press Syndicate of the University of Cambridge
The Pitt Building, Trumpington Street, Cambridge CB2 1RP
40 West 20th Street, New York, NY 10011–4211 USA
10 Stamford Road, Oakleigh, Victoria 3166, Australia

First published 1987
Reprinted 1988, 1993

Printed in Great Britain at the Athenaeum Press Ltd, Newcastle upon Tyne

British Library cataloguing in publication data

Gellner, Ernest
Culture, identity, and politics
1. Social change
I. Title
303.4′01   HM101

Library of Congress cataloguing in publication data

Gellner, Ernest.
Culture, identity, and politics.
Bibliography.
Includes index.
1. Political sociology. 2. State, The.
3. Social change. I. Title
JA76.G38 1987   306′.2   86–26444

ISBN 0 521 33438 1 hardback
ISBN 0 521 33667 8 paperback

Transferred to
Digital Reprinting 1999

Printed in the
United States of America

RB

Contents

Preface

The nineteenth century was the age of nationalism. It was also the age in which the great secular ideologies emerged, and it was the period during which the social sciences came into being. The three events are not unrelated. The turbulence and instability which were undermining the old order naturally led some men to try to understand what was happening, to investigate the very foundations of society, to grasp the principles of the new social forms which were emerging. It led others to try to change the world, or specify the directions in which it should change.

The present essays are primarily concerned with the theories and reactions provoked by fundamental social change in this and the last century. But they are also concerned with the deep structure of that change itself. One essay deals with the nature of the new political principle of nationalism, and relates it to the ideas of the foremost French theorist of social cohesion, Émile Durkheim. Another one deals with a man who has been unjustly forgotten, but who provided Durkheim with one of his central ideas: Émile Masqueray. This Frenchman carried out most of his important work in Algeria, and his ideas exemplify the impact of the new colonial experience on European thought. The ideas themselves have had an enormous, though as yet unacknowledged, impact on modern social anthropology.

Durkheim's theorising neither underwrote nor repudiated modern nationalism. Bronislaw Malinowski, the main founder of contemporary anthropology, in effect used the social sciences as an alternative to nationalism. Recent Polish research into his youth and the intellectual dilemmas and influences which formed him have made this plain. He fused romanticism and positivism in an altogether new way, which made it possible to investigate the old communities in the round, but which at the same time refused to accord political authority to the Past. His famous synchronicism was not merely a charter of intensive fieldwork and a means of repudiating evolutionist speculation, but also a way of rejecting that nationalist manipulation of the past for current purposes which was so characteristic of Central and Eastern Europe. The essay on Hannah Arendt analyses another and more complex attempt by an intellectual to come to terms with romanticism and its frequently lethal political implications.

Two of the essays are case studies, attempts to observe what happens in a post-revolutionary situation in our age. One of the revolutionary regimes is a communist one, the other, a Shi'ite Muslim fundamentalist one. The real conditions prevailing under socialism provide an interesting check on our theories concerning the potential of industrial society; so does the Iranian revolution. The former illuminates the strain between a society based on cognition and technological growth, and the imposition of a unique social ideology; the latter corrects any facile theory of the secularisation of our world. The third essay which belongs in this group investigates the moral problems which face any researcher into authoritarian societies. These problems have to be faced, whether or not they have neat or satisfying solutions: we must needs try to understand our authoritarian neighbours, and to do so, we must talk to them. How far may we go in attempting to explore and understand, without endorsing the unacceptable?

Finally, four essays deal with substantive problems or aspects of contemporary industrial society: its egalitarianism, its celebrated 'disenchantment', and the social and philosophical difficulties it faces in its endeavours to secure legitimation. One of these is highly abstract, and considers what kind of logical schema could possibly be available for the self-vindication of our social order. What premisses remain at our disposal which could serve for the legitimation of our moral order?

All the essays circle around the troubled relationship of state, civil society, identity, culture and legitimacy. These relationships have assumed a radically new form in our time, a form which also varies from place to place, and which continues to develop. The preoccupation with the range of our options, and with what constrains them, gives these essays their unifying theme.

Ernest Gellner
Cambridge, 1986

1 A blobologist in Vodkobuzia

Make no mistake about it, Vodkobuzia is a breathtakingly beautiful country. In the autumn, the wooded slopes which sweep down from the Carbunclian Range to the lowlands of the Manich Depression are ablaze with a colour which not even Hampshire or Liguria can match. (There actually *is* a geographical location called the Manich Depression, believe it or not, which you can find on the map if you look hard enough. But do not suppose you can identify the country I am talking about from the location of that Depression. This is a composite portrait, based on various lands drawn from a *number* of ideological culture circles, as you might say.) It is also from this area that the most plaintive, most moving folk songs come, commemorating as they do the devastation wrought by the invasions of the Rockingchair Mongols.

It is this beauty which makes it so hard to cut oneself off from that land. Hence the brutal coup, and subsequently the ideological straitjacket, imposed on that country over a quarter of a century ago by Colonel Shishkebab was not merely a tragedy for the natives of the country, but also a sadness for those outside it who love it and its culture. Colonel Shishkebab did not hide his firm conviction that a New Man was to be forged in the light of the principles of Revolutionary Populism, to which his country now adhered under his leadership, and that an ideal which was, all at once, so elevated and yet so arduous – going as it does against various well-known, deeply rooted, quite endearing but not altogether edifying traits of the national character – did not allow for half measures if it was to have any prospects of effective implementation. A Trauma, as the Colonel referred to it, was required, in order to shake the people out of their engrained habits, and a Trauma was duly administered.

This was most unfortunate for those who were, as the phrase went, Trauma-Resistant (the execrable TRs, as they were known at the time), and rather extreme measures were required to make them socially and morally more sensitive. Mind you, quite a few of those who were executed during the Trauma have now been posthumously rehabilitated, and their widows on occasion receive a small pension. Even their children, who at the time were forbidden access to education, have now been issued with certificates confirming that their illiteracy is not wholly their fault but a consequence of the temporary Deformation of the principles of Revolutionary Populism. Historians now refer to that time as the Period of the Trauma. It has of course been disavowed by Shishkebab's successors, though with different degrees of emphasis and nuance, and correspondingly the term Shishkebabist – an adherent of an *à outrance* application of the principles of Revolutionary Populism, as practised in the days of Shishek, as he was affectionately known among his intimates if they survived – has become pejorative, while to be a TR has become all at once more glamorous and less dangerous.

At that time, in fact, I faced no moral problem. I was far too insignificant to be invited to the country and to be used to legitimise whatever it was up to. The few articles on aspects of Vodkobuzian folk music (rather a hobby of mine), which have since earned me some invitations were at that time not written, let alone published. So no moral problem arose, and problem No. 1 which I wish to offer for your consideration is quite hypothetical. If you had been invited, at the time of the Trauma, would you have gone?

Consider the circumstances. Shishkebab had imprisoned most of the best men in my main field (blobology), had had some of them tortured, and had imposed on the Institute of Blobology, as its Director, a party hack whose knowledge of the subject would soil the back of any postage stamp on which it could easily be inscribed. (In fairness, it must be said that during the Shishkebab regime, postage stamps were very large, portraying glorious events in the national past in great detail.) To have gone would have meant, among other things, shaking the hand of this Director, an ignoramus who had benefited from the incarceration, and worse, of his predecessors. Moral problem No. 1 is simple: in these circumstances, would you accept an invitation to go? The question answers itself. No decent man would go, and I wish no decent man had gone.

But now it is more than a quarter of a century later. The regime has softened. Above all, all kinds of internal cross-currents and strains can be discerned, and some of those internal currents earn one's respect both by what they stand for and by the courage of those who represent them. Take once again the situation in my field. The old hack appointed by Shishkebab has long since retired, and the Institute is in the hands of his successors, who are not hacks, or at any rate not all of them and not altogether. Even the man who runs the place and who is consequently too busy politicking to do any real work in the subject (a fate not unknown even in the most liberal societies), and whose public pronouncements are the very height of innocuousness (that can happen here too) has an admirable record in securing jobs and facilities for good scholars even when endowed with dubious TR pasts, and with a regrettable tendency to shoot their mouths off in a TR manner.

But there is more to it than that. Inside the subject there is a complex and confused struggle between those who would liberalise it and heed scholarly criteria (whatever they may be) and those who drag their feet, or even wish to march in the opposite direction. But do not be misled into supposing that the moral line-up is simple, or that the alignment of individuals is self-evident. Here, as elsewhere, life is full of moral ambiguities – perhaps rather more so, or perhaps they matter more because more is at stake. No one is ever quite what he seems, and when the veils come off, you never know whether you have seen the removal of the last one.

Let me give you some examples. Take the guilt-ridden liberal. X has impeccable values and has *never* soiled his hands with Shishkebabism. He paid his price in the days of the Trauma; more ironically, he also paid a certain price in the heady days of de-Traumatisation, for de-Traumatisation was carried out above all from within the Movement. Those who were not in it were deprived, at least until very late, of any base from which to take part in the process. Ironically, the ex-Shishkebabists who turn against the unpalatable aspects of their faith, are often terribly fastidious about cooperating with those who had never committed the same errors: or who abandoned them too soon or too late. Though Errors they be, it seems that one must have committed them to be eligible for political participation, and the Timing of Repentance is of great importance. By a further irony, X, deprived of full participation for his consistent TR-ism, did not suffer too much when the pendulum swung back again towards orthodoxy, and scores were settled among and between ex- and neo-Shishkebabists. Consequently he is left more or less alone, his professional life is relatively satisfactory (though not deeply fulfilling), and he is abandoned to his Inner Emigration, within which he is haunted by guilt, knowing full well the contempt in which he is held by those who are suffering more, and who despise him as the regime's Parade-Liberal.

For contrast, take Y. Y is a toughie, physically and otherwise. He has what is known as a good profile, excellent prefect or officer material in erstwhile British terms, combined with evident devotion to the principles of Revolutionary Populism. He is trusted and can travel abroad. But eventually – is it because he trusts me, or was he trying it on? – he let himself go, as we are walking through those lovely forests which sweep down from the Carbunclian Mountains to the Manich Depression, where bugging is hardly feasible. Y is not going to waste himself on some five minutes of pointless and expensive protest: he will make it *when it counts*. Was he apologising to me for having failed to make it yet (though heaven knows I do not presume to sit in judgement on him, and I shudder to think what I would have done, or failed to do, in X's or Y's shoes)?

Now consider moral problem No. 2. The moment *when it counts* has come at last. The TRs are struggling, more or less openly, with the half-cowed neo-Shishkebabists. The current Director of the Institute of Blobology (admittedly once a Shishkebabite, and owing access to his present position to docility or even enthusiasm in the days of Trauma) now struggles for liberalisation. He invited me over to lecture on some recent developments in Blobology, and to help develop contacts between his Institute and blobologists the world over.

Would I go? Of course I would go. I like going. I fancy myself as rather suitable for this kind of mission. In the capital, I am in fact seldom taken for a foreign visitor. My accent in the language is appalling, but I think they usually attribute this to my belonging to some kind of ethnic minority within the country. In fact, my kind of squashed-dago looks are quite common in the country (especially in the south, where the Carbunclian hills sweep down, etc.). But above all, it must be the poor quality of my clothing. Tourists are usually approached by touts offering them local works of art or fakes thereof (which it is illegal to export) in exchange for their suits, but no self-respecting member of the Vodkobuzian elite, let alone their swinging youth, would be seen dead in the kind of suit I wear, and so I am never accosted on that account.

But I need not really explain or defend myself. In situation No. 2, when decency and oppression have joined in battle under reasonably well-defined banners, most men would go and help. Few would be put off by the Shishkebabite record, in the Trauma days, of some of those who are now sponsoring the invitation and soliciting moral aid. The Trauma was a quarter of a century ago: what regime, what individual, can bear having its or his record examined very far back? Here once again the question more or less answers itself, though not perhaps for everyone. At the distance of twenty-five years, a situation has arisen which calls for a different, and, now, a positive answer.

Here comes the rub: there are many lands whose moral situation, or the response they evoke, is not at either end of the spectrum schematised in my argument as situations 1 and 2, and separated, in my hypothetical example, by a neat quarter of a century. If you allow, for the sake of argument, the passage of time to correspond neatly to the moral situation (the real world is always more complex), then moral clarity prevails at either end: a year or two or three after the Trauma, *of course* you still would not go; a year or two or three before the Moment of Truth, of course you *would*, and be eager and proud to help that moment along, to recognise it before it becomes obvious.

But in the real world you never know how far off that moment is, or which way the pendulum is swinging. The country looks, not close to either end of the spectrum, but somewhere in the middle. A dozen years or so away from Trauma, perhaps, and as far again from Rebirth. The ambiguity surrounds not merely the overall situation but also the role of individuals within it.

Some of the bravest, most admired TRs have a Shishkebabite past. Some present seeming Shishkebabites are biding their time (or were they having me on?). Some apparent TRs may be *agents provocateurs*. In brief, the present situation, unlike the two which I have constructed, does not evoke a clear moral reaction. If you go, you shake the hands of practitioners and beneficiaries of Shishkebabism and it is said that you strengthen them, as the price of possibly also aiding TRs, including some latent TRs within the breasts of outward conformists.

There is no simple or reliable answer, perhaps no answer at all. I cannot feel at home either with the holier-than-thou puritans (who never compromise at all) or the blasé practitioners of *realpolitik* (always willing to go). Yet one must also try not to be complacent, even at the second level, about one's lack of complacency (shared in different forms by the puritans and by realists). There is a certain seductive regress, seeming to offer one moral clearance by virtue of one's anxiety. I am not complacent, or even complacent about my non-complacency, and so on. Yet in the end one still risks patting oneself on the back. The fact that I am recursively anxious about using my own anxiety as a justification still does not give me clearance. The danger lies in supposing that being a Hamlet excuses everything, which is one further twist of complacency – and so is saying this in turn, if it were meant to excuse anything. There really is no clear answer, and I leave the question with you.

2 Nationalism and the two forms of cohesion in complex societies

The role of amnesia in the formation of nations is perhaps most vigorously affirmed by Ernest Renan: 'L'oubli et, je dirais même, l'erreur historique sont un facteur essentiel de la création d'une nation...'[1] Renan, like other theorists of nationalism, does also invoke common memories, a shared past, as one of the elements which bind men and help form a nation. But a deeper and more original perception is to be found in his view that a shared amnesia, a collective forgetfulness, is at least as essential for the emergence of what we now consider to be a nation. Antiquity, he had noted, knew no nations in our sense. Its city states knew patriotism, and there were of course imperial and other large agglomerations: but not nations.

Renan believed nations to be a peculiarity of Europe as it developed since Charlemagne. He correctly singled out one, perhaps *the*, crucial trait of a nation: the anonymity of membership. A nation is a large collection of men such that its members identify with the collectivity without being acquainted with its other members, and without identifying in any important way with sub-groups of that collectivity. Membership is generally unmediated by any really significant corporate segments of the total society. Sub-groups are fluid and ephemeral and do not compare in importance with the 'national' community. Links with groups predating the emergence of the nation are rare, tenuous, suspect, irrelevant. After listing various *national* states – France, Germany, England, Italy, Spain – he contrasts them with a conspicuously un-national political unit of his time, Ottoman Turkey. There, he observes, the Turk, the Slav, the Greek, the Armenian, the Arab, the Syrian, the Kurd, are as distinct today as they had been on the first day of the conquest. More so, he should have added, for in the early days of conquest, it is highly probable that Turkish-speaking tribes absorbed earlier Anatolian populations; but when the Ottoman empire was well established, a centrally regulated system of national and religious communities excluded any possibility of a trend towards an ethnic melting-pot.

[1] Ernest Renan, *Qu'est-ce qu'une nation?*, Paris 1882.

It was not so much that the ethnic or religious groups of the Otto-man empire had failed to forget. They were positively instructed to remember:

> The Ottoman Empire was tolerant of other religions... But they were strictly segregated from the Muslims, in their own separate communities. Never were they able to mix freely in Muslim society, as they had once done in Baghdad and Cairo... If the convert was readily accepted, the unconverted were excluded so thoroughly that even today, 500 years after the conquest of Constantinople, neither the Greeks nor the Jews in the city have yet mastered the Turkish language... One may speak of Christian Arabs – but a Christian Turk is an absurdity and a contradiction in terms. Even today, after thirty-five years of the secular Turkish republic, a non-Muslim in Turkey may be called a Turkish citizen, but never a Turk.
>
> (Bernard Lewis, *The Emergence of Modern Turkey*, 2nd edn, Oxford, 1968, pp. 14 and 15)

Yet overall, Renan's perception of what it is that distinguishes the modern nation from earlier collectivities and polities seems to me valid. His account of how nations came to be important seems to me inadequate and incomplete. It is basically historical, and seeks to explain why the national principle prevailed in Western Europe, and not yet (at the time he wrote) in Eastern Europe and elsewhere. He invokes the circumstances of the Teutonic conquests: Franks, Burgundians, Lombards, Normans often arrived without a sufficient number of women, and eventually intermarried with the locals; moreover, they adopted the religion of the conquered. Next, powerful dynasties imposed the unity of large societies; the King of France, he notes, did so by tyranny and by justice. Switzerland, Holland, America, Belgium were formed by the voluntary union of provinces, even if in two cases the union was subsequently confirmed by a monarchy. Finally, the eighteenth century changed everything. Though he had ironised the idea that a large modern nation could be run along the principles of an ancient republic, he nevertheless retains a good deal of the return-to-antiquity theory of the French Revolution: 'L'homme était revenu, après des siècles d'abaissement, à l'esprit antique, au respect de lui-même, à l'idée de ses droits. Les mots de patrie et de citoyen avaient repris leur sens.'

To sum up: that crucial required amnesia had been induced by wifeless conquerors, willing to adopt the faith and often the speech of the vanquished; by effective dynasties; sometimes by voluntary association; and the principle of amnesia and anonymity within the body politic was finally confirmed by the eighteenth-century revival of the ideas of rights and of citizenship. And it is the glory of France, he observes, to have taught mankind the principle of nationality, the idea that a nation exists through itself and not by grace of a dynasty. It is also the case that he exaggerated somewhat the extent to which France had become culturally unified in his time. Eugen Weber tells us convincingly[2] that the process was far from complete. But the fact that it was in the process of completion is significant. Whether it supports Renan's explanation, or a modified one, is another matter.

Renan's theory of nationality and nationalism in effect has two levels. His main purpose is to deny any naturalistic determinism of the boundaries of nations: these are *not* dictated by language, geography, race, religion, or anything else. He clearly dislikes the spectacle of nineteenth-century ethnographers as advance guards of national claims and expansion. Nations are made by human will: une nation est donc une grande solidarité,... elle se résume ... par ... le consentement, le désir, clairement exprimé de continuer la vie commune. L'existence d'une nation est un plébiscite de tous les jours... This is one level of his argument: a voluntaristic theory of nationality and the nation state. Paraphrasing T. H. Green, he might have said: will, not fact, is the basis of a nation. Green, when he said that will, not force, was the basis of the state, then had to go on to say that Tsarist Russia was a state only by a kind of courtesy. Renan was obliged to concede that the ethnic groups of antiquity and pre-modern times generally, often barely conscious of themselves, and too unsophisticated to *will* a cultural unity or to crave state protection for it, were not really 'nations' in the modern sense – which is indeed the case.

The second level is the answer to the question, how did the nations which he did have in mind, roughly European nations west of the Trieste–Königsberg line, come into being? He notes the anonymity which prevails in these large collectivities and their shared amnesia, and credits them to the wifelessness of Teuton conquerors, the brutality of centralising monarchs, direct affirmation of will amongst the Swiss and Dutch, and a belated affirmation by the Italians...

Be it noted that the theory is profoundly unsatisfactory at both levels, and yet at each level it contains an important and valid insight. Will, consent, is not an exclusive characteristic of modern nations. Many utterly un-national groups or collectivities have persisted by consent. Amongst the wide variety of kinds of community or collectivity which has existed throughout history, consent, coercion, and

[2] *Peasants into Frenchmen*, London 1979.

inertia have co-existed in varying proportions. Modern national states have no monopoly of consent, and they are no strangers to inertia and coercion either.

Similarly, at the second level, the processes invoked – wifeless and conversion-prone conquerors, strong ruthless centralising rulers – are in no way a speciality of Western European history. They have occurred elsewhere, and plentifully. No doubt they had often had the effects with which Renan credits them in Europe, destroying kin-links, eroding continuities of social groups, disrupting communities, obliterating memories. But, after the cataclysm and trauma, when the deluge subsided, when social order was re-established, internal cleavages and discontinuities reappeared, justified by new, probably fictitious memories... New ones are invented when the old ones are destroyed. Most societies seem allergic to internal anonymity, homogeneity, and amnesia. If, as Renan insists, Frenchmen have obliterated the recollection of Gaulish, Frankish, Burgundian, Norman, etc. origins, this does not distinguish him from those whom he singles out for contrast: the Anatolian peasant also does not know whether his ancestor had crossed the Syr-Darya, or whether he had been a Celt, Greek, Hittite or any other of the local proto-inhabitants. His amnesia on these points is at least as total as that of his French peasant counterpart. An Islamic folk culture stands between him and any fond memories of the steppes of Turkestan. And his ancestors too had known invaders and centralising monarchs – on occasion more effective ones than those who had ruled and unified France. The Orientalist Renan should have known better than that.

What distinguished Western Europe are not those invasions and centralising efforts which happen to have preceded the modern national state – though they may have contributed to a situation which, accidentally, resembled in some small measure that fluid anonymity which characterises membership of a modern 'nation', and have helped prepare the ground for it. What distinguishes the areas within which nationalism has become the crucial political principle is that some deep and permanent, profound change has taken place in the way in which society is organised – a change which makes anonymous, internally fluid and fairly undifferentiated, large-scale, and culturally homogeneous communities appear as the only legitimate repositories of political authority. The powerful and novel principle of 'one state, one culture' has profound roots.

If Renan was misguided about the origin of the phenomenon which he correctly identified, his hand was also a little unsure in tracing its central feature, in his famous 'daily plebiscite' doctrine. Religiously

defined political units in the past were also recipients of the ritually
reaffirmed loyalty of their members; they were the fruit, if not of a plebiscite of every day, then at least of the plebiscite of every feast-day –
and the ritual festivities were often very frequent. Conversely, even
the modern national state does not put its trust entirely, or even overwhelmingly, in the daily plebiscite and the voluntary reaffirmation of
loyalty; they are reinforced by a machinery of coercion.

And yet here, too, Renan discerned something distinctive and important. The modern nationalist consciously wills his identification
with a culture. His overt consciousness of his own culture is already,
in historical perspective, an interesting oddity. Traditional man
revered his city or clan through its deity or shrine, using the one, as
Durkheim insisted so much, as a token for the other. He lacked any
concept of 'culture' just as he had no idea of 'prose'. He knew the
gods of his culture, but not the culture itself. In the age of nationalism,
all this is changed twice over; the shared culture is revered *directly* and
not through the haze of some token, and the entity so revered is dif-
fuse, internally undifferentiated, and insists that a veil of forgetfulness
should discreetly cover obscure internal differences. You must not
ignore or forget culture, but oblivion must cover the internal differen-
tiations and nuances *within* any one politically sanctified culture.

Can we go further and complete his account, developing his
insights and avoiding his misunderstandings?

The present lecture commemorates A. R. Radcliffe-Brown. My contention is that the problem highlighted and solved only in part by
Renan does indeed have a definitive solution, and moreover one
which can be reached only by a systematic use of a distinction which
pervaded Radcliffe-Brown's thought, and dominated the anthropological tradition to which he had contributed so much. Renan had correctly singled out a problem: there is something quite distinctive
about the principle of cohesion and of boundary-definition which animates the modern national state. He identified the distinctiveness
(correctly) in terms of internal amnesia, and a little misleadingly in
terms of voluntary assent: and he explained it, somewhat irrelevantly,
by invoking its allegedly unique historical antecedents, rather than in
terms of persisting social factors which perpetuate it. It seems to me
that we can go further and do better, and that we can best do so with
Radcliffe-Brown's tools, applying them to a problem which had not
preoccupied him.

The tools I have in mind are simple, indeed elementary, and pervasively present in the discourse of anthropologists: they are, essen-

tially, the distinction between structure and culture. It may perhaps be said that Radcliffe-Brown's contribution here was more towards giving his students a sense of what a social structure was, and why it was important, and how it should be investigated, rather than in helping to formulate a logically satisfactory verbal definition of it. But he did not consider this matter of definition to be trivial. On the contrary:

> While I have defined social anthropology as the study of human society, there are some who define it as the study of culture. It might perhaps be thought that this difference of definition is of minor importance. Actually it leads to two different kinds of study, between which it is hardly possible to obtain agreement in the formulation of problems.
>
> (*Structure and Function in Primitive Society*, London, first published 1952, p. 189)

'Structure' he defined as a system of relatively, though not completely, stable social 'positions', to be distinguished from more volatile 'organisation', seen as a system of more transitory activities.[3] Thus in his view, the system of military ranks forms a structure, whilst the temporary deployment of this or that soldier on a given task merely exemplifies 'organisation'. Their switches from one activity to another constituted a kind of Radcliffe-Brownian motion which did not affect the overall structure. His terminology was not altogether consistent: in the general essay on social structure, 'role' occurs in the definition of structure itself; whereas in the subsequently written general introduction, roles are said to distinguish organisation as distinct from structure.

I do not think this terminological instability matters much. The underlying idea is clear, simple, and forceful and, as Radcliffe-Brown saw and stressed, had profound implications for the whole practice of social inquiry. Karl Marx is credited with the observation that if appearance and reality did not diverge, science would be unnecessary. The trouble is – how are we to distinguish appearance and reality, and to identify reality? The importance of the structure–culture distinction, so pervasive in the tradition to which Radcliffe-Brown contributed, springs from the fact that it implicitly contains an entire programme for locating this boundary in the social life of men.

The distinction between structure and culture has profound affinities both with the contrast between primary and secondary qualities, so important in British empiricist philosophy (and surviving in other

---

[3]   *Ibid.*, p. 11 and the whole of ch. X.

terminological guises), and also with the central Marxist distinction between base and superstructure. It indicates the areas which the investigator is bidden to seek out, and the areas accessible to comprehension, comparison and generalisation. The implicit programme and recipe are: structure, the relatively stable system of roles or positions, and the tasks and activities allocated to them, which really make up a society. It is in this area that we may hope to compare one society with another, and perhaps discern generalisations valid for a whole range of societies. By contrast, the system of tokens which, in the idiom of one society or another, constitute the signals by means of which these various roles, positions, or activities are brought to the attention of its members is of only secondary importance.

Though this stratified approach to phenomena has a certain very broad affinity to Marxism, it also differs from it in at least two very important ways. Marxism possesses a relatively specific, highly contentious, and interesting theory of what constitutes that system of primary elements: they are constituted by the means and relations of production. The kind of structuralism exemplified by Radcliffe-Brown never drew any such sharp and restrictive boundary around the system of primary roles or positions. This is a matter of considerable importance, in so far as the crucial difference between the Marxist and others hinges on whether or not, for instance, the means of coercion and relations of coercion are *also* allowed to be independent determinants of a social order. Are they part of the basic structure? A coherent Marxism precludes it, and indeed derisively refers to the 'Idealist theory of violence'; but there is nothing whatever, on the other hand, in Radcliffe-Brown's theory or practice to exclude it.

The second great difference is that Radcliffe-Brown's position contains no theory whatever of a historic sequence of social structures and of the mechanisms by which they replace each other. The two contrasts are linked: the Marxist identification of the deep or primary structure is at the same time meant to be a specification of the area within which those processes take place which lead to the substitution of one structure by another. Marxist interest in social structure is inspired by an interest in change, which it holds to be a law of all things: it is consequently in some embarrassment when facing social structures (for instance nomadic ones, or the 'Asiatic mode of production') which appear to be stagnant.

My contention is that the problem which intrigued Renan, the emergence of that distinctive social unit, the national and often nationalist state, is a precise example of this kind of replacement of one structure by another; and that it cannot be explained by invoking historical events alone, but only by highlighting the difference between the two contrasted structures.

The argument is, in a way, paradoxical. It employs the structure–culture contrast; it pays heed to the Radcliffe-Brownian admonition that attention to either of these two elements will lead us to quite different problems. But it argues that the essence of this particular *structural* change is, precisely, that in the course of it, the role of *culture* itself in society changes profoundly. This is not a matter of replacing one culture, one system of tokens, by another: it is a matter of a structural change, leading to a totally new way of using culture.

One might put it the following way. Culture mirrors structure – but not always in the same kind of way. There are radically different *ways* in which the system of tokens and signals (culture) can be related to the system of roles or positions constituting a society.

Let me make the argument concrete by sketching contrasted models of two different kinds of society:

(1) Consider first a fairly stable, but complex, large and well-stratified traditional society. At its base, there is a large number of rural, servile, inward-turned food-producing communities, tied to the land, and obliged to surrender their surplus produce. Above them, a self-insulated ruling elite of warriors/administrators controls the means of coercion and the channels of communication, and is legally entitled to act as a cohesive body (a right denied to the peasant category). This enables it to maintain its domination. Alongside it, there is a parallel religious hierarchy, comprising both monastic communities and individual officiating priests, who provide ritual services to other segments of the population. In between the rural communities on the one hand and the military-clerical elite, there is a layer of craftsmen and traders, some settled in small pockets in the countryside, or living as perpetual migrants, and others living in more concentrated urban agglomerations.

The technological and administrative equipment of this society is fairly stable. Consequently its division of labour, though quite elaborate, is also fairly constant. In the majority of cases, the recruitment to the many specialised positions within this intricate structure is by birth. Though the skills required are often considerable, they are best transmitted on the job, by a kinsman to the junior member of the group, sometimes by master to apprentice. They do not presuppose an initial *generic* training by an unspecialised centralised educational system.

The clerical hierarchy possesses a near-monopoly of literacy, and the language which it employs in writing is not identical with any living spoken idiom, and very distant from some of the dialects employed in daily life by various social groups. This distance and the resulting unintelligibility to non-initiates constitutes no disadvantage, but, on the contrary, enhances the authority of the doctrine and the rituals which are in the care of the clerisy. It strengthens the aura which surrounds the spiritual arcana. A stratified intelligibility reinforces a stratified society.

In this overall situation, there are no factors making for linguistic and cultural homogeneity, but there are on the contrary various factors making for diversity. The immobility and insulation of the rural peasant groups encourage the diversification of dialects, even if initially neighbouring settlements had spoken the same tongue, which often they had not. The manner in which the polity had expanded – by conquest – meant that in any case it contained peasant communities speaking diverse languages, but the rulers are completely indifferent to this, as long as the peasants remain docile. Higher up in the structure, there is a complex proliferation of diverse ranks and statuses, in principle rigid and hereditary, and in fact fairly stable. The externalisation of this relatively stable and accepted hierarchy, by means of differences in speech and cultural style, is a considerable convenience for the system as a whole and for its members: it avoids painful ambiguity, and constitutes a system of visible markers which underwrite and ratify the entire hierarchy and make it palatable.

Systems of this kind sometimes experience clerisy-led and inspired campaigns for religious unification. The clerisy wishes to affirm its monopoly of magic, ritual, and salvation and to eliminate free-lance shamanism, which tends to persist, especially amongst the rural population. Religious monopoly may be as precious for it as coercive and fiscal monopoly is to the political elite. But what is virtually inconceivable within such a system is a serious and sustained drive for linguistic and cultural homogeneity, sustained by universal literacy in a single linguistic medium. Both the will and the means for such an aspiration are conspicuously lacking.

(2) Consider now a wholly different kind of social structure. Take a society with the following traits: it too has a complex and sophisticated division of labour, but one based on a more powerful technology, so that food-production has ceased to be the employment of the majority of the population. On the contrary, agriculture is now one industry amongst others, employing a fairly small proportion of the population, and those employed in it are not locked into inward-looking rural communities, but are fairly continuous with other occupational groups, and occupational mobility from and into agriculture is roughly as common and as easy as other kinds of lateral occupational mobility.

The society in question is founded on a realistic and well-based expectation of economic growth, the material betterment of all or most of its members. The power of its technology has not merely enabled a small minority in its midst to grow enough food to feed everyone: it also possesses an inherent potential for growth which, over time, allows everyone to become richer. This anticipation plays a central part in securing social consensus and assent: the division of spoils loses some of its acerbity if the total cake is growing. (It also constitutes a grave danger for this society when, for one reason or another, this growth is arrested.) But compared with many previous societies, this one is often permissive and liberal: when the Danegeld Fund is growing steadily, when you can bribe most of the people most of the time, it may be possible to relax the more brutal traditional methods of ensuring social conformity.

A society that lives by growth must needs pay a certain price. The price of growth is eternal innovation. Innovation in turn presupposes unceasing occupational mobility, certainly as between generations, and often within single life-spans. The capacity to move between diverse jobs, and incidentally to communicate and cooperate with numerous individuals in other social positions, requires that members of such a society be able to communicate in speech and writing, in a formal, precise, context-free manner – in other words they must be educated, literate and capable of orderly, standardised presentation of messages. The high educational level is in any case also presupposed both by the type of highly productive economy and by the expectation of sustained improvement.

The consequence of all this is the necessity of universal literacy and education, and a cultural homogeneity or at least continuity. Men cooperating on complex tasks involving high technology must be able to read, and to be able to read the same idiom. Men on the move between diverse jobs, in enterprises with distinct and independent hierarchies, can only cooperate without friction if the base line assumption is one of a rough equality: all men as such are equal, and ranking is *ad hoc* and task-specific. Inequality is temporarily vested in individuals, in virtue of wealth, role-occupancy, or achievement; it is not permanently vested in entire hereditary groups.

This is the general profile of a modern society: literate, mobile, formally equal with a merely fluid, continuous, so to speak atomised inequality, and with a shared, homogeneous, literacy-carried, and school-inculcated culture. It could hardly be more sharply contrasted with a traditional society, within which literacy was a minority and specialised accomplishment, where stable hierarchy rather than mobility was the norm, and culture was diversified and discontinuous, and in the main transmitted by local social groups rather than by special and centrally supervised educational agencies.

In such an environment, a man's culture, the idiom within which he was trained and within which he is effectively employable, is his most precious possession, his real entrance-card to full citizenship and human dignity, to social participation. The limits of his culture are the limits of his employability, his world, and his moral citizenship. (The peasant's world had been narrower than his culture.) He is now often liable to bump against this limit, like a fly coming up against the window-pane, and he soon learns to be acutely conscious of it. So culture, which had once resembled the air men breathed, and of which they were seldom properly aware, suddenly becomes perceptible and significant. The wrong and alien culture becomes menacing. Culture, like prose, becomes visible, and a source of pride and pleasure to boot. The age of nationalism is born.

It is worth adding that, at the very same time, it becomes increasingly difficult for men to take religious doctrine seriously. This is ultimately a consequence of that very same commitment to sustained economic and hence also cognitive growth which also leads to social mobility and homogeneity. Perpetual cognitive growth is incompatible with a firm world-vision, one endowed with stability, authority, and rich in links with the status-system, ritual practices, and moral values of the community, links which reinforce all parts of the system. Cognitive growth cannot be fenced in and insulated, it is no respecter of the sacred or of anything else, and sooner or later it erodes all the cognitive elements of any given vision, whether by outright contradiction or merely by placing them *sub judice*, thereby destroying their standing. So at the very same time that men become fully and nervously aware of their culture and its vital relevance to their vital interests, they also lose much of the capacity to revere their society through the mystical symbolism of a religion. So there is both a push and a pull towards revering a shared culture *directly*, unmediated in its own terms: culture is now clearly visible, and access to it has become man's most precious asset. Yet the religious symbols through which, if Durkheim is to be believed, it was worshipped, cease to be serviceable. So – let culture be worshipped directly in its own name. That is nationalism.

Nationalist theory pretends that culture is *given* to the individual, nay that it possesses him, in a kind of ideological *coup de foudre*. But, in the love of nations as in the love of men, things tend to be more complex than the mystique of spontaneous passion would allow. The industrial world had inherited from the agrarian age an endless wealth of dialects, of cross-cutting nuances of speech, faith, vocation, and status. For reasons which I have tried to sketch briefly, those elaborate, often baroque structures had served agrarian humanity very well. The multiple cross-cutting links helped give the system such stability as it enjoyed. But all these nuances and ambiguities and overlaps, once so functional, become obstacles and hindrances to the implementation of the newly overriding imperative, a literate homogeneous culture, and of an easy flow and solid mobility, a seamless society. Not all the old cultures, let alone all the old subtleties and shading, can conceivably survive into the modern world. There were too many of them. Only some survive and acquire a new literate underpinning, and become more demanding and clearly defined. The new primary ethnic colours, few in number and sharply outlined against each other, are often *chosen* by those who adhere to them, and who then proceed to internalise them deeply.

So Renan was right. There is indeed a perpetual plebiscite, a choice rather than fatality. But the choice does not ignore the given cultural opportunities and resources. It takes place, not every day perhaps, but at each *rentrée des classes*. And the anonymity, the amnesia, are essential: it is important not merely that each citizen learn the standardised, centralised, and literate idiom in his primary school, but also that he should forget or at least devalue the dialect which is *not* taught in school. Both memory and forgetfulness have deep social roots; neither springs from historical accident. Renan boasted that it was the French who taught the world through the Revolution that a nation can will itself, without the benefit of a dynasty. He had not really gone far enough. A culture can and now often does will itself into existence without the benefit not only of a dynasty, but equally of a state; but in this situation, when devoid of a political shell, it will then inevitably strive to bring such a state into being, and to redraw political boundaries so as to ensure that a state does exist, which alone can protect the educational and cultural infrastructure without which a modern, literate culture cannot survive. No culture is now without its national theatre, national museum, and national university; and these in turn will not be safe until there is an independent Ministry of the Interior to protect them. They constitute, as does an independent rate of inflation, the tokens of sovereignty.

Our argument is that there are two great types or species of the division of labour, of social structure, *both* of them being marked by very great complexity and size, but which differ radically in their implications for culture, in the manner in which they make use of culture. Bipolar theories of social development, or dualistic typologies of human societies, have tended to confuse and conflate them. Yet when it comes to understanding the kind of social solidarity associated with nationalism, this distinction is of paramount importance.

One of these, which may be called advanced agrarian-based civilisation, makes for great cultural diversity, and deploys that diversity to mark out the differential situations, economically and politically, of the various sub-populations found within it. The other, which may be called growth-oriented industrial society, is strongly impelled towards cultural homogeneity within each political unit. When this homogeneity is lacking, it can be attained by modifying either political or cultural boundaries. Furthermore, this social form is marked by the overt use of culture as a symbol of persisting political units, and the use of its homogeneity to create a sense (part illusory, part justified) of solidarity, mobility, continuity, lack of deep barriers, *within* the political units in question. In simpler words, agrarian civilisations do not engender nationalism, but industrial and industrial societies do.

This relationship is supremely important, but to assert it is not to claim that it is absolute and free of exceptions. Pre-industrial political units use all kinds of diacritical marks to distinguish their adherents and subjects from those of their neighbours and enemies, and from time to time they may also use cultural differences for this end. But this is contingent and accidental, and constitutes an exception rather than a rule. They may also on some few occasions display a tendency towards that anonymity and individualisation which in our argument only receive their stable social base with industrialism; and it may well be that it was precisely those societies which acquired the cultural traits of industrialism by accident, and prior to the coming of industrial production, which also constituted the social matrix of industrial society. The argument linking scripturalist Protestantism with the coming of modernity owes much of its great plausibility to this very point: a population of equal individuals/clerics, each with a direct line to the sacred, and free of the need for social and stratified mediation, seems particularly well suited for the newly emerging world. The fact that this universalised private line uses a written text favours that general diffusion of literacy and of a standardised idiom which the modern world in any case requires.

Just as pre-industrial societies may contingently acquire some traits of industrial culture, so some industrial societies may lack them. The factors which make for the implementation of the 'one state, one culture' principle are indeed strong and pervasive, but they are not the only factors operative in our world, and sometimes other forces may prevail or lead to some kind of compromise. On occasion, mobility, continuity and communication may be attained despite differences of language, in the literal sense. People may 'speak the same language' without speaking the same language, for instance. Sometimes, sheer force may impose a solution; and sometimes the advantages conferred by preserving a well-established polity may outweigh the disadvantages of a partial violation of the nationalist principle. But these are exceptions: in general, we live in a world in which the new type of division of labour engenders a powerful and, in most cases, successful nationalist groundswell.

If this is so, it is curious that this supremely important side-effect seems to have escaped those two supreme theoreticians of the division of labour, Adam Smith and Émile Durkheim. Let us take them in turn and chronological order.

Both of them are of course very preoccupied with the growth of towns, the natural home of an advanced division of labour. Adam Smith has for very long been stolen by the economists and treated as their proprietary founding father. Social scientists who are not economists have, it seems to me, been somewhat too complaisant about this appropriation. So the idea has spread that Adam Smith's Hidden Hand is primarily concerned with *economic* effects: it augments production and wealth, but if we are concerned with other social benefits, we had better look to later, more sociological thinkers. For Smith, according to this misleading image, the free operation of the Hidden Hand in the economy needs to be protected from harmful political interference: so the crucial relation between economy and polity is a negative one, hinging on the harm which the political interference may do to the economy.

This *laissez-faire* lesson is indeed present in Smith, and it is the one which has been most heeded. But it is very far from the full story. His Hidden Hand is at least as active and significant in political sociology. It is not, as you might expect, that a strong yet liberal state, by terminating feudal anarchy and permitting relatively untrammelled trade, has made the growth of wealth possible: the real connection is the other way round. The growth of manufacture and trade destroys the feudal order. On this point Smith, like his disciple Marx, is an economic determinist: it was the base, the relations of production, which allegedly modified the political superstructure:

commerce and manufactures gradually introduced order and good government, and with them, liberty and security of individuals, among inhabitants of the country, who had before lived in a continual state of war with their neighbours, and of service dependency on their superiors. This, though it has been the least observed, *is by far the most important of all their effects.*

(*The Wealth of Nations*, bk. III, ch. iv.
The italics are mine)

Adam Smith goes on to remark that, to his knowledge, only he and David Hume had noticed this supremely important connection.

The basic mechanics of this development are, in his view, simple. In barbarous conditions of low productivity and ineffective government, rural proprietors are, it appears, pushed into the employment of retainers for the simple and negative reason that there is nothing else on which they can spend their surplus. The resulting power-relations are ratified, not caused, by feudal law.

But happily, cities emerge in the interstices of the feudal system. Initially, their inhabitants are almost as servile as those of the countryside. But, as it is advantageous for the monarch to grant them liberties in return for their becoming their own tax-farmers, they eventually prosper. The more the king is in conflict with the barons, the more he protects the townsmen. Eventually, they prosper so much as to supply the market with luxuries which seduce the barons and destroy their power. The barons, in Smith's view, seemed to have lacked all political sense, and were easily corrupted:

All for ourselves, and nothing for other people, seems in every age of the world, to have been the vile maxim of the masters of mankind. As soon, therefore, as they could find a method of consuming the whole value of their rent themselves, they had no disposition to share them with any other persons. For a pair of diamond buckles perhaps, or for something as frivolous and useless, they exchanged the maintenance, or what is the same thing, the price of the maintenance of a thousand men for a year, and with it the whole weight and authority which it could give them.

(*The Wealth of Nations*, bk. III, ch. iv)

Smith seems to have anticipated the Highland Clearances. His theory of the reduction of the feudal class by trinkets and baubles is not entirely convincing. Were they really such fools? Were they really willing to sacrifice their power base, even before it had been demonstrated to them that they were unable to use it anyway? A page earlier, Smith himself had commented that

It is not thirty years ago since Mr. Cameron of Lochiel, a gentleman of Lochabar in Scotland, without any legal warrant whatever ... used ... nevertheless to exercise the highest criminal jurisdiction over his own people ... That gentleman, whose rent never exceeded five hundred pounds a year, carried, in 1745, eight hundred of his own people into the rebellion with him.

One suspects that such gentlemen did not begin to buy diamond buckles, even if available on £500 a year, till the failure of the rebellion had brought home to them the uselessness of their retainers. In a society in which you may not use your retainers, but can readily convert diamonds into other forms of wealth which do exercise social leverage, it is perfectly rational to prefer diamond buckles to thugs. The buckles were not a seduction of the gullible, they were a perfectly appropriate substitute for the old forms of influence, a good way of indulging a rational liquidity-preference.

Though this part of Smith's argument is unconvincing or incomplete, his main point is entirely cogent. It is this: if the laird uses his money to maintain a man, he thereby builds himself a power-base. (Such rural power-bases then set off the vicious circle of weak central government and strong local power.) If, on the other hand, he spends the same money on luxury articles, the multiplicity and anonymity of the craftsmen and traders who had contributed to the final products create no political bond between them and him whatsoever. The *kind* of trade he had in mind engenders no patronage links. Thus it is the anonymous, single-shot and many-stranded, nature of market relations which is the true foundation of liberty and good government.

the great proprietors ... (h)aving sold their birthright ... for trinkets and baubles, fitter to be the playthings of children than the serious pursuits of men ... became as insignificant as any substantial burgher or tradesman... A regular government was established in the country as well as in the city, nobody having sufficient power to disturb its operations in the one, any more than in the other.

(Bk. III, ch. iv)

In the previous chapter, Smith expresses surprise that the rot, from the viewpoint of the feudal rulers and the monarchy, should ever have been allowed to start. Why should kings have granted those liberties to towns, which were eventually to shift the entire basis of the social order? A good question. His answer is that it was in their short-term interest. In anarchic circumstances, where taxes were hard to collect, urban centres, grateful for some protection, might be glad to pay them to the monarch voluntarily. They gained some protection and he was spared the toils and perils of tax-collection. Clearly this account of the involuntary conception of urban capitalism in the womb of feudalism was largely taken over into Marxism.

What is interesting, however, from our viewpoint, is a certain insularity on the part of Adam Smith. He is most sensitive to the difference of ethos and structure between Glasgow and the Highlands, between economically enterprising townsmen and economically timid lords (so that the former make far better rural developers); but ethnicity does not attract his attention. Neither the ethnic distinctiveness of the Highlands nor the (far more significant) ethnic *continuity* between the burghers and government elicit any comments from him.

Strangely enough, in one as well informed as he was, he does not comment on one extremely well-diffused device which had once been open to the monarch, when he granted trading privileges and even internal legal autonomy to the trading burghers. There exists a political device which will provide the ruler with a docile and taxable town, but will also ensure that, even when it prospers, it can be no threat to him. Why not grant such rights only to ethnic, linguistic or religious minorities, preferably such as those endowed with a stigma, and thus excluded from political aspirations, and who can be relied upon to remain, in all probability, in great need of royal protection? This method had served well in other parts of the world, and prevented that conquest of rural society by the urban, in whose beneficial political consequences Smith rightly rejoiced. Perhaps the expulsion of the Jews made its contribution to the development of medieval England, by ensuring that the burghers who remained were culturally continuous with the majority and the rulers, and so unhampered by political disability.

Smith did notice some of the traits and contrasts which enter into our account of the new order: anonymity and mobility. We have seen his comments on the latter. Old families, he notes, are very rare in commercial countries. By contrast, amongst uncommercial nations, such as the Welsh, the Highlanders of Scotland, Arabs, or Tatars, they are very common. Why, he exclaims, a history written by a Tatar Khan (Abulghazi Bahadur Khan, brought back and translated by some Swedish officers imprisoned in Siberia during the Northern War and published in Leyden in 1726) contains scarcely anything *other than* genealogies! Here Smith may have been supplied with some misleading information: fortunes amongst Eurasian nomads are most unstable and precarious, because of vagaries of weather and the fates of flocks. This precisely is a key argument against the 'feudal' interpretation of their societies. They can only talk in terms of genealogies, but fortune is most fickle with their lineages for all that. But Smith's overall conclusion was sound.

Having seen so much, why did he fail to link the new division of labour to ethnicity? I can only suggest that he was misled by the fact that the milieu he knew best and was most interested in had entered the new division of labour *already* well endowed with a very fair measure of ethnic homogeneity.

Perhaps the error of Durkheim is the same as Smith's: both see the progress of the division of labour in bipolar terms. It is not enough to contrast a well-developed division of labour with its absence, with mechanical solidarity and homogeneity. If we make this contrast, we face the extraordinary paradox that it is in the modern world, within which in one sense the division of labour has gone further than anywhere else, that we also find the powerful drive towards cultural homogeneity which we call 'nationalism'. These societies are not segmentary, yet they display a marked tropism towards cultural and educational similarity.

Hence, genuinely homogeneous traditional societies, displaying a 'mechanical solidarity' within which everyone does much the same and men do not differentiate themselves much from each other, must be contrasted with *two* quite different rival options. One is a large society within which diverse groups of men do quite different things, and within which this group diversification is neatly confirmed by cultural differences between the groups in question. Groups complement each other and fit into an interdependent whole, but do not identify with each other culturally. The other is the kind of society which we have entered or which we are entering, in which a very special kind of acute diversity of occupational activity is accompanied, surprisingly, by a strongly felt push towards cultural similarity, towards a diminution of cultural distance. Activities are diversified, but they are all codified in writing in a mutually intelligible idiom. Communication between men is intense (which is what interested Durkheim), and this presupposes that they have all learned the same code. This facilitates not merely their contacts, but also their mobility and job-changes: retraining is feasible if each skill is recorded in the same style and language. In this kind of society, cultural distance becomes politically and socially offensive. Once, it had been nothing of the kind – quite the reverse. It had helped everyone to know his own place. Now, in a musical-chairs society, it only inhibits a movement which is essential to the life of the society.

The phenomena in which the division of labour, alias organic solidarity, manifests itself, are borrowed by Durkheim from both kinds of division of labour at once.[4] He fails to distinguish them. Intensity of

---

[4]   *De la division du travail social*, 10th edn, Paris, 1978, II, ch. ii.

interaction, urbanisation, the augmentation of the means of communication and transmission, specialisation of function... The
trouble was perhaps that Durkheim's treatment was abstract, theoretical, and unhistorical (whereas Renan was too historical and not theoretical enough). But the tacit implication of Durkheim's abstract
approach is that all progressions towards the division of labour are
basically alike; and that they are reasonably continuous. In other
words, what is excluded is the possibility of radically diverse paths,
leading to different *kinds* of division of labour, and also the exclusion
of *jumps* in the history of the division of labour. In fact, bifurcations
and discontinuities are most important for the understanding of the
distinctive nature of modern, nationalism-prone society. Smith had
been more concrete, more historically anchored than Durkheim: but
he also seemed to assume that laggard societies would either remain
backward, or follow the same path of development as the one he had
analysed.

Durkheim apparently had an aversion to Renan.[5] But he might have
benefited from following Renan, at least so far as to spare a thought
for Ottoman Turkey, or indeed for India and for caste. In the chapter
in which he considers the causes of the division of labour, he does
reflect on Russia and China – but only to say that great populousness
and genuine social density (an elusive notion) are not one and the
same thing. Imperial China and Tsarist Russia, it would seem, are but
cases of mechanical solidarity writ large. The same is implied for
ancient Israel, notwithstanding the fact that, in the fourth century BC,
it was more populous than contemporary Rome, which, however, was
more developed. Durkheim's observations about Russia were at any
rate congruent with the views of the Populists, though they were made
in a very different spirit. The aversion of Kabyles to specialists (which
can easily be paralleled in other societies of the same very broad
region) is also invoked, and of course fits his argument admirably.
The deep contempt and distaste which members of the dominant
stratum of segmentary societies feel for the specialists whom they tol-
erate in their midst (even for the religious specialists whom they
nominally revere) reappears in the nineteenth-century romantic cult
of the peasant and the simple soul, preached by intellectuals with a
kind of self-hatred. Durkheim stood such populism on its head and
endeavoured to give specialisation a higher moral dignity by making it
the basis of a superior form of social cohesion. But he failed to see that
it achieved such dignity only when professional specialisation *and*
mobility were fused with cultural standardisation. The mobility made

[5]   See Steven Lukes, *Emile Durkheim: His Life and Work*, London, 1973, pp. 71, 72.

the standardisation necessary; the standardisation made specialisation, at long last, morally acceptable. That is our social condition.

One feels he should have paid more heed to societies containing groupings such as castes or *millets*, in which the division of labour is great, but does *not* engender all that social density, that cumulative and historically continuous interaction, which are central to his picture. Both these great thinkers are, in their own way, unilinearists, or at any rate bipolarists. They argue in terms of one line of development, or of one grand opposition. From the Highlands (paralleled by Tatars, Arabs, and early European barbarians) to Glasgow; or from the Hebrews, Kabyles, Greeks, and Romans to France. If this be an error and these two giants committed it, no wonder that variants of it reappear in so many of their successors.

Forms of complex division of labour can and do exist which, though they may help a social system to survive, do not engender a feeling of community – rather the reverse. The distinctive, mobile, and literacy-sustained division of labour, which does lead to the modern sense of national community, is historically eccentric. Some of Durkheim's perceptions about the role of interaction and 'density', misguidedly applied to complex societies in general, but in fact only applicable to their modern industrialising variant, seem to receive interesting confirmation from perhaps the most thorough attempt yet made to apply quantitative historical methods to early nationalism, namely the work of Miroslav Hroch.[6]

Hroch investigated the origins of early nationalists in a whole set of small European nations – Czechs, Lithuanians, Estonians, Finns, Norwegians, Flemings, and Slovaks. His findings[7] certainly confirm Durkheim's views, if we treat nationalist activists as indices of organic solidarity. But an interesting aspect of Hroch's conclusions is that these activists were most heavily concentrated in small towns with artisan productions, centres of prosperous agricultural production beginning to supply a distant market; but *not* in areas directly affected by industrialisation proper. This finding does not destroy the theory linking nationalism and industrialisation, but may well require some refinement of it.

Having consigned the Tsarist Russia of his day to a segmentary stage (remarking that 'the segmentary structure remains very marked, and hence, social development not very high'), one wonders what

---

[6] See *Die Vorkämpfer der nationalen Bewegung bei den kleinen Völkern Europas*, Prague, 1968; also Hroch's 'K otázce územní skladby narodního hnutí', *Československý časopis historický*, 1972, 513.

[7] *Die Vorkämpfer*, p. 168; 'K otázce', 535.

Durkheim would have made of the Soviet Union. Its national policy and aspirations, and to some extent its achievement, conspicuously highlight my central contention that the division of labour and 'organic solidarity' are multi-dimensional notions, and cannot be plotted along one single continuum. The professional division of labour has obviously increased enormously since the Tsarist days when the overwhelming majority of the inhabitants of the Russian Empire were peasants. But, at the same time, public policy is obviously eager to counteract any *ethnic* division of labour, and to strive for and demonstrate that the composition of diverse Soviet republics and nationalities is parallel rather than complementary. Consider, for instance, a volume which is the first of the fruits of a major study of ethnicity in the USSR, and is in a study of the Tatar ASSR:

In the contemporary stage the social structure of the Tatar nation has attained correspondence with the all-Union social-class and social professional structure.

The approximation of the social structure of Tatars to that of the Russians expressed itself in the equalisation of the proportions of basic social groups...

> *Sotsial'noe i natsional'noe*, ed. Yu. V.
> Arutyunyan, L. M. Drobizheva, O. I.
> Shkaratan, Moscow, 1973, p. 311.

Clearly, policy does not seek the extreme amnesia noted by Renan, but does very much aim at avoiding the kind of ethnic specialisation which marked the Ottoman empire and perpetuated ethnic distinctiveness. If Soviet policy and aspirations in this sphere can be summed up briefly, it is that ethnicity should be cultural, and should not reflect structural differences.[8]

The aspiration is to endow the total society with the fluid type of organic solidarity, ensuring that ethnic-cultural boundaries within it should cease in any way to be structural markers. This would mean organic solidarity for the Union as a whole, and for each constituent republic, but mechanical solidarity for the relationship *between* republics. This aim is clearly reflected in the main orientation of Soviet social anthropology ('ethnography' in the local terminology): at a time when many Western anthropologists react to the diminution of the archaic world by turning themselves into micro-sociologists, and making micro-structures into their speciality, their Soviet colleagues single out *culture* as their distinctive field in the modern world.[9]

[8] See, for instance L. M. Drobizheva, *Dukhovnaya obshchnost' narodov SSSR*, Moscow, 1981; V. I. Kozlov, *Natsional'nosti SSSR*, Moscow, 1973.
[9] Cf. Yu. V. Bromley, *Etnos i etnografiya*, Moscow, 1973.

The division of labour, or social complementarity, is then something pursued at the level of individuals, and avoided at the level of ethnic groups, of social sub-units. It is precisely this crucial distinction which fails to be highlighted by Durkheim's work. The alternatives facing mankind are not simply binary, between being alike and being members of similar sub-groups on the one hand, and being both individually and collectively differentiated and complementary on the other. There are at least three options: being alike and members of similar groups; being different in virtue of being members of differing and complementary groups; and being different *individually*, in virtue of the absence of any significant sub-groups. Adam Smith thought primarily in terms of a transition from the first to the third stage, and largely ignored the second. Durkheim thought in terms of a transition from the first stage to something which combined features of the second and third.

My main point is very simple. Advanced agrarian societies with a fairly subtle technological equipment and status system, and industrial societies oriented towards growth and endowed with a fluid system of roles, *both* have a complex division of labour. But their form of social cohesion and their use of culture to enhance it are almost diametrically opposed. Any sociological theory or typology which fails to highlight this difference cannot be adequate.

Bipolarism will not do in this field. The division of labour can only be plotted on an (at the very least) bifurcated diagram, with possibly only one starting-point, but two quite different paths and end-points. No doubt some paths lead through *both* kinds of complex division of labour. But a stable, agrarian-based division of labour has cultural consequences which are sharply different from those of a growth-addicted and industrial society. There is only one kind of society which really permits and fosters that amnesia which Renan rightly singled out as an attribute of modern nations, and which overlaps with Durkheim's 'density'. It is engendered, not by the division of labour as such, but by one distinctive species of it. It may be that both Smith and Durkheim were misled by the fact that the society which engendered industrialism was already endowed by some strange historical freak with its cultural corollaries before the event.[10] Perhaps this is indeed a clue to the understanding of the emergence of industrialism.

But to return to Radcliffe-Brown. He was right when he said that concern with society, and concern with culture, lead to quite different questions. But the problem of nationalism obliges us to ask both of them. We have to ask what kind of structure it is which does, and does

[10]   Cf. Alan MacFarlane, *The Origins of English Individualism*, Oxford, 1978.

not, lead to a self-conscious worship of culture, no longer mediated by an externalised Sacred, *and* to the compulsive standardisation of culture within the political unit. To answer that question we need to operate with the Radcliffe-Brownian structure–culture opposition, but we also need radically to rethink our assumptions about the division of labour.

3 The roots of cohesion

Emile Masqueray's study, first published in 1886, is a minor master-piece.[1] Its significance lies in the penetration and originality of its ideas, its thorough and unique documentation, and its crucial position at the crossroads of sociological ideas. It provided an overall picture of the social organisation of the three main Berber regions of Algeria, supplemented by one of the earliest European accounts of the societies of central Morocco. It is probably the single most important book written about North Africa in the nineteenth century. At the same time, its ideas made a major contribution to the general debate concerning the roots of social cohesion.

But it is a work which has been largely forgotten, and which had become virtually unobtainable. It is true that an inter-war collection of readings in sociology, used as a textbook for training French school-teachers, favours Masqueray with coverage similar to that accorded to Fustel de Coulanges. But this merely acquainted French schools with his ethnographic *material*, and does not seem to have disseminated his *ideas*. These were used by anthropologists, but without an awareness or recognition of their point of origin. Hence this beautifully executed republication (under the auspices of CRESM in Aix-en-Provence, one of the main French research centres on North Africa), aided by an excellent introduction by Fanny Colonna, is a major service to scholarship.

Fanny Colonna herself is one of the leading contemporary experts on Algeria: of *pied-noir* (French settler) background, with a lineage connection with Algeria dating back over a century, she retained Algerian citizenship after the coming of Algerian Independence. She has established her reputation with a study of the Algerian schooltea-cher class during the colonial period (see Colonna 1975), and is at

[1] Émile Masqueray, *Formation des cités chez les populations sédentaires de l'Algérie: Kabyles du Djurjura, Chaouïa de l'Aouras, Beni Mezab*. Réimpression de l'ouvrage publié en 1886 chez l'éditeur Ernest Leroux à Paris. Présentation par Fanny Colonna. Centre de Recherches et d'Études sur les Sociétés Mediterranéens, and Edisud, La Calade, 13090 Aix-en-Provence, 1983.

present working on a social history of the Aures mountains in the nineteenth century. No one could have been better equipped to introduce Masqueray's work.

The republication should do a great deal to correct the history of social ideas, from which he has been unfairly excluded. It is not so much that he has left no traces. Rather, no one so far seems to have had the motivation to follow up the scent, which is plainly there for all to follow.

Two lines at least lead from Masqueray to our intellectual world. One leads through a crucial footnote in Émile Durkheim's *De la division du travail social*. This is, of course, one of the Founding Texts of modern sociological thought. It is organised around the distinction between mechanical and organic solidarity. What Durkheim had done was to try to take away the appeal of human interdependence and cooperation, of social integration, from the romantics and reactionaries who attributed it to *earlier* societies, and who deplored its decline in modern societies. He did so by pointing out that it was primitive man who was standardised, and that it was modern man who attained, through a more highly developed division of labour, a far greater complementarity and interdependence with his fellows. Thus, it seemed, *togetherness* was the coming thing, rather than something which we were losing. This approach also meant the theft of the idea of division of labour from the economists: its real function was not to produce more and better pins, but to make us depend on each other, in a manner more effective and altogether superior to the one which had prevailed before. When we were alike we had little to offer one another. Now we have come to differ, we need each other. It stands to reason.

In the Durkheim version, increased population density seems to lead to a greater division of labour; the Adam Smith picture tended to suggest the opposite connection, from specialisation to productivity and hence populousness. So Durkheim inverted conventional wisdom twice over. What is relevant here is Durkheim's documentation of the primitive 'mechanical' or 'segmentary' element of his opposition. At a certain point (1893: 152) of his discussion of mechanical (i.e. primitive) solidarity, he announces that we are about to leave the domain of prehistory and conjecture. We are entering the realm of contemporary ethnographic fact. The facts he invokes, before returning to biblical and classical antiquity, are those drawn from Algerian Berbers. His sources are two-fold: a much-used study of Kabyle customary law by Hanoteau and Letourneux, and Masqueray's book. Hanoteau and Letourneux have fared better than Masqueray:

throughout the French period in Algeria, administrators continued to use them as a guide. Kabyle villages never lost (certainly up to and including the Algerian War of Independence) their habit of self-administration by customary law, and their three volumes no doubt underwent the transformation from being descriptive to becoming actual sources of law. But Masqueray's work was too theoretical to have this kind of use, and fell into oblivion.

Within segmentary society, Durkheim distinguished two sub-species: there is the more primitive kind, in which a set of internally undifferentiated hordes become clans by being juxtaposed, as he puts it, like a linear series (a model which he thought applied to many North American Indians); and a second, more elevated mode of or-ganisation, in which various elementary groups come to unite once again, with a shared name and life (whilst retaining their separate identity), and where these larger groups-of-groups again fuse into larger groups still, and so on. In this kind of segmentary society, simi-larity is not merely lateral but also vertical: it is not simply that groups resemble their neighbours at the same level of size, but it is also the case that groups resemble, organisationally, the sub-groups of which they are composed, and the larger groups of which they are members. This is totally unlike the organisational principle on which our own society is based; the independent national state, for instance, hardly resembles either its own sub-units, or the larger associations which it enters.

Later, Edward Evans-Pritchard, who really diffused the idea of segmentation in anthropology, made this 'vertical' similarity into an integral part of the notion. For Durkheim, though he was clearly aware of this possibility, it remains a kind of optional extra. This trans-formation of the concept has considerable implications. Durkheim still relies on the interesting but contentious and perhaps mystical idea of solidarity engendered by resemblance. But must I really feel at one with people who resemble me? Who would wish to join a segment which lets in people like himself? Evans-Pritchard by contrast trans-formed segmentation into a much more earthy theory of how social order is maintained, even in the absence of an effective and central-ised state: if rival groups exist, *at each level of size* at which conflict can arise, they can, inspired by mutual fear, restrain and police their own members, even though no specialised order-maintaining agency exists, either within or without all these nested units. This was, in effect, the adaptation of the idea of balance of power to tribal societies, though with some considerable refinement.

The contemporary examples of this form of social life which Durk-

heim invoked were drawn from Masqueray. Yet Steven Lukes's massive and authoritative study *Emile Durkheim* (1973) does not even
mention Masqueray, and treats this part of Durkheim's ideas as deriv-
ing directly from Fustel de Coulanges. Moreover, it stresses Fustel's
ideas on religion far more than his account of social organisation,
though of course the two are linked. Durkheim's characterisation of
segmentary society was, as indicated, transformed and improved by
Evans-Pritchard, and has become one of the commonest ideas in
anthropology. It has spread to political sociology, where it is applied
rather loosely to any form of imperfectly centralised social order. But
one of the key springs of this major river is Masqueray.

There is a certain irony here. In his postscript to the second edition
of his study of a Berber society in Morocco which was inaccessible in
Masqueray's day, Professor Jacques Berque (1978: 480–1) of the Collège de France, a leading contemporary North Africanist and Arabist,
offers the following explanation of why anglophone anthropologists
are attracted by his own predecessor, Robert Montagne:

L'hypothèse segmentariste, qui devait être mise en oeuvre au Maghreb par
des ethnologues anglais et américains ... a salué, comme une sorte d'anticipation d'elle-même, ce que Robert Montagne avait écrit...

When scholars disagree about the origin of an idea, normally each
claims it for his own country. Here on the contrary Berque seems to
credit the Anglo-Saxons with an idea initially worked out by a series of
Frenchmen: Fustel, Masqueray, Durkheim...

One fertile line leads from Masqueray through Durkheim to
Evans-Pritchard. Why were the origins of the idea ignored or recognised only selectively? Part of the answer may lie, as Fanny Colonna
suggests, in Evans-Pritchard's at best ambivalent feelings towards
Durkheim. She notes that he does not cite Durkheim in his own positive work on order-maintenance in acephalous societies, where his
debt to him might be expected to be greatest. He only polemicises
with him on the subject of religion, where it seems he found Durkheim's implicitly reductionist attitude irritating. Evans-Pritchard
declared 1864, the publication year of Fustel's *Ancient City*, a 'dividing
point' in the history of anthropology (1981: 172), but he refrained
from making any such claim for Durkheim's *Division of Social Labour*.
One who was not eager to stress his own debt to Durkheim was unlikely to dig deep into Durkheim's sources.

One might suppose that the French themselves would follow this
up. But this does not seem to have happened. When France re-
entered the big league of anthropological thought in the age of Lévi-

Strauss, it did so under the leadership of a thinker who was overtly uninterested in political structures. The anthropological Marxists who emerged in France soon after, on the other hand, were plainly distrustful and suspicious of the notion of segmentation. It was meant to explain how a certain harmony was maintained, whilst they were extremely doubtful whether there was any harmony there to be explained in the first place. As far as they were concerned, far from being a powerful explanatory idea, it was all part of the eyewash, obscuring real conflict rather than explaining a fictitious equilibrium.

In North African studies, in a manner curiously parallel to Lévi-Strauss, Berque announced in his study of Berber tribal organisation that he was not concerned with political sociology, and so the great problem of 'ordered anarchy' was firmly put outside his terms of reference. In sociology proper, Raymond Aron was certainly interested in the problem of political order. But he was not interested in tribes, and as he tells us in his inaugural lecture at the Collège de France, he found the whole Durkheimian tradition boring, and thought that it led to the formulation of the wrong questions. Its preoccupation with consensus and cohesion, both conspicuously absent from the Europe of the first half of the twentieth century, was irrelevant. Here for once he was in agreement with the Marxists. But people who thought that Durkheim had got his questions wrong were unlikely to show zeal to dig up the bits and pieces from which he had constructed his answers.

The one scholar who did unambiguously acknowledge his own debt to Masqueray, which was indeed enormous, was Robert Montagne. (It was his book which aroused my own interest in Masqueray.) Montagne's *Les Berbères et le Makhzen* (1930) is probably the best study ever of the relationship between a weak state and strong tribes. It is one of the most important books ever written about North Africa, and deserves to be far more widely known than it is. Montagne took over (with full and generous acknowledgement) most of Masqueray's ideas, and applied them to an even richer range of contemporary and historical material, such as happened to be available to a naval officer seconded for intelligence work in the course of the protracted, and often political rather than military, conquest of Morocco.

But here something odd happened. Montagne, unlike his successor Berque, *was* interested in political sociology. The problem of order-maintenance, in an uncentralised (or intermittently or imperfectly centralised) society, was at the centre of his attention. He saw, very clearly, the applicability of the idea of balance of power to tribal units. But he made rather selective use of it. How is order maintained in regions in which the Sultan's writ does not run?

One of the two central themes of Montagne's great book is that this is done by the *leffs*, two great and opposed leagues. These constituent cantons were distributed like black and white squares of a chessboard, right over the countryside. This solution has a grave theoretical defect, which Montagne never really faced. The balance of power between two such moieties can indeed explain why and how peace is maintained, more or less, between the two grand leagues, and between the units which constitute them. But it cannot explain how order is maintained *within* each of those units, and their sub-units, and so on. After all, the constituent cantons are just as devoid internally of specialised order-enforcing agencies, just as lacking in centralised authority, as are the big two leagues which face one another and keep one another in check... Although Montagne's empirical material lends itself admirably to a segmentarist interpretation, his theoretical analysis does not really allow one to enlist him as an adherent of, or contributor to, the mainline theory of segmentation, contrary to a suggestion made in a remarkable recent book by Jack Goody (1983). Montagne in fact does not use the term 'segmentation'; he uses but a fragment of the idea contained in it, and he does not mention Durkheim. He is a direct, unmediated intellectual descendant of Masqueray.

Apart from this theoretical problem, there is also an empirical disagreement between Masqueray and Montagne, which may or may not be explicable in terms of differences between the regions which were their respective stamping grounds: Masqueray does speak of binary leagues, but finds them to be fluid and opportunistic in composition, whilst Montagne seems to endow them with a kind of stability and rigidity (not confirmed by subsequent researchers in the region, such as Jacques Berque or Abdallah Hammoudi).

So whilst taking over Masqueray's picture of North African tribal organisation, Montagne's handling of the problem of 'ordered anarchy' obscured, in a way, its explanatory power. Masqueray had found the multiple-level nature of these groups, the neat 'nesting' of units, though he continued, in a Europo-centric way, to look for the *real* unit, the *cité* (as Fustel de Coulanges had done, and as Montagne continued to do). It was Evans-Pritchard who really made clear that the whole point was that there was *no* crucial unit of size, that all units were in some measure *ad hoc* and were galvanised into existence only by conflict. (Evans-Pritchard, in connection with the Nuer, implausibly and unnecessarily assumed that there was a kind of upper ceiling to the segmentary units, beyond which there was no way of activating solidarity. The history of religious movements amongst segmentary populations does not support such an idea. Religious Messianism enables them to bring about temporary fusions well above the ceiling provided by the uppermost and broadest genealogical or tribal names, or other pre-existent symbols of potential unity.)

In her introduction, Fanny Colonna affirms that Masqueray did not use the – still unchristened – idea of segmentation for the purpose for which it is now used, because he was not, on her reading, interested in the *opposition* of segments. Nothing interested him less, she says. I am not at all convinced by her on this point. He *liked* fusion better, but that is another matter. He was too good a scholar not to perceive and document fission when it accompanied fusion, as it did conspicuously and dramatically. It is true that fusion was his first concern, and that even, in a very strange passage which she invokes (and which is in conflict with his own material), he affirms that the tribal *cité* only recognises individuals, and no sub-groups, within itself. His evidence for this is odd – the fact that the group assembly is not content with a mere majority vote. But this only shows that in this kind of grouping, decisions must in the end be endorsed unanimously, for otherwise the group ceases to be one. It does not spring from some respect for the individual. Masqueray himself, after he had rhapsodised in this passage over the transcendence of internal kin factions, then proceeds to wake up and admit that this transcendence is only attained *par instants*... But in fact he documents, only too amply, often with regret, the persistence and vigour of sub-groups, and the ferocity of their conflicts (notably in Mzab, notwithstanding the fact that in his view the formation of civic consciousness had made most progress there). I do not wish to say that Masqueray himself was clear about this matter: his material, rather than all his interpretations (torn by conflicting requirements), *is* superbly clear.

In any case, it was not the errors (if such they be) of Montagne which prevented Masqueray from becoming visible through Montagne. It was rather that Montagne himself was unjustly ignored after his death in the early 1950s. Post-Independence scholarship, understandably if illogically often in pursuit of the not quite lucid aim of intellectual de-colonisation and expiation, was not attracted by a man associated with colonial conquest. Moreover, the problems which had pervaded this part of Montagne's work had ceased to be topical. The post-colonial state was strong enough to prevent private warfare and self-administration amongst tribal segments, and Morocco became a country within which unsymmetrical, dyadic patronage relationships largely replaced the symmetrical ones of the segmentary *républiques des cousins*, in Germaine Tillion's phrase. Scholars who only arrived at

this stage were sometimes misled into treating the new situation, recently engendered by more effective centralisation, as the permanent
condition. In any case, Montagne was now largely ignored, and hence
no one was much concerned with his intellectual ancestry.

So, though Masqueray stands at the start of two powerful currents,
one leading through Durkheim and Evans-Pritchard to the mainstream of anthropological theory, the other through Montagne to contemporary students of North Africa such as Raymond Jamous (1981),
and, in an American offshoot, to Carleton Coon and his intellectual
offspring, nonetheless there has as yet been little by way of pilgrimage
to this ancestor.

There remains, however, the puzzling and significant question of
Masqueray's relation to the other (and far from forgotten) source of
these ideas – Fustel de Coulanges. In his remarkable history of
French Algeria, Charles-Robert Ageron plausibly remarks (1968:
275):

Masqueray voulut être le Fustel de Coulanges de la 'Cité Africaine'; et il le
fut en quelque façon, dogmatisme inclu...

The parallels between Fustel de Coulanges and Masqueray are
indeed obvious and striking. Each is concerned with the same problems. Each is preoccupied with the *cité* and its growth. Each has a
three-stage theory of the emergence of civic consciousness. There are
also biographical connections between the two men. But the contrasts
and silences are perhaps more important than the overlaps. One
should add that Ageron, notwithstanding his allusion to the dogma-
tism which the two men shared, also stresses that Masqueray has
remained unrecognised and yet is one of those who has contributed
most to our understanding of Algeria (p. 422).

How exactly can Ageron know that Masqueray *wanted* to be the
Fustel de Coulanges of the African city? Had he said so? Of course it
is hard to think of him in any other way, and I had always done so, long
before reading Ageron's remark. Their similarity leaps to the eye. But
the matter is not so simple. They were interested in strikingly similar
problems, and took part in the same continuing debate about the
foundations of social order, in which Renan (whom Masqueray does
quote) and later Durkheim also took part. Nonetheless, as Colonna
most relevantly points out, *Masqueray never refers to Fustel*. The omission is so striking, so odd, and so contrary to all logic, that it *must* have
a reason. When I first went to do fieldwork, Raymond Firth's parting
advice was: at any reunion, always note who is and who is not present.
There is always a reason why those who are present are present, and

why the absent are absent. The principle applies with special force to references.

Fanny Colonna has done some research on this and gone through the library of the École Normale Supérieure. Masqueray himself was a *normalien*; Fustel became the Director of the School in 1880; and, Colonna tells us, Masqueray had severed all contacts with the school in 1876 or soon after. The library only possesses his three published books, but none of his offprints except for the first. There are hints here of a troubled relationship with which Colonna intrigues us, and one must hope that someone will dig up the full story. But Colonna is surely right when she says that Masqueray's work must not be seen as ammunition assembled for some long-term debate in the rue d'Ulm. Masqueray was not trying to make his mark on the Parisian scene, or if he was, he failed lamentably. As Colonna tells us, references to his work were either strangely absent (except for Durkheim's use of his material, unaccompanied by any evaluation), or patronising, until the coming of Montagne's masterpiece of 1930, which hailed him as master.

Fustel's account of the origin of 'the city' (by which, as he stressed, he meant a community and not its habitation) is so similar, in merits and defects, to Masqueray's that the absence of any reference by the later writer, Masqueray, to the earlier one, is strange indeed. Leaving aside the possibility of a personal intrigue in the high temple of French humanist education, an explanation must be sought, in the first place, in the implications of Masqueray's work either for a general theory of society, or for the problems of French policy in Algeria. Colonna considers both these fields but not, in my view, in a sufficiently close relation to one another. My hunch is that this is precisely where the answer is to be found.

In his 1864 classic, Fustel has a three-stage theory of the *Ancient City* which made *religion* into the prime determinant of social order. The cult of family and lineage deities had engendered the early kin communities, which combined and grew upwards along what could later be called the segmentary scale, till they formed a 'city', which likewise had to be sustained by its own specific worship. Later, the internal conflicts within the city, which Fustel views with the same disaste as Plato, led to its transformation under Roman domination. Christianity, which separated religion from polity, law and family, brought in a third stage. Fustel has some difficulty in fitting his second, middle stage into his thesis of the primacy of religion; he cannot quite bring himself to say that religious change actually engendered the Roman empire, and contents himself with saying that it helped it along.

Now Masqueray, without citing Fustel, is strongly opposed to this particular idea. He is more wholeheartedly opposed to it than Durkheim was to be later, when he observed that M. Fustel de Coulanges had mistaken the cause for the effect. The social order explains the force of religious ideas, and not the other way around, says Durkheim. And here Masqueray was very much on Durkheim's side. In fact he went much further than Durkheim was to go. For Durkheim the social role was fundamental, but religion played an essential part in it. For Masqueray the social role is not merely essential but self-sufficient. He believed that he had found the original and secular basis of social order and cohesion, in the way in which the larger genuine unit (the 'city') grew out of the family. The family he seemed to take for granted. He did not think that this principle was the prerogative of any one race or tradition, and it did not seem to need religion in order to function.

Colonna, like Ageron, is interested in the contemporary political role of Masqueray and his ideas. And here she and Ageron are in headlong collision. Both see him as liberal and pro-native, by the standard of the time. His popularity was not enhanced by such an attitude, and his political influence was short-lived and limited. But Ageron sees Masqueray's views as the product of the fashionable Berberophilia of the time, plus a classical education. Colonna affirms categorically, indeed somewhat defiantly, that Masqueray was innocent of being a supporter or co-inventor of that pro-Berber policy. This issue must be considered jointly with his mysterious failure to refer to Fustel.

The evidence and logic of the situation seem to me to be on Ageron's side. It is true, as Colonna stresses, that Masqueray decided to use the term 'Africans' rather than 'Berbers', and also that he considered the conventional contrast between (Berber) sedentaries and (Arab) nomads to be overdrawn, and that he held it to be a matter of relative stress rather than of a sharp dividing-line. He implied (as is indeed most plausible) that many nomads in Algeria were arabised Berbers. But the terminological point cuts the other way. The really conspicuous omission in the book (in addition to the lack of reference to Fustel) is the total lack of interest in the *Arab* city. Constantine, Kairouan, Fes, Meknes, Marrakesh, might just as well never have existed. Tunis and Tlemeen are only contemptuously referred to as places where there were Sultans.

Now all this is strange. It would have been most natural for a man who traces the growth of civic consciousness from Aures via Kabylia to Mzab at least to *ask* himself whether this path might in the end not lead to the Muslim city, to the great pre-industrial towns of North Africa. The question is *never* asked. The real force of writing about 'Africans' seems to be that the culturally quite distinctive Arab city is morally expelled from Africa, is implicitly treated as an intrusion. It doesn't belong in Africa at all, but is a displaced fragment of Syria or the Yemen...

Masqueray had good reasons for ignoring both Fustel and the Arab city, and they were the *same* reasons. If Fustel was right in his religious determinism, then the kind of social organisation which Masqueray found in the berberophone parts of Algeria should only be possible on the basis of clan and family deities and their worship. No segmentation without *lares et penates*! Masqueray does in fact find and note parallels to classical religion, in clan-linked saints and clan-linked rituals. But he is eager not to push this too far, and above all not to make it a condition of a form of social organisation which he explicitly says is rooted in the secular needs of men, 'independently of any religious idea'. He also notes that for the 'Africans', Islam is not the 'elevated doctrine, resembling our Catholicism', which would make all Muslims into one family, but rather a version which subdivides the faith into a multiplicity of micro-churches. This religious fragmentation, consistently enough, he does not attribute to organisational need (which is the real explanation, as can be documented from his own work): he prefers to invoke the survival of ancient Donatism under a Muslim guise, as if the local saints represented diverse levels of spiritual perfection, which emphatically is not the case.

In brief, he was most eager *not* to make the social organisation, for which he had so much sympathy, depend *either* on a religion which the Berbers ought to have had if Fustel were right (but which they only had, at most, in a residual and camouflaged form), *or* on the religion which they nominally did have, but which they would only see correctly if they turned to a version of it more elevated than the one they actually practised. When the time eventually came for Algerians to repudiate clan-linked saints, and embrace a reformed Islam which for the first time defined them all as one unit as against non-Muslims, the days of the French rule were numbered. Masqueray did not prophetically spell this out, but he did seem to sense the logic of it. He wanted to see their social organisation as independent of all religion, unlike Fustel and Durkheim. Durkheim used his material and ignored his secularism. He found Masqueray useful for *The Division of Social Labour*, but would have found him awkward for *The Elementary Forms of Religious Life*. Fustel had made religion essential *and* primary. Durkheim made it essential but not primary. For Masqueray, it was *neither*.

There is another interesting triangular contrast here, from which Masqueray preferred to avert his gaze. There is the ancient city as seen by Fustel, there is the Arab city as it continued to be, and as best analysed by Ibn Khaldun, and there is the community of sedentary Berbers as seen by himself. Fustel gives us an account of the ancient segmentary city, in which both the segments, and the city as a whole, are confirmed or, according to him, actually engendered by a shared ritual and worship, and where a semi-incorporated plebs is kept in place by the effective device of exclusion from the rites. The Arab city is virtually a mirror image of all that. Religion includes *all* Muslims in moral citizenship. The lower orders are more, not less, specifically *encadré*, through religious brotherhoods and saint cults, than the upper classes, with their greater tendency to an unmediated, universalistic, 'elevated' version of the faith. *Neither* level is allowed much political participation or organisation. Masqueray's Berber *cité* (which, with the possible exception of Mzab, is never actually a city) did not contain much in the way of an excluded plebs, took little notice of the elevated and all-embracing version of the Faith (again with the possible exception of Mzab), and was sharply articulated in its sub-units; it enjoyed a very high degree of political participation, and its sub-unit articulation was only ambiguously dependent on religious markers. (The saints were clan-linked, but seldom, if ever, exclusively. They were more often mediators between groups than symbols of any one group.)

Fustel had said about the ancient world:

Between priests of two cities, there were no links, no communication, no exchange of teaching or of rites. Passing from one city to the next, one found new gods, new dogmas, new rituals.

Whether or not this is fully true of the ancient Mediterranean, it is wholly inapplicable to traditional Muslim tribal North Africa. Local saints were indeed local: but passing from one locality to the next, one remained firmly within the same continuous system. The saints recognised, and did not dispute their dependence on, a unique God, whose authoritative (if not in fact fully familiar) Word was in the keeping of literate urban scholars. The saints themselves were linked to each other by a wealth of genetic, spiritual and organisational links, which helped to maintain cultural and economic contacts even in regions which were politically fragmented. This unity-through-religion, combined with organisational fragmentation, was of the essence of the situation, and it was quite incompatible with Fustel's theory, which required that the gods should replicate social units and divisions. Moreover, whilst preserving that fusion of law and faith which Fustel credited to antiquity, Islam ambiguously separated them from social and family units. As the French discovered and stressed in North Africa, it knew two layers of law: one divine, theocratic, centralist and urban-based, and the other customary, communal, pliable. The French supported the latter against the former.

There is a certain irony about Fustel's position. His central point is that classical antiquity is *so* different from us, in its religious and organisational assumptions, that interpreting classical politics in our terms, or vice versa, is a dreadful anachronism. Nonetheless, though he is eager to teach us the differences, it is virtually impossible to read many passages in his book without also seeing them as parables on nineteenth-century France. As in Flaubert's *Salammbô*, the parallels are only too conspicuous. When Fustel discusses just how much political concession had to be accorded to the plebs, so as to ensure its military usefulness against external enemies, it is impossible to suppose that he was thinking only of the past.

This element seems to me largely absent from Masqueray. When he speaks about the Berbers, he is speaking about the Berbers, perhaps about the early human condition in general, but he is not squinting at France. He wants France to teach the Berbers, and not the other way round. In this he was Durkheim's predecessor: Durkheim used his material to highlight not the mechanisms of cohesion operative in nineteenth-century European societies, but the mechanism we have left behind, and which illuminates our condition only by contrast.

The French 'Berber policy' in North Africa consisted of favouring customary law and the community which sustained it and was sustained by it, against the encroachment of divine, Koranic law, linked to urban learning and to centralisation. It presented this custom as pliable, moderate, secular *wisdom*, opposed to rigid, if not fanatical, potentially theocratic and xenophobic leanings. If Fustel was right, such an opposition was nonsensical. A form of religion would have to underlie *each* of the opposed social types. Secular tribal wisdom opposed to religious functional universalism was an absurd confrontation. If Fustel's doctrine was valid, Berber customary law and community had to be a fragile plant indeed, sustained only by a residual and camouflaged religious base. Working out the implications of Fustel's views for French policy in North Africa would lead to piquant results. Should the *Bureaux Arabes*, and possibly the White Fathers, be asked to set up clan deities, perhaps to give instruction in their worship? Should France, following the Roman example as described by Fustel, transport maraboutic shrines to Paris, and install them in the Pantheon? Should the President be deified?

Enough of all this. If these thoughts passed through Masqueray's head, which they probably did, he kept them to himself. He might of course have used his Algerian material for a major onslaught on Fustel and his ideas. But one can think of at least three good reasons against such a course. For one thing, what chance did a provincial prof have against a Parisian star? For another, Masqueray clearly liked, and was eager to use, one *half* of Fustel's theory, namely his account of social organisation, even though he had little use for its link-up with religion. The two issues would have got muddled up. And thirdly, Masqueray was genuinely interested in Algeria and the fate of the Berber communities, and a theoretical battle in Paris about the general issue of society and religion would have obscured what concerned him. Who knows what he might have said later, had he not died prematurely at the age of fifty-one in 1894? But at the time, the most sensible thing seemed to be to use Fustel's organisational ideas, simply and totally ignore his theory of religion with its bizarre implications for North Africa, and mention neither him nor the Arab city. This is precisely what Masqueray did, and it makes sense.

But it does not seem to me that he can be disconnected from the 'Berber policy' which is claimed with emphasis and confidence by Fanny Colonna. At the very least, he made the premisses of that policy coherent, which they could not have been had Fustel's theory of religion been accepted. At the same time, he made manifest the institutional framework of Berber customary law, and he did so admirably, using Fustel's insights into social organisation. Fustel's faith-saturated theory of society was destined to please the French Right at home, but it was awkward for French colonial policy in North Africa. The French wanted tribal secularism to be the opium of the North Africans, reserving the opium of religion for themselves. The accusation levelled against them by early nationalists, that they wanted to convert the Berbers to Christianity, was an exaggeration of this strange vicarious secularism.

It was all very well to use Fustel's vision to provide a social buttress for Catholicism in France, but quite another thing to do the same for Islam in Algeria. Masqueray took over Fustel's ideas on social structure, fused them with superb ethnography, and ignored both Fustel's name and his ideas on the social role of religion. This made it possible for colonial administrators, however Catholic in the context of their own society, to be at the same time secularist *and* traditionalist on behalf of the Berber tribal communities, whose alliance they sought, and whose custom they were eager to sustain. (Tribal law was not really secular in the sense of being free of magical elements. It was only secular in being disconnected from and spurned by the urban high theology of Islam, and being anti-centralist, modifiable by consent, and in the hands of tribal assemblies rather than urban scholars.) Whether those who implemented this policy were really anxious about the logical consistency of their sociological premisses may perhaps be doubted; but if they were, Masqueray made it possible for them to be so.

It should be stressed that what Masqueray helped to discover was the *fact*, and not the *theory*, of segmentation. To a large extent he was repelled by segmentary organisation, and only accepted, and superbly documented, the facts which make that theory mandatory, *à contre-coeur*. In flat contradiction of indigenous ideas, he liked to stress the discontinuity between family bonds and wider social ones. Community was good, particularist bonds within it were suspect. If he was one of the first theoreticians of segmentation, it was *malgré soi*. Some Jacobin centraliser within his soul, some follower of Rousseau who will not allow factions within the body politic, makes him seek the 'real' city, where citizens transcend special ties within it, and even to talk himself briefly into having found it, and then proceed to document with regret the undeniable persistence of segmentation within it. Masqueray's *cité* is defined by a sense of co-citizenship, preferably direct and unmediated – but he settles for the mediating sub-groups when they refuse to disappear – and by shared legislation. He is delighted to note in Mzab that, though the intervening sub-groups will not go away, at least they are deprived of independent legislative power. He notes with approval that meetings between two sub-groups are forbidden, to stop plots and alliances – though all this really documents is the vivacity of the sub-groups themselves.

He contrasts the real city, which is a genuine unit, with the mere confederation, of which he speaks disparagingly. A confederation is, as the Swiss say about Lebanon, *eine Eidgenossenschaft auf Widerruf*, a revocable sworn brotherhood. His theory of the difference between three Algerian groups is articulated in terms of this distinction. The Chaouia of the Aures only have a city at a low level, and nothing above that. The Kabyles have a city low down and two levels of organisation above that: a middle one, which is a cross between a real city and a confederation, and above that, a mere ephemeral confederation. The Mozabites have two layers of real city, no less, topped by the merest of confederations.

The abortiveness of this pursuit of the 'real city', of the really operative social level, never dawns upon him, though it is highlighted by his own superb material. In this weakness he is followed by Robert Montagne, who saw the potential which conflict has for engendering cohesion, but applied this to one level of organisation only, and continued to seek the really crucial social level, where the action is, and complained of 'decadence' when he failed to find it. Neither drew the moral from the fact (which they lucidly perceived) that sub-groups are never dissolved or swallowed up by the larger group in this kind of society, and that the larger groups generally depend on an external threat for their crystallisation. One of the few points, incidentally, on which Masqueray and Montagne disagree is that Masqueray was a trinitarian and Montagne a binarist. Montagne thought that binary opposition between *leffs* worked tolerably well, whereas Masqueray thought that it worked badly, and could be enormously improved by bringing in a third party. He thought that the success both of ancient Rome and of Beni Sgen (in Mzab) was due to their triple segmentation.

A further irony of the whole situation is that Fustel's theory of the religion–society tie-up is admirably suited for interpreting the subsequent history of modern Algeria, always provided one reads it in its transformed Durkheimian version, which gives priority to society rather than to religion. In the days when Algerians lived largely within the bounds of their segmentary communities, their Islam was the Islam of marabouts, of saintly mediators between tribal segments. When the modern world brutally transformed most of them into an anonymous pulverised mass, they shifted with impressive speed to a universalist, scripturalist, 'Reformist' Islam, which damned the erstwhile mediators (between men and God in theory, between social groups in fact), declared them to be frauds, and for the first time turned Algerians into a single community, more or less. Paraphrasing the final and culminating sentence of Fustel's famous book, one might say that a society emerged and brought forth its religion. It underwent a series of revolutions, and its faith was modified. The old society disappeared and the religion was transformed.

So Masqueray had excellent cause to ignore Fustel. Fustel's theory of religion, as it stood, made nonsense of everything Masqueray was commending. He admired the Berber community but did not wish to see it rooted in religion. We cannot expect him to anticipate the development of Algeria half a century later, still less to interpret it in terms of Durkheim's modification of Fustel, which was only published a year prior to his own premature death.

Masqueray shared some of Fustel's weaknesses. Like Fustel, he confused the developmental cycle of a community *within* an overall social order with the emergence of that order itself. The way in which a sub-community develops within a broader social system is most unlikely to be identical with the emergence of the social order as a whole from a previous condition. That could only arise if the constituent sub-communities had lived, and been roughly the same, before they combined with each other to form the overall social order. This is highly improbable. (Folk beliefs about the developmental cycle of sub-communities need correspond with neither the real cycle nor the true manner of emergence of the overall social order, of course.) In consequence, like Fustel, Masqueray sees the emergence of the order with which he is concerned as occurring from below upwards, by fusion. But this is partly a matter of exposition, and does not really lead him to ignore conflict between groups.

But when it came to the organisation of North African tribal groups, he basically got it right. He did so astonishingly early, with little aid, and whilst hampered by some of his own theoretical preconceptions. He saw the manner in which nested communities co-existed with each other, in fusion *and* in conflict. He understood the role of saintly lineages, in which he was partly anticipated by Tocqueville. (I cannot accept Fanny Colonna's charge that he underestimated their importance, for it is contradicted by evidence from within the book: he may have failed to report on the importance of a *sherif* in the Aures rising of 1879, but amongst other pieces of evidence, he describes the great importance of a saintly lineage in the very same region which had come over to the French, and he does so with both sympathy and irony.) He saw the co-existence of multi-layered egalitarian institutions with oligarchic practice; he described the manner in which personal fiefs could be built up, and the way in which they disappeared again. He observed the system before a more effective and interfering state replaced segmentation by opportunist patronage. His perception was amazingly accurate, and he is an important intellectual ancestor of modern social anthropology, whose conceptual genes are disseminated far and wide, though almost totally unrecognised by his own posterity. The resuscitation of his book by Fanny Colonna is a worthy and pious act, which deserves our gratitude. Those of us interested in social organisation of uncentralised societies, and those interested in the history of European ideas, should jointly take part in the homage at his shrine.

REFERENCES

Ageron, Charles-Robert 1968. *Les Algériens musulmans et la France*, 2 vols. Paris.

Berque, Jacques 1978. *Structures sociales du Haut-Atlas* (2nd edn). Paris.

Colonna, Fanny 1975. *Instituteurs algériens 1862–1939.* Paris.

Durkheim, Émile. 1893. *De la division du travail social.* Paris

Evans-Pritchard, E. E. 1981. *A History of Anthropological Thought*, ed. Andre Singer.

Goody, Jack 1983. *The development of the Family and Marriage in Europe.* Cambridge.

Jamous, Raymond. 1981. *Honneur et baraka.* Cambridge.

Lukes, Steven 1973, 1975. *Emile Durkheim: His Life and Work.* Harmondsworth.

4 *Zeno of Cracow* or *Revolution at Nemi* or *The Polish revenge*
A Drama in Three Acts

From the late eighteenth century onwards, the central, crucial fact facing the European mind, both perturbing and exhilarating, was the uniqueness of the newly emerging social and intellectual order of Western Europe. Europeans were struck primarily by the veritable chasm which was opening up between themselves and their own past. They also became aware of the similar gulf between themselves and the rest of the world. The two oppositions seemed linked, and it was only natural that, in due course, Europeans should come to think of their non-European contemporaries as *backward*, that is as resembling their own past. The difference and the inferiority were eventually classified as *retardation*, as a consequence of a slower progression along what might be one and the same path. One single path towards better things, along which all humanity moves, albeit at diverse speeds: that is the idea of Progress. Thus backwardness replaced evil as the generic characterisation of that which is undesirable. To call something 'evil' has come to sound archaic and vaguely comic. But *backwardness* is a form of denigration which now makes sense. It is a usable moral category, because it fits in with the way in which we see the world functioning.

The alleged fact of Progress of course also constituted a problem. It required explanation and justification. What exactly are the criteria in terms of which the world is getting so much better? – and just what might validate those criteria? These questions constitute the central preoccupation of European thought since the middle of the eighteenth century.

Two main answers are available: the Historic Plan theory, and Positivism. Historic Plan theories affirm that global development is governed by an ultimately beneficent design, and they also specify the mechanism(s) which control(s) this design. The global plan itself becomes the fount of morality and honour. These theories differ from the religious visions which may well be their ancestor, in that the mechanism(s) which they invoke operate *inside* this world, and make use of worldly forces.

By contrast, positivism (in a very generic sense) does not look at history much. Starting out from the perception that modern Europeans are superior to their own ancestors and to contemporary non-Europeans above all in their *knowledge*, it looks at knowledge itself rather than at general history. The answer it offers is in terms of what makes one particular cognitive style superior and effective. Allegedly, it is the sovereignty of experience, the eschewing of transcendent entities and explanations, which made modern knowledge so very powerful. This is the positivist explanation. Note that positivism in the narrower sense, as preached by Comte, who disseminated the term, combined the two answers. A Plan of History was articulated, its stages defined in terms of cognitive styles, with the 'positive' spirit constituting a kind of culmination of historical development.

Unquestionably, the greatest conceptual poet of history seen as a 'meaningful', purposive, upward-striving, achievement-oriented design was Hegel. World History was for him not merely world-judgement but also a world-career, a justification of human striving and suffering by a sustained upward progression – in brief, a projection of the bourgeois conception of individual life, as a career-plan of mankind; and the success of this collective career justifies all the tribulation along the way:

the only thought which philosophy brings with it is ... the idea that reason governs the world, and that world history is therefore a rational process.

The sole aim of philosophic enquiry is to eliminate the contingent... In history, we must look for a general design, the ultimate end of the world... We must bring to history the belief and conviction that the realm of the will is not at the mercy of contingency. That world history is governed by an ultimate design ... whose rationality is ... that of ... a divine and absolute reason ... is a proposition whose ... proof lies in the study of world history itself, which is the image and enactment of reason.

(*Lectures on the Philosophy of World History*, translated by H. B. Nisbet. Introduction by Duncan Forbes, Cambridge, 1975)

All this is clear enough. Whether it is also true is another matter.

Hegel brings (or codifies) the good news: history is not a pointless and chaotic story of suffering, a tale told by an idiot ... signifying nothing, but on the contrary well planned and designed, with a good end in view, so that all suffering en route is, in the end, amply justified. In this way, the belief in Progress constitutes a new theodicy, a justification of the ways of God to man, and it was and remains by far the most important theodicy of modern times. But, and here's the rub, the good news is not equally good for all of us. All humanity is saved, but some sections of it are saved more than others.

> Freedom is nothing more than knowledge and affirmation of ... law and justice, and the production of a reality which corresponds to them – i.e. the state.
> Nations may have had a long history before they finally reach their destination – i.e. that of forming themselves into states – and may even have developed considerably in some respects before they attain this goal. But ... this *pre-historical period* lies outside the scope of our present investigation, irrespective of whether a real history followed it or whether the nations in question never finally succeeded in forming themselves into states.
>
> (*Ibid.*)

This also is clear. So the good news of the purposive directedness of history is not quite so good for all men alike. Some men are not really within proper history at all, if genuine history is defined by the possession of a state of one's own, and it is by no means certain that they will ever enter it. Members of nations which have failed to form their own states are either outside history, or if within it, only enter it by courtesy of other, *echt* historical, state-endowed nations.

> To us pre-war Poles, nationality meant allegiance to the language, the traditions, the customs and the ideas of our forefathers, as distinct from any political obligations and loyalties. By two at least of the powers who had divided and annexed our territory and absorbed our population, the whole political machinery of the state was directed towards de-nationalization.
>
> (Preface by Bronislaw Malinowski, pp. vii and viii, to *The Cassubian Civilisation*, by Fr. Lorenz, Adam Fischer, and Tadeusz Lehr-Splawinski, London, 1935)

So, in this realm of rational history, there clearly are second-class citizens, fellow-travellers endowed at best with a kind of immigrant's probationary visa or entry-permit into rationality and meaningfulness, eagerly and anxiously waiting to see whether full citizenship will be conferred on them. They acquire it, if at all, by courtesy of their betters, by being generously incorporated in *their* more successful careers. Much later, Jean-Paul Sartre, who was very much a Hegelian on this matter, was rightly chided for similar arrogant ethnocentrism by Claude Lévi-Strauss in the final chapter of *The Savage Mind.*

The question which faces us here is this. How did the second-class citizens of World History react? Well, they had a number of options open to them. They could reallocate themselves individually, leave the ethnic category which consigned them to second-class status, and join one of those historic and state-endowed nations which really did belong to the mainstream of life. Or, if they could not join them, they could strive to beat them. Perhaps history had made a mistake, in excluding their own nation from front political rank, in failing to include their own ethnic group, and with a bit of a struggle, history might be obliged to mend its ways. In brief, they could become irredentist nationalists.

Either of these paths could be and was trodden by many. The assimilation of ethnically diverse populations into an educationally dominant, literate High Culture makes up much of the social history of nineteenth- and twentieth-century Europe, and Malinowski[1] for one thought that, as long as it was not done in a 'forced, regimented' manner, it took place 'spontaneously and naturally ... with an amazing ease and speed'. The establishment of new or revived national states, which turn erstwhile stateless and hence non-historic nations (by Hegel's criteria) into full members of the community of nation-states, and thus into fully paid-up participants in History, was an alternative possibility.

However, these two options do not exhaust all the available alternatives. A man might also simply repudiate the worship of history, of states, of nations. (Or some, i.e. Marxists, might revere history, but not states or nations.) Men could turn to internationalism, cosmopolitanism, seek to identify with humanity and not some segment of it, and endeavour to detach government and the maintenance of order from any links with special national interests and culture. It is obvious that, at the political level, Malinowski was attracted by this option.

This path has also been trodden by many. It may perhaps appeal specially to individualists, culturally self-made men living in a complex and mobile environment, and therefore given to identifying such a situation with the human condition in general: men who feel either that this is what human life is like, or that this is what it ought to be. But this internationalist, individualist, 'cosmopolitan' option, the cult of the Open Society, is perhaps less likely to constitute the *whole* answer for a man who knows full well, professionally, that the human condition in general is *not* like that – who knows, in virtue of his professional expertise and commitment, that a great part of mankind lives or lived in absorbing, relatively self-contained communities. In other words, can an anthropologist whole-heartedly adopt the 'cosmopolitan' model of man? He may well be cosmopolitan himself, but can he conceivably see the human condition in general in such terms? And if indeed he cannot, is he therefore condemned to embrace its best-

[1] Preface to Lorenz *et al.*, *The Cassubian Civilisation*, p. ix.

known and most favoured alternative, and indulge in the 'organic' sense of historic communities and of continuity? What if it is awkward for such a man to be a Hegelian, and yet also difficult for an anthropologist to be a positivist? What if indeed the *pan* in question is a Pole wishing to be an anthropologist? Must he choose between cosmopolitanism and Hegelianism? On the surface it would seem to be so. Or rather, it did seem so until the 1920s.

But at that point another option, subtler and more complex, came to light. It became possible to have an acute sense of community and its role in human life, or *Gemeinschaft*, and yet at the same time firmly repudiate the cult of history and any equation of full membership of humanity with the possession of a state-of-one's-own. The discovery and orchestration of this new option was a major achievement, and a most significant event in the history of European ideas.

I am trying to offer a theory of both the inner logic and the genesis of this new option, in sharp and no doubt simplified outline, and of its double role in the history of anthropology and of European sensibility. I do it largely on the basis of the two Malinowski centenary conferences in 1984, one in London, the other in Cracow. I had the good fortune to attend both conferences, and learned a vast amount from the papers which were presented. The present argument is heavily indebted to them, and I only hope that I have not misinterpreted any of the contributors.

I should like to lead you back some twenty years to an old Slavonic university town ... I could then show you a student leaving the medieval college buildings, obviously in some distress of mind, hugging, however ... *The Golden Bough*.

I had just then been ordered to abandon for a time my physical and chemical research because of ill-health, but ... no sooner had I begun to read this great work than I became ... enslaved by it. I realised then that anthropology, as presented by Sir James Frazer, is a great science, worthy of as much devotion as any of her elder and more exact sister studies, and I became bound to the services of Frazerian anthropology.

(Address delivered by Malinowski in
Liverpool in November 1925, reproduced in
Magic, Science and Religion and Other Essays,
London, 1974, 1982, pp. 93–4)

Here we have Malinowski's own account of his vision on the road to Damascus. However, if my diagnosis of the predicament of a member of a then stateless and hence un-historical nation is valid and applicable to Malinowski, even in part (was the distress of that young student due only to ill-health?), then it is far from clear why he should have found his salvation in the service of Frazer and enslavement to *The Golden Bough*. Frazer, it is true, was no Hegel. Though fascinated by divine kingship, there is no question of state-worship in his work. But on the other hand, it is obvious that his anthropology is firmly locked into an evolutionary vision. Malinowski himself tells us

[Frazer] works by the comparative method ... combined with the evolutionary approach [which] implies certain assumptions. Men ... develop gradually from a primitive level and pass through various stages of evolution ... the concept of survival is essential to the evolutionist ... As we move down the various levels of development we find the most primitive level accessible ...

(A *Scientific Theory of Culture and Other Essays*, New York, 1960, p. 187)

For such an approach a 'survival' becomes a tool of discovery, indeed *the* tool of discovery. It consists of using a fragment of something past which, precisely, was *not* fit to survive *properly*, in its full original function or essence as crucial evidence of a past condition. Once the alien is seen as the *retarded*, a science of retardation is required, and anthropology becomes that science. Those most retarded leave no records, because they are too retarded to know how to document themselves. Thus they can only be reconstructed from 'survivals', which become the main or perhaps even the only tool of investigation.

What was a strong and flourishing belief at one level, becomes a superstition in the next one.

(*Ibid.*, p. 187)

A 'survival' is a kind of fraudulent survivor, unfit and undeserving of surviving in its proper role, but remaining with us nevertheless for some accidental reason extraneous to the purposes which had originally moulded it. Like a traitor who survives from a defeated army, by performing some new service for the victors, it allows us to reconstruct an eliminated past. The turncoat may be the only witness, invaluable as an informant but not otherwise admirable. For instance, it is only thanks to Josephus' treason that Israeli nationalists know in detail just what happened at Massada, and distaste for the traitor has to fuse with gratitude to the informant. Was there not moral distaste as well as epistemological distrust in Malinowski's characterisation of 'survivals'?

Though Frazer's pervasive evolutionism is clearly inspired by

Darwin rather than by Hegel, nonetheless he too sees the global pattern of development as passing an ultimate moral verdict. *Weltgeschichte* still remains *Weltgericht*. Reason, though of a British empiricist variety this time, still guides history, albeit loosely. How pleasing can these world-historical verdicts be to a member of a nation whose political institutions have apparently *not* been fit to survive? The historic Polish state, an elective monarchy which had conferred excessive powers on the gentry, especially the notorious *liberum veto*, had conclusively demonstrated its own unfitness to survive in the eighteenth-century age of centralisation. All this being so, why should Malinowski find so much joy in Frazer?

This might be a troubling question, were it the case that Malinowski saw himself as a simple perpetuator, faithful guardian of Frazerian views. But of course he was not. He succeeded Frazer, and he also supplanted and killed him. Malinowski himself is eloquent:

> The death of James George Frazer, on May 7, 1941, symbolizes the end of a epoch. Frazer was the last survivor of British classical anthropology.
>
> *(Ibid.,* p. 179)

If the King was dead, there could be no shadow of doubt about the identity of the new King. Quite obviously Malinowski conceived his own relationship to Frazer to be that of the successive priests at Nemi, as Ian Jarvie pointed out long ago. If the Frazerian regime perished with Frazer, then the identity of the new priest-king was manifest. A new regime was due to be inaugurated at Nemi. Note the weapon with which the old priest was slain. The concept of *survival* had been the cornerstone of the Frazerian edifice. Its exclusion was equally central to the Malinowskian style.

> The real harm done by the concept of survival in anthropology consists in the fact that it functions ... as a spurious methodological device in the reconstruction of evolutionary series... Take any example of 'survival'. You will find, first and foremost, that the survival nature of the alleged cultural 'hangover' is due primarily to an incomplete analysis of the facts... The real harm done by this concept was to retard effective field-work. Instead of searching for the present-day function of any cultural fact, the observer was merely satisfied in reaching a rigid, self-contained entity.
>
> *(Ibid.,* pp. 29–31)

It is important to repeat that *survival* is not merely a tool of discovery, it is also an implicit evaluation. That which is a 'survival' has not really survived, not in its real essence; it is but an echo of something that was not fit to survive. By destroying the methodological tool, Malinowski also in effect destroyed the philosophy of history and the ethic which was implicit in it and inextricably bound up with it. Should we see him as deliberately doing both these things? At that point, anthropology ceases to be the science of retardation. A tool of investigation – 'survivals' – and an evaluation intimately linked to it are jointly disregarded.

It is also worth looking carefully at just how he managed to do it, and yet be or remain an anthropologist. Now, after Malinowski, his characteristic fusion of a sense of culture and of the interdependence of institutions, with a-historicism, may not seem so difficult or implausible. But it indicates a lack of historical imagination, a kind of ethnocentrism-in-time, not to see just how difficult and eccentric this combination of ideas must have seemed once.

The quarrel between diachronists and synchronists did not begin with Malinowski. On the contrary, it pervaded the famous *Methoden-streit*. Roughly speaking, the synchronists were those imbued with the kind of approach associated with neo-classical economics: societies are the by-products of the intentions and beliefs of individuals, rather in the way in which a market price results from the demand and supply schedules of individuals. The interaction of present needs with present resources is all we really need. By contrast, the diachronists had a sense of historic continuities, or 'organic' interdependence and of latent, hidden functions, of the unconscious cunning of institutions, of moral climates working *on* individual choices. As long as this was the line-up, it was not at all easy to be an anthropologist *and* a synchronist. Anthropologists were then by nature diachronists, just as formal economists were impelled towards synchronicism. Anthropology was *born* of an attempt to use the present as evidence of our past. At the same time, it was also not easy to be both a diachronist and a Pole, for reasons stated. Yet Malinowski was a Pole, and he wanted to be an anthropologist. So each of the two available options was closed to him, twice over perhaps. What was to be done?

There was a way out, and Malinowski found it. In his essay in *Man and Culture*,[2] Edmund Leach credits Malinowski with an intellectual lineage, that of Jamesian Pragmatism.

It is my thesis that Malinowski found this body of theory in the Pragmatism of William James. It was precisely in the period around 1910, when Malinowski first came to England ... that James' philosophy had its maximum vogue ...

(p. 121)

As a piece of history, this would seem to be highly speculative: is there

---

[2]   Ed. R. Firth, London, 1957, p. 121.

much evidence that Malinowski studied William James? Nevertheless, a valid insight is contained in Leach's claim. He correctly identifies the ideas which Malinowski seized on, but attaches the wrong person's name to them.

A recent extremely perceptive commentator [Gallie 1952, p. 25] has summarized James' position thus: 'First, from the plausible thesis that biological interests underlie ... all our thinking, he [James] passed to the more exciting ... thesis that the sole function of thought is to satisfy certain interests of the organism, and that truth consists in such thinking as satisfies those interests.' Substitute *behaviour* and *behaving* for *thought* and *thinking* in this quotation and we have in a nutshell the whole essence of Malinowski's functionalism.

(p. 122)

But it does not matter too much whether Malinowski had really read and been influenced by William James. James had no monopoly of these views. Similar ideas are also to be found in Ernst Mach, and the great influence of Mach on Malinowski is fully documented. Leach spotted the right intellectual connections, even if he attached the wrong personal name to it. By 1910, Malinowski had completed and presented his dissertation on Ernst Mach, and thus had thoroughly familiarised himself with ideas which he could have later obtained from William James; but it is obvious that he did not need to receive them from that source. He arrived fully equipped with them.

Whilst there appears to be no evidence that Malinowski was influenced by James, Andrzej Paluch, Andrzej Flis and others have now clearly shown and analysed Malinowski's preoccupation with Ernst Mach.[3] Two of Mach's ideas are specially relevant. They are not altogether independent of each other. The first is an idea not specially stressed by Flis, but familiar to anglophone philosophers, who are liable to think of Mach as an ultra-positivist, a man who influenced Bertrand Russell, a man who preached the replacement of *surmised* unobservable entities by *constructs* out of observable ones. The bricks of our world were to be made out of accessible data, rather than be precariously *inferred* from them. Mach taught a kind of extreme immanentism or anti-transcendentalism, and this of course earned him a book-length critique by Lenin, who linked him to Bishop Berkeley.

The second idea conspicuously present in Mach is also absolutely central to Malinowski's doctoral dissertation of 1908, as Flis underscores. It is, he says, the second feature of the neo-positivistic school of Avenarius and Mach which preoccupied Malinowski. It is the view, as Flis puts it, that knowledge

3 Cf. especially *Miedszy Dwoma Swiatami* ('Between Two Worlds'), ed. Grazyna Kubica and Janusz Mucha (Warsaw and Cracow, 1985); translation forthcoming, Cambridge.

does not reflect, does not ... contemplate the world; [it] is a response to bio-logical human needs. Cognisance means active adaptation, a practical-vital activity throughout.

A further, third idea, as listed by Flis, is very closely linked to the second. In Flis's words again:

The problem of the validity of knowledge does not refer to the transcendental relation between knowledge and the acting man. Valid knowledge is ... knowledge attained by the least effort and permitting the fullest possible adaptation to the world.

I am inclined to lump together the second and the third idea, which Flis and presumably Malinowski separated out into two distinct points, and to refer to them jointly as the Pragmatist Assumption. It is of course precisely this that, according to Leach, Malinowski had found in William James. We now see that the Jamesian-origin hypothesis not merely lacks supporting evidence, but is unnecessary: these ideas were clearly present in Mach, and constituted the central theme of Malinowski's doctoral dissertation. William James, like the deity, is a redundant hypothesis.

If we call this part of Mach (subdivided into the two points by Flis) the Pragmatist Assumption, then the anti-transcendentalist, instrumental-constructivist part of his views can be called the Positivist Assumption. The two assumptions are closely linked. Positivism insists that abstract concepts should *not* be treated as names of transcendent entities; Pragmatism insists that they should be treated as names of adaptive functions, of devices satisfying the organism's needs. One of these tendencies deprives abstract concepts of their old status, the other endows them with a new role. It is in fact rather hard to see how these two assumptions could manage without each other. Positivism without Pragmatism is sadly incomplete: if abstract terms are not names of entities, why do we use them so much and find them so indispensable? Pragmatism without positivism is otiose: if abstract terms really were names of real and important entities, what need for invoking biology and adaptation to explain why our thought is so pervasively haunted by them?

Malinowski's thought was indeed pervaded, not to say dominated, by *both* the Positivist and the Pragmatist assumptions. That this was so when he was writing his dissertation is amply established by what Flis tells us. But if we assume that it continued to be so thereafter, we can simultaneously explain (a) how he reached the kind of position in social anthropology which in fact he did reach, and (b) how he provided a way for coping with the general problem situation facing European thought in his age.

It must be remembered that in central and Eastern Europe, the past was profoundly problematic. In the West, Ernest Renan perceptively pointed out how France was made, not by shared memories, but by a shared amnesia, and he opposed the intrusion of ethnology in politics: will, not ethnography, was to be the basis of the state, and Malinowski clearly thought much the same. The English, likewise, did not feel that their identity was at the mercy of mediaevalists. But in the eastern half of Europe, things were different. The Czechs, for instance, tried to buttress their own identity and existence by a mediaeval epos which was shown to be a forgery during the period when Malinowski was growing up. The Russians possess a similar piece of literature whose status continues to be disputed to this day. The manipulation of the past for current political purposes pervaded scholarly disputes, and Malinowski must have been thoroughly familiar with these debates. His comments on the political significance of Cassubian ethnography are clear and explicit.[4]

There cannot be much serious doubt concerning the motives of his a-historicism in anthropology: it enabled him to dispose of the historicising magpie Frazer twice over, by instituting synchronist functionalism as the new dominant style. Frazer was past-oriented *and* atomistic, fragmentary in his methods: 'survivals' isolated from their context and each other were interpreted so as to reconstruct the past. By negating him on both scores – denial both of their isolability and the relevance of the past – one could end up with a synchronist-holistic position that was radically new. Mach's anti-transcendentalism underwrote the synchronicism, his biological position underwrote the holism, by urging one to see the meaning of activities in the service they rendered to a biological or social whole. As an anthropologist, Malinowski used and fused both these elements. Did he do the same as a Pole?

We may speculate whether or in what way Malinowski also welcomed the implications of a-historicism for his home situation, so to speak. There can hardly be any doubt but that he saw what those implications were, and understood the way in which the new vision erased certain judgements and imperatives. He *might* have had either of at least two motives, a national or a personal one. His view of history firmly cancels any Hegelian judgement on an 'un-historical nation',

---

[4] Preface to Lorenz *et al.*, *The Cassubian Civilisation*, p. vii.

and obliterates the stigma. Equally, it deprives history of its authority as taskmaster, a taskmaster who, in Poland, spoke with an irritatingly Delphic ambiguity. In the First World War, some Poles formed a legion to help the Austrians drive out the Muscovites, but others considered doing the very opposite. A man who does neither, and goes to the Trobriands instead, might welcome a rationale for cocking a snook at history. We do not know whether either of these motives actuated him. We do not know whether he wished to remain loyal to Poland or to the *Imperator* under whose *auspiciis* his dissertation on Mach and the economy (in effect, functionality) of thought had been so well received and honoured. Unless documents exist which make his motives clearer, we may never know. But the Preface to *The Cassubian Civilisation* tells us a fair amount:

I should like to put it here on record that no honest and sincere Pole would ever have given anything but praise to the political regime of the old Dual Monarchy. Pre-war Austria in its federal constitution presented, in my opinion, a sound solution to all minority problems. It was a model of a miniature League of Nations.

(p. viii)

Malinowski strove to separate love of native culture from political obligation. As Andrzej Flis[5] puts it: 'Thus, in *Freedom and Civilisation*, Malinowski contrasts ... the culture of a national community with the aggression and destruction rooted in the state organisation.' If History prefers to act through states and spurns state-less cultures, such a distinction becomes difficult to uphold. Can a culture really survive unless endowed with its own state organisation?

What is clear in any case is that very good reasons were available, which Malinowski must have fully appreciated, whether or not they actually motivated him, for seeing history as the corrupt servant of present interests, rather than as an Authority. Long before Orwell, he had taught us how the present controls the past. These reasons for seeing this were also rooted in the European, and not just the Trobriand, situation. Malinowskian themes continue to be very conspicuous in the streets of Cracow to this day. A massive granite statuary commemorates the victory of the Poles over the Teutonic Order at Tannenberg. After their victory in 1939, the Germans demolished the monument. The Poles rebuilt it after 1945. You may say that the

---

[5] 'Bronislav Malinowski's Sociology and Social Anthropology', in P. Sztompka (ed.), *Masters of Polish Sociology*, Wrocław, 1984, p. 159.

objective events of 1410 are unaffected by the demolitions and recon-
structions. But the *visibility* of those events is a function of the *present*
distribution of power.

The speculation about his motives is of course related to another
debate, concerning the relative influence of positivism and 'modernism' on Malinowski. Paluch and Flis have stressed the positivistic,
Machian element, which is easy to document from Malinowski's dissertation; their picture has been, not opposed outright, but amended
by I. Strenski[6] and by Jan Jerschina. Modernism or neo-romanticism
was an intoxicating witches' brew made up of many diverse elements;
whereas the neat and crisp logical connection between Mach's central
ideas, his immanentist and functional view of cognition, and Malinowski's anthropological practice, are easy to demonstrate. Given the
clear logical nexus, it almost does not matter whether or to what extent
Malinowski spelt it out to himself.

By contrast, it is difficult to trace clear and exclusive links between
the protean and turbulent neo-romantic sentiments and Malinowski's
views or indeed any other position. Certainly, the holistic view of culture might be traced to this source. (Paluch has challenged the suggestion of Hegelian influence, stressing that there is no evidence for
it. This may well be so. But Hegelian-type ideas, implying a holistic
reification of culture, were so well diffused in the nineteenth century
that it hardly matters just which one of the many formulations
specially marked Malinowski. The use of 'Hegel' as a code word for
these ideas seems to me a reasonable practice.) But if we accept Jan
Jerschina's plausible claim that the modernist movement had a great
hold over the feelings of the intellectuals in Cracow and Zakopane,
and that the repudiation of Hegelian historicism was an important
element in it, this does strengthen the surmise that Malinowski's
synchronism was rooted not merely in the methodological problem
situation in the Trobriands, but equally in the cultural and political
situation of Poland.

The past is a foreign country; they do things differently there. But it is
not merely a foreign country. It is also, when you come to think of it, a
hidden and inaccessible one. You can know it only through the marks
it has left in the present. But how do you know that those marks are
really linked to the past? To establish that such a link truly obtains, you
would need to have before you *both* the past *and* its marks in the present, so as to check their congruence. But, on your own admission, you
only have the marks in the present. As that is *all* you have, you can

never really check whether the connection truly holds. So, the past is for ever hidden and inaccessible.

The proof is entirely cogent. Bertrand Russell at one time toyed with the conundrum 'How can one know that the world was not created five minutes ago, complete with records and memories?' The answer is that you cannot possibly know that this is not so. (Some anti-Darwinian Creationists uphold, with perfect consistency, a version of precisely this position: God created the world, complete with the as-if pattern of fossils, and even endowed Adam with a navel, *as-if* he had been born in the normal way, rather than created as an adult without benefit of a genitrix.)

This is but one of a group of structurally similar arguments, which positivists must raise against the use and invocation of unobservables. The past is merely one species of unobservable. The rejection of the unobservable substrate of matter leads to phenomenalism: 'matter' is no more than the permanent possibility of sensation. The rejection of unobservable other minds leads to behaviourism: 'other minds' merely are the observable behaviour pattern of other people. And so on.

The past is just as unobservable as other minds or 'substance', the alleged persistent carrier-substrate of observable properties. It deserves the same reductionist treatment, the same elimination. One positivist who endeavoured at one stage to be fully consistent on this point was A. J. Ayer.[7] Statements about the past were to be reduced to statements about the present phenomena, such as are normally treated as 'marks' (*survivals?*) of the past. Statements about the Battle of Hastings are really statements about what you may find in archives or on tapestries at Bayeux, etc. Ayer found it impossible to maintain this view, and in due course reformulated his position.[8] We feel we *know* that the past once was the present, and that it once 'really' happened, just as we feel we know from our own experience that one mind at least is more than mere behaviour. It is psychologically more difficult to uphold such positivist reductionism with respect to either the past or other minds than it is with respect to material substance.

Ayer, as far as I know, had no motive to seek the elimination, the reduction of the past, other than a general striving for a consistent positivist, Machian position. Ayer did not in any way have it in specially for the past. If the past were allowed to have an independent existence after all, his consistency and hence his logical amour propre might suffer in some small measure, but that was all. The past as such was no more noxious than any other species of unobservable. One more or less, what's the odds?

7 A. J. Ayer, *Language, Truth and Logic*, Harmondsworth, 1971, p. 135.
8 *Ibid.*, p. 29.

Suppose, however, that there is a man independently known to be an ardent Machian, and who does have strong and multiple motives for wishing to be rid of all the past, to make the past unreal or irrelevant. Suppose such a man lives in an intellectual climate in which both history and the state are revered and conjoined to each other, and that he belongs to a nation whom history has deprived of its own state and thus relegated to sub-historical status. Suppose furthermore he wishes to make his mark in a field – anthropology – where evidence about the past is often of very poor quality, and in which the speculative exploitation of it has been pushed as far as it can usefully go (and probably much further), but where, on the other hand, a resolute synchronicism would constitute a striking new style and a dramatic innovation, and one admirably fitted to displacing sharply and for ever the dying king of a historicising anthropology (Frazer) by highlighting his methodological inadequacy? What then? Would not such a man remember, and deploy to the utmost, those very Machian ideas on which he had worked so hard, and with such outstanding recognition, in his doctoral dissertation?

But there is more to it than that. Such a man would not restrict himself to the use of the negative, reductionist, transcendence-eliminating positivist constituent of the Machian doctrine. He would be just as attracted by the positive, pragmatist, instrumental element in it. The King is dead, long live the King. The past is irrelevant, and the past is supremely important. But it is no longer the same past. It is not the past as an echo, mark, 'survival' of the past: it is the real past, real in the sense of being endowed with a function in the present. Quite literally, it has a *presence*. Sir Raymond Firth writes in what I take to be the absolutely authentic Malinowskian spirit when he says

Malinowski was ... careful to distinguish his approval of 'real history' from his rejection of 'speculative history' so often current at the time. In 1938 he wrote ... 'I should be, of course, very interested in ... all the real history the Agoni still know ... my dislike of the historical method does not in any way touch real history. In fact, if you take the Master's [i.e. Malinowski's own] theory of myth and legend, whether it be true or not, you will see that the influence of historical tradition on present life is of the greatest importance.'

('Malinowski and the History of Social Anthropology', in *Miedszy Dwoma Swiatami* and forthcoming translation.)

The phrase 'speculative history' in this passage leads one at first to expect that it will be contrasted with documented, accurate history.

Not a bit of it. As the passage proceeds, it becomes manifest that accuracy of history as a set of statements about the past is neither here nor there. What makes history *real* is its genuine influence on present life.

But if that influence is genuine, accuracy is redundant; if that influence is absent, accuracy is insufficient. Either way, genuine reference to past events is irrelevant. And just in case there is any doubt left in anyone's mind, Malinowski explicitly assimilates *real* history to myth and legend, as interpreted by himself, i.e. as a set of charters from present practices. All this of course is an application of the Machian attitude to unobservables in general: they are to be seen in terms of their impact on observables, and in the end, in terms of that impact alone, which exhausts their essence. The unobservable is and ought to be a slave of the observable. (It is a construct from it.) The past is but the living role of the past in the present.

Note that there is nothing in the very least opportunistic and *ad hoc* about Malinowski's Machismo here. He does not fish out a philosophical theory about the irrelevance of the past, just because he happens to be interested in the ethnographic present, and happens to be working on an illiterate society. Far from it: he is behaving as a consistent Machian, as one whose thesis on Mach has been received *sub auspiciis Imperatoris*, and was the only dissertation to be so honoured in Cracow in 1908, and one who knew and admired what Mach had said, and understood what it implied. His philosophical heritage was ready and ideally suited for his anthropological tasks. He was not meting out one kind of treatment to history and another one to more favoured kinds of knowledge: history was valid in virtue of – and only in virtue of – satisfying a current need. It was not treated either less or more favourably than any other kind of cognitive claim. In the light of such a philosophy, we can see that it is not at all paradoxical to use the phrase '*real* history' not for accurately documented statements about the past, but on the contrary for statements effectively functional *in the present*, even though purporting to be about the past. Thus current functionality overrules and renders irrelevant historic veridicality. Present function trumps historic reference.

Malinowski's 'Charter' theory of myth and legend must in all consistency be applied to all statements about the past. It is strongly suggested both by the positivist elimination of explanations in terms of unobservables *and* by the positive pragmatist account of truth as functionality. The essence of statements is not that they refer to external realities, but that they fulfil a function in social life. In his dissertation of 1908, he had commented on both these doctrines; in his anthropological practice, he came to implement them.

The inaccessibility of the past is the application of a familiar positivist-reductionist formula: X is inaccessible, though the manifestations of X are important in our life. The manifestations are important, but the entity *of which* they are the alleged manifestations is out of our cognitive reach: does it not follow that the manifestations themselves are all that really matters, and that the alleged Essence Beyond is but a useful notational device, a mere functional convenience?

The philosopher Saul Kripke has called this strategy the reversal of priorities,[9] and listed a whole series of its applications. Malinowski dramatically reversed the priorities between great historical events and current practices. We do not perform the acts we perform because we believe that certain things had happened: we believe that certain crucial events had happened because we do what we do. England does not have a great landed aristocracy because of the Battle of Hastings. The Battle of Hastings is invoked and remembered because England has a great landed aristocracy.

But Malinowski did not merely reverse some priorities *within* a discipline: he turned a whole discipline on its head, by reversing its central and defining priorities. Anthropology was no longer to be a time-machine for visiting the past, a study of retardations, fuelled by survivals: it was to be a tool for investigating the ethnographic present, in which beliefs about the past are seen as functionally subservient to current, present needs. Anthropology had previously been survival-oriented twice over. Its interest in simpler societies, which defined the subject, had been inspired by seeing them as survivals from our own past. But, imbued with this spirit, if something required explanation *in* an archaic society, it was seen as a survival twice over, a left-over from something more archaic still, in a kind of historic pluperfect tense. Malinowski eliminated both kinds of survival-hunting with one stone. Neither simpler societies nor institutions within them were to be seen as survivals. The reasons for his synchronism were different from (and I think better than) those which can be credited to *structuralisme* later.

The argument from inaccessibility of the past is only one of a number of ways towards the desired conclusion. Malinowski's position is a bit confusing because here, as at other points, the co-presence of a number of not always fully compatible considerations muddies this issue.

One complication is that the inaccessibility of the past is both contingent, empirical, *and* also necessary. It is just a contingent fact that pre-literate societies have few if any reliable records of the past. It is a

[9] *Wittgenstein on Rules and Private Language*, Cambridge (Mass.), 1982.

necessary truth (if true at all) that the past can only be apprehended through the marks it leaves in the present, whatever they may be (documents, monuments, institutions), and that these marks can then be treated as existing and operating here/now, thereby making the past-proper redundant.

But another path to a similar conclusion leads through the demonstration of the impossibility of change. As is well known, cogent proofs exist showing that change is impossible. They were elaborated by Zeno of Elea in the fifth century BC. Take this by way of example: any body occupies a space equivalent to its own size. Whilst it occupies that fixed space, the body is, naturally, at rest. An arrow in flight (or indeed at any time) can only occupy such a limited space at any given moment, i.e. a space equivalent to its own size. But whilst occupying this delimited and fixed space, it cannot be in motion, it cannot be in flight. It cannot occupy a space larger than itself. Ergo, it cannot be in motion. Q.E.D. As a character in a Tom Stoppard play wrily observes, evidently Saint Sebastian died of fright.

Social change is presumably but a species of motion, so this argument (and the others deployed by Zeno) could simply be applied to social change as a sub-species of change or motion in general. But it is more illuminating to work out a variant of Zeno's argument directly in terms of social motion. At any given time, a society is a system of institutions, practices, relations or whatever which at that particular time mutually constrain each other to be what they are, or if you like, occupy the available social space. The things that are done at that time are the things that are done; so, at any given time, a society is what it is, and it is not changing. But as this argument applies equally to any time, it follows that societies never change, just as arrows never fly.

Now all this is not simply a logical paradox, a mind-twister: the impossibility of change is a doctrine which has often been credited to functionalism, usually by its critics, with a view to using it as a reductio ad absurdum. Here we face the bewildering conflation of a formal and of a substantive argument. It is an empirical claim (presumably true of some occasions and false on others) that social systems are self-maintaining, that they contain mechanisms ensuring their own fairly stable self-perpetuation; and there also exists a formal argument, sketched out above, showing that stability is the law of all things at all times...

Curiously enough, it is the formal argument, with its unacceptably paradoxical conclusion, which may well be the more valuable, important and illuminating. To my knowledge, it was never formally elaborated by Malinowski himself: if it had been, he would have had to distinguish between his formal and his empirical claims, and I don't think he ever did that. Yet, though not formally elaborated, the spirit of this formal argument pervades his attitude to society and to its investigation. It really constitutes the point of the quotation invoked by Firth above. It is the present which constrains the present: it is only the present which can do so, for only the present *is* present, is real. The past-within-the-present can be significant, and indeed is significant and receives praise, as 'real' history; but the past that is gone is dead and absent and cannot constrain anything.[10]

This consideration pervades the spirit of synchronist, Malinowskian anthropology. The fact that it can be articulated, in its simplest form, as an absurdity – there is and can be no social change – should not lead one to ignore the fact that, when formulated properly, it contains an important element of truth. The location of situations in a temporal sequence, as such, neither explains nor constrains anything. Forces or laws (whichever terminology is employed) alone can explain why one situation can account for a subsequent one, irrespective of whether the two situations are identical (thus exemplifying stability) or not (thus exemplifying change). The forces (or laws) must be operative *at the time* at which the effect-to-be-explained actually occurs. Thus in one very important sense, all explanation is synchronic, whether or not the situation-to-be-explained is a stable or an unstable one.

Malinowskian a-historicism or synchronism is complex and multi-layered. The strata that are buried under the surface deserve to be seen separately. There are, as far as I can see, at least four distinct strata:

(1)   The Argument from Rigour. In pre-literate societies, records are lacking, and hence, to explain current institutions in terms of the past is speculative, and above all circular.

(2)   The Functionalist Argument. Many societies, but in particular some simpler societies, are stable, and in a condition of self-perpetuating equilibrium. Hence their social condition is best explained by highlighting the manner of that self-perpetuation.

(3)   The Machian or anti-transcendentalist Argument. The past as

---

10   This formulation, which I have come across on occasion amongst Malinowskian anthropologists, contains the quite mistaken suggestion that the past can only act in the present through memory, through being remembered. This of course is not so. The plausible, and perhaps tautological suggestion, that the past can only operate on the present if incarnated in it, is represented by some kind of intertemporal ambassador, should not be confused with the false suggestion that this ambassador can speak only through memory, whether individual or collective.

such is inherently unobservable. *Only* its marks in the present, the past-in-the-present, are observable. Hence the-past-in-the-present is the 'real' past, the only kind of past acceptable to a good empiricist.

(4)   The Zenonic Argument. Any system is responsive only to contemporary constraints, which can and do act on it, but it cannot be responsive to the past or the future, which are both literally absent. (Even the threat of future deterrents can only act if *perceived* now, in the present.) Hence any system can only be explained synchronically

The four intertwined positions can be represented on a diagram, which follows. There are two epistemological considerations (concerned with the nature of available evidence), and two substantive ones (concerned with the nature of societies). There are two formal arguments (valid *a priori* if valid at all), and two contingent ones (dependent on how things turn out in this world). These two oppositions cut across each other, giving us four distinguishable arguments.

	Epistemological	*Substantive*
Contingent	(1) Argument for Rigour	(2) Functionalism proper
Formal	(3) Mach	(4) Zeno

Arguments (1) and (2) are contingent, depending, in the case of (1), on what kind of evidence is available in pre-literate societies, and, in the case of (2), on how or whether things actually function, on whether a given society is indeed self-perpetuating or not. Arguments (3) and (4) are formal or necessary, if valid at all. Arguments (1) and (3) are epistemological, and concern the nature of the available *evidence*. Correspondingly, (2) and (4) are substantive, and concern the nature of *society*.

Arguments (1) and (2) are in brazen contradiction to each other.[11] You cannot both say that societies are stable, which is to say covertly (though not even very covertly) that their past is like their present, *and* say that you are not entitled to make assertions about their past for lack of documentation. Either one or the other. Malinowski's functionalism is open to the charge that it covertly indulges in just as much speculation about the past as Frazer ever did: it just happens to be different speculation (one attributing stability rather than change), that is all. Moreover, the two affirmations apply, as plausible approximations, to whole classes of societies, but *not to the same ones*: not all

[11]   This was noted by Edmund Leach. See *Man and Culture*, ed. R. Firth, p. 126.

simple pre-literate societies are stable. Not all literate societies are unstable. Some societies, however, are both stable and pre-literate.

Affirmation (4) contains a valid and important insight – only contemporary constraints, in one sense, can ever be operative – but it does lead to an absurdly paradoxical corollary – that change is impossible, because, if the currently operative constraints impose a given situation now, they must also do it at the next instant, and so on for ever. This absurd corollary must somehow be detached from the valid premisses. It will presumably be no harder to do this in social studies than it was in natural science. There was·no reason to suppose that the study of society would be exempt from Zeno's arguments. We'll have to live with them, or ignore them, just as natural scientists do.

So the famous paradoxes of Zeno, in their general form, apply to social reality as much as to any other; but in their general form we may as well leave them to the philosophers of mathematics who normally handle them. But the paradoxicality of the denial of change is perhaps more acute in the social sphere than elsewhere. What does it mean to say that a *society* is 'stable'?

In nature, 'stability' has an intuitive and literal meaning. Heavy objects deposited on a firm and level surface are normally expected to remain where they were placed. If they retain the same position and shape as they had when they were deposited, this normally calls for no further explanation: their stability is self-explanatory. Had they been moved, or had dents appeared in them – now, that *would* have required explanation. Within the common-sense physics that is built into daily speech and life, stability of heavy objects, made of firm materials, constitutes a kind of conceptual base-line: conformity to it requires no further explanation, but deviations from it do. But what is the situation in the social realm? What base-line do we have there?

Note first of all that the stability in the social sphere simply does not mean, as it does in the physical realm, literal inertness. Heavy material objects are literally inert unless a great deal of force is applied to them. But when we attribute stability to social institutions or practices, what we mean is that the same *activities* are performed repeatedly, though sometimes separated by considerable intervals of time. If it is the case, for instance, that the Christmas ritual in a given country has remained 'stable' for a long time, this does not mean that a set of people have remained inert: it means, on the contrary, that some people actively *do* the same or similar things, come December, having done quite different things for the previous eleven months. Furthermore, there is a turnover in the performing personnel. Some constraints must be operative to make them return to the same activity, and to get themselves replaced by new participants, and to keep the activity within such limits as to ensure that it resembles the corresponding activity of previous years. Stability manifestly requires explanation. It is an achievement rather than a gift of nature.

In natural science, it took a certain sophistication to perceive that inertness is not self-explanatory, that it requires explanation just as much as change does. In social life it is immediately obvious, once one reflects on it. And this perhaps brings us closest to appreciating the real achievement of synchronist functionalism: its doctrine of stability (in so far as it is empirical at all), though false (or at best a very partial half-truth), by requiring anthropologists, field-workers, to account for the present situation in terms of contemporary constraints (instead of circular historical just-so stories), *in effect obliged them to treat stability as a problem which requires explanation.*

Under the apparent dogma of stability and self-maintenance, there is in reality a most *un*dogmatic requirement *that stability be explained*. It placed very salutary restrictions on the way in which such explanations might be constructed. Evolutionism had explained change in a circular fashion, and it had barely explained stability *at all*. Malinowski's implicit requirement that the present be explained by the present was at least as valuable as Durkheim's explicit injunction that the social be explained by the social. In the form of a dogma, he had in reality highlighted a problem. Evolutionism or historicism had been content to locate institutions in a grand Series of developments, to see societies at any given time as rungs on an evolutionary ladder. They had very low standards of explaining either each rung or the links between them.

Evolutionist anthropology had, naively, inherited the base-line expectation of stability from traditional visions, which had treated stability as both a moral and conceptual norm. Led into social theorising by the perception of radical change, it had, many times over, rather low standards of what was to count as an explanation. Stability continued to be treated as self-explanatory, and change was explained by evolutionary schemata which had a variety of defects: they were too abstract to handle the constraints really operative in daily life; the relationship of evidence to theory was circular, with the theory inventing the evidence which then sustained it; and they were uncritical in their invocation of the forces or laws which were supposedly responsible for the changes. A synchronistic approach then raised the level of explanatory rigour immensely.

There is a profound irony about all this. Functionalism has been accused of being politically reactionary because it inculcated a sense of social stability. By encouraging people to seek out hidden latent functions, it was said, it encouraged them to accept social situations which at the merely manifest level might have aroused indignation and even resistance. A science which delights in the discovery of latent functions cannot pretend to be value-free, the argument runs. Every irrationality, inequality, oppression which is ascribed its latent purpose is thereby given a kind of clean bill of health and sheltered from reform... On the surface, no doubt there is an element of truth in all this. But the deeper and more permanent effect of the functionalist vision seems to me to be the very opposite: the problematic nature of stability is highlighted. It ceases to be a base-line that is more or less taken for granted. Synchronicism was a mistake of genius.

I am very sceptical about the frequently made charge that functionalist anthropology served colonialism. If imperialism required an ideology with which to justify indirect rule, it could always find the notion of latent function, with which to whitewash otherwise repugnant institutions, *nur mit ein bisschen anderen Worten*, in Edmund Burke. In the French Empire, the Gallieni/Lyautey tradition developed similar ideas without any help from the London School of Economics.

But if anthropology did not serve colonialism, there can be no doubt but that colonialism served and suited anthropology. The period between the wars was the time when the overseas empires were at their most stable and secure. (Only Spain, then a poor-white nation, managed to suffer a colonial defeat in this period.) The empires provided a safe reservoir of many well-preserved cultures. A technique for tapping this intellectual wealth was badly needed. It is a striking fact that not a single anthropologist who ventured among the savages in this period lost his life in the process. (This ceased to be true when decolonialisation came.) Anthropologists were effectively helped as well as safe: a fieldworker of my acquaintance told me once how he overcame lack of cooperation amongst his informants. He gave a cocktail party to which he also invited the colonial Governor, with whom he naturally had a university link. After the party, informants became eagerly cooperative. Though its political usefulness *to* imperialism seems to me eminently doubtful, there can be no doubt that Malinowskian anthropology was ideally suited for making the best possible use *of* the research potential of empires. Evolutionist research would have led to much speculative nonsense. The value of functionalist fieldwork is unquestionable.

Of course, this half-dazzling, half-confused medley of ideas about time, change and history would not have had the impact that it has had, nor would it have deserved it, had it not been presented in the context of outstanding fieldwork, which highlighted the kind of fruit that the synchronic functional method could yield. Once the lesson is learned, however, the stability hypothesis can easily be dropped. Once properly practised, this kind of synchronistic accountancy of the way in which diverse institutional constraints keep a society either stable *or* unstable can be applied whether or not stability obtains.

This was the real achievement of Malinowski. The historicising or evolutionary outlook had widely disseminated a new conceptual base-line, replacing the old paradigm, which had given the impression that it could explain social institutions and structures above all by locating them along an alleged evolutionary path. Though it had some ideas about what the mechanics of propulsion along that path were, its prac-titioners tended to take those mechanics far too much for granted, and failed to scrutinise them very carefully: locating the alleged path of de-velopment took up most of their time. Take Frazer as an example: the mechanics of the supposed changes in belief Frazer basically took over from Hume's associationist psychology. Frazer was shockingly lax when it came to demonstrating the solution to what officially was his main problem, the mystery of the rule of succession at Nemi: he was content with showing certain possible associations which would lead gradually to the reported practice.

He starts with the problem of how can one explain the strange rule of succession which decrees that only he who kills the priest at Nemi may succeed him. That the rule existed is historically documented. Frazer ends by inferring an even earlier stage, which is not documen-ted, when the priest had to be not merely killed but ritually burned. An institution we do not understand is explained by an earlier one still for which we have no evidence!

Now grounds have been shown for believing that the priest of the Arician grove ... personified the tree on which grew the Golden Bough... It is, therefore, easy to understand why, before he could be slain, it was necessary to break the Golden Bough... And to complete the parallel, it is only necessary to suppose that the King of the Wood was formerly burned, dead or alive ... and thus it would be in a great fire of oak that the King of the Wood formerly met his end.

(J. G. Frazer, The Golden Bough, abridged
edition, London, 1957, p. 921)

The explanans is parasitic on the explanandum which it is meant to illuminate... If there is any mitigation of this brazen circularity, it is in the accumulation of evidence showing that if the earlier practice had indeed prevailed, it would have exemplified principles of reasoning, which Frazer also claimed to find in many other beliefs and institutions, concerning which evidence was available. But the double pliability, of selection and interpretation, makes it easy to find the principles required. Frazer himself used Humean psychology, but his material fits in even better with a Jungian approach. The circularity remains even if slightly mitigated, but the explanation is also curiously vacuous: in what way was the candidate for the perilous hieratic position constrained or influenced by an earlier situation, of which he was presumably quite ignorant, as Frazer had to reconstruct it speculatively on the basis of distant comparative data?

There is a two-dimensional cardboard quality about Frazer's explanations when put alongside those of Malinowskian anthropology. Not everything pre-Malinowskian was cardboard, of course, and Malinowski was not the only thinker to contribute to the overcoming of the facile two-dimensionality of historicist schemata. Nevertheless, he was the most dramatic instance of this switch, and the one which was crucial in anthropology.

It is of course possible to attack Malinowski's positivism without being a Hegelian or a historicist of any kind.[12] It could be argued that Malinowski's assault on the circular invention of fact also undermined the theoretical impulse: is there room, within functionalism, for more than a series of idiographic studies of the functional interdependence found in this, that or the other social order? Flis plausibly defends Malinowski from having any such intention. But it is arguable that, whether from logical considerations, or as of a consequence of the great emphasis on the fieldwork experience among Malinowskians, theoretical imagination was somewhat atrophied at the same time as observational sensitivity was heightened. Was there a danger of a new kind of two-dimensionality? Perhaps the a-historicism, like the stability assumption, comes to be shed once the positive lesson has been learned.

Within the wider context of European thought, Malinowski can be seen as a unique phenomenon: a thinker who fused epistemological Machismo, the here-now positivistic orientation (giving it a specifically anti-past twist), with the organic sense of institutional interdependence and of functionality; these he might equally well have derived from either historicising romantics or from the biologising pragmatists. Probably he obtained it from the latter; but he could

[12] This is the viewpoint of Ian Jarvie's *The Revolution in Anthropology*.

equally have taken it from either. He managed to be a romantic positivist or a holistic synchronist; he used positivism to exorcise the past, and pragmatism to give a living, organic interdependence to the present. Thus he reshuffled the cards played in the fundamental European debate between Reason and Community. Like Hegel he saw the Cunning of Reason in institutions, but unlike him, he failed to revere the Authority of Time. His position defied the customary alignments, and did so with a new cogency and elegance.

This particular combination was specially suited to ethnographic material, with its intricate richness and its lack of historic depth. So, the particular set of cards dealt to him and others in Cracow in the early years of the century was ideally suited both to shrug off the insult and injury meted out to Poland by history, or to seek exemption from the obligation to reverse and invert it; *and* to kill and supplant Frazer, and thus to become the new King of the Sacred Grove of Anthropology.

He played his hand superbly. He was a cultural nationalist and a political internationalist. His holism vindicated the importance of culture, whilst his positivism firmly countermanded the nationalist political imperative, allegedly issued by History. So, the *very same* combination of elements found in Mach which enabled him to succeed Frazer also provided a coherent charter for his cultural and political attitude. Frazer can be slain with ideas which can equally be used to pay homage to Franz Josef. Down with Frazer and up with Franz Josef. Malinowski did unto the Past what positivists habitually did unto the Transcendent. The ideas drawn from Mach were now applied to the Trobrianders, and taught at the LSE. History was not to be our judge or taskmaster or reservoir of explanations. She was a multi-faced meretricious lady and spokesperson of current interests, used by men to impose their own views on others for contemporary ends; she could legitimately be ignored. The present was explained by the present. History was doubly immolated on the Machian pyre. Historic insults lost their sting, and a new anthropological style emerged from the ashes.

Though he was offered a chair in Cracow, before anyone had perhaps properly understood what he was up to, inter-war Poland did not take too much of an interest in the compatriot who had become Anthropologist Laureate to the British Empire. Inter-war Poland was nationalist, and used history to buttress its sentiments, as did its neighbours. What use had it for a theorist who taught that history is manipulated to serve current concerns? No wonder he attracted little attention in his homeland. How could such ideas appeal to the colonels of Warsaw?

But what would happen if, later, history came once again to treat Poland harshly, imposing a deplored verdict in the name of one variety of evolutionist metaphysics? A romantic positivist, who had taught that history had never been endowed with any such authority in the first place, would then acquire a conspicuous new relevance. In his own case, we can only speculate to what extent political motives accompanied the methodological one. He spoke clearly of his methodological concerns; the others may have been secondary. About his latter-day students, we may ask ourselves whether this priority has not now been reversed.

Of course, one could always ask how a synchronist such as Malinowski can be influential nearly half a century after his own death, without so to speak pragmatically contradicting his own views. How dare a voice from the past exhort the present? Let the dead bury their dead. Does he not realise that what is now past has no authority to constrain our present? The answer is simple: there is a conspicuous new role for his ideas in the current, contemporary situation. In Malinowski's day, Poland was divided into three parts. In one of the three, Malinowski's own, Polish culture was respected, and political conditions were good. Malinowski concluded that loyalty to culture and to political authority need not be linked and, it seems, that History is not to be revered. Today, Poland is united, and the integrity of Polish culture is not in peril. The political condition is identical but less than ideal in each of the three parts of Poland. In this situation, Malinowski's latter-day disciples have cause to be attracted by Malinowski's conclusions.

REFERENCES

Ayer, A. J., *Language, Truth and Logic*. Harmondsworth, 1971.
Flis, Andrzej, 'Bronislaw Malinowski's Sociology and Social Anthroplogy', in P. Sztompka (ed.), *Masters of Polish Sociology*, Wrocław, 1984.
Firth, Raymond (ed.), *Man and Culture*. London, 1957.
Frazer, J., *The Golden Bough*. Abridged edn, London, 1957.
Gallie, Bryce, *Peirce and Pragmatism*. London, 1952.
Hegel, G. W. F., *Lectures on the Philosophy of World History*. Cambridge, 1975.
Jarvie, Ian, *The Revolution in Anthropology*. London, 1964.
Kripke, Saul, *Wittgenstein on Rules and Private Language*. Cambridge (Mass.), 1982.

Kubica, Grazyna and Mucha, Janusz (eds.), *Miedszy Dwoma Swiatami* ('Between Two Worlds') (Warsaw and Cracow, 1985); translation forthcoming, Cambridge.

Lévi-Strauss, C., *La Pensée Sauvage*. Paris, 1962.

Lorenz, Fr., Fischer, A., and Lehr-Splawinski, T., *The Cassubian Civilisation*. London, 1935. Preface by B. Malinowski.

Malinowski, B., *A Scientific Theory of Culture and Other Essays*. New York, 1960.

Malinowski, B., *Magic, Science and Religion and Other Essays*. London, 1974, 1982.

Paluch, Andrzej, 'The Polish Background to Malinowski's Work'. *Man*, 16, no. 2, June 1981.

Strenski, I., 'Malinowski; Second Positivism, Second Romanticism'. *Man*, 17, no. 4, December 1982.

5 From Königsberg to Manhattan (or Hannah, Rahel, Martin and Elfriede or Thy Neighbour's *Gemeinschaft*)

If Hannah Arendt had not existed, it would most certainly be necessary to invent her. Her life is a parable, not just of our age, but of several centuries of European thought and experience. Providence, however, in its wisdom has decided that Hannah Arendt should actually exist, so there is no need to invent her for the sake of the parable. All that needs to be done is to write her biography, which Elizabeth Young-Bruehl has duly done.[1] The parable might have been more economical; but the copious facts assembled by Miss Young-Bruehl are not uninteresting.

Hannah Arendt was born in 1906. But the biography does not begin then. It begins, in effect most fittingly, in the Königsberg of the late eighteenth century. Max Arendt, Hannah's paternal grandfather, was descended on his mother's side from people who had already moved to Königsberg at the time of Immanuel Kant and Moses Mendelssohn, who died in 1786. One of the excellent photographs in the volume shows Königsberg *c.* 1900, and conveys something of the cold northern light and beauty of this Baltic port.

So the parable which Hannah Arendt was destined to live out does indeed begin long before her birth and upbringing in that city in the eighteenth century. It was in Königsberg that the torch of the Enlightenment burned with its most fierce flame, in the thought and person of Immanuel Kant (who was a universal mind without ever having left the city); and it was there too that the Jewish followers of Moses Mendelssohn systematically transmitted the new secular European wisdom to the East European Jewish communities. The acceptance of the new Enlightenment by them and by their Gentile neighbours meant that eventually, political emancipation was to follow cultural and social fusion. The real full consequences of that emancipation, and of the ideas which warranted and required it, were only due to be played out nearly two centuries later, precisely within the

---

[1] Elizabeth Young-Bruehl, *Hannah Arendt: For Love of the World*, New Haven and London, 1982, 563 pp.

75

span of Hannah's life. She was destined to live out those delayed effects, and to try and understand them, to be personally well placed for such an effort, and to acquire fame in the process. *This* is the parable of which her life is the concrete embodiment.

It is not just Hannah Arendt herself, but her native and ancestral city of Königsberg, which constitutes a parable. In more than one sense, the city literally no longer exists. The place where the Prussian city of Königsberg had stood is now occupied by the Russian city of Kaliningrad. This town is part not merely of the USSR, but of the Russian Socialist Republic itself. The Russians are averse to discontinuous, colonial-type possessions, and voluntarily returned to the Finns the Soviet peninsular Gibraltar controlling entry to the Gulf of Finland which they had taken after 1945; but they do not seem so averse to discontinuous possessions *within* the USSR. So the isolated pocket around Kaliningrad is politically attached to the Russian republic, and not to the neighbouring Lithuanian one.

All this is not merely a matter of a change of name. Of the 5000 or so Jews who lived there at the turn of the century, or their descendants, most were no doubt killed, and the rest exiled; of the remaining, German population, most were no doubt exiled, and many killed. But this total discontinuity between the Königsberg of Kant and Mendelssohn and the Kaliningrad of today (whose illustrious sons, if any, remain unknown to fame), is not a contingent, external, accidental fact. No extraneous Genghis Khan had emerged from central Asia to wipe out the inhabitants. Their elimination, liquidation, was the work of two political movements and systems which were unambiguously and conspicuously the fruits, whether directly or by reaction, of that very Enlightenment which had shone on that Baltic shore at least as brightly as it had done in Berlin, Paris, Glasgow or Edinburgh.

The ideas and the eventual killing and exiling were intimately linked. Hannah Arendt was to rethink and relive those ideas, in exile, whilst the killing took place, in a multiply personal, involved manner. Königsberg/Kaliningrad is of course not the only city in Europe to symbolise the delayed explosive power of the ideas of the Enlightenment; but it is perhaps the one in which the symbolism is most conspicuously blatant. In her childhood already, the young Hannah and her family fled from Königsberg because the Russians were advancing on it: 'The Cossacks are coming!' was the cry. As it happened, the Cossacks were turned back at Tannenberg and did not, on that occasion, arrive. It is worth noting that had they made it, it would not have by any means been their first visit, and that in the eighteenth century, there had been no need to flee when they came. The Russians occupied Königsberg during the Seven Years War, and it was actually the Russian Governor who confirmed Kant's chair. *Cuius regio, eius cathedra.* When Frederick the Great recovered the town, Kant did not have to face any de-Russification tribunal. Things were different then. The age in which the Enlightenment ideas were formulated was more restrained than the one in which they and the reaction they unchained were fully played out.

What were those ideas, with their concealed time-bomb destined to blow a whole world to smithereens? In fact, of course, the Enlightenment was an attempt to codify and legitimate that totally new world which was emerging in Europe, and whose most conspicuous birth-pangs were the Industrial and the French Revolutions, and which is probably the biggest single event in all the history of mankind. But that was not how the Enlightenment actually saw itself. It saw itself as the Revelation, rational, not supernatural this time, of a *universal* human truth, valid for all men at all times. In Kant's version, the basic and sufficient elements of that truth are incapsulated in the mind of every single man (every rational being in fact, if there be others).

If this truth was so universally and easily accessible, why did it need to be revealed and taught? An awkward question (to which Hegelianism and other systems were soon to offer their solutions), but the rough answer seemed to be that somehow or other, the manifest truth had been lost or obscured during the Dark Ages, though it had previously been available, at least in a kind of early proof edition, in some of the ideas of antiquity and in at least the ethical teachings of the great religions. (This enabled some of the preachers of the Enlightenment, such as Kant himself, to believe that they were not really cutting themselves off from their religious roots.) The central political implication of this vision was quite obvious: equal rights for all rational men.

So, as far as the Enlightenment itself was concerned, the implications were the same for everyone, Gentile or Jew. It also posed the very same problem for everyone: when embracing the new wisdom, is he also to disavow the old faith which, if taken literally and with the seriousness which had previously been accorded to it, was plainly incompatible with the new secular revelation? But when it came to facing this problem, there was an important difference between Gentile and Jew. For a Gentile, the problem was only intellectual: abjuring the old faith did not also mean abjuring the old community. For a Jew, it did mean precisely that. The fact that the community to be abjured was a pariah one, endowed the decision with a moral ambiguity which it has never lost: was one choosing the truth and incidentally gaining an advantage, or pursuing an advantage and, as a means, changing a doctrinal cloak? As they used to say in a different (but related) context in Palestine in the 1930s, *kommen Sie aus Ueberzeugung oder kommen Sie aus Deutschland?* (Do you come from conviction or from Germany?)

In the first generation of the full impact of the Enlightenment, some went one way and some another, and many temporised between the two extremes, and it goes without saying that ideologues soon appeared ready to prove that a Middle Way existed which made the best of all worlds. (As the American joke has it, some prayed to the God of the Old Testament, some to the God of the New Testament, and some To Whom It May Concern.) There was some perfectly reasonable justification for leaving the minority community which was also a closed one, quite apart from the lure of advantage: the new emerging society was not merely due to be more rational than the *ancien régime* it was replacing, it was also destined to be more mobile, *open*. (Karl Popper's famous phrase, whatever other important functions it also performs, contains an implicit justification of the abandonment of minority communities.) This being so, the new order absolutely needed a *shared* cultural idiom, rather than a multiplicity of in-group jargons. It was only natural that this idiom should be that of the majority group, especially if it *already* contained a powerful literature of Enlightenment. So the dilemma which the Enlightenment imposed on its converts was somewhat more acute for the members of the minority group; but it was not *yet* so terrible. The situation was due to become much more serious with the romantic reaction to the Enlightenment.

'Romanticism' has no doubt many meanings, but the one that is relevant and important here is this: the romantic reaction taught that a religion of humanity *an sich*, beyond all cultural or ethnic specificity, led to a bloodless cosmopolitanism, and that the concrete earthy, folksy cultures, with all their idiosyncrasies (above all with their idiosyncrasies) were to be esteemed and preserved not simply as the convenient idioms for a universal truth, but as supremely valuable in themselves.

Now if this is so, it presents no great problem for the members of the majority culture, or for those who can enter it unobtrusively and without fuss; but it constitutes what is a virtually insoluble problem for the members of the minority group, who had occupied what is now seen to be an intolerably oppressive ghetto in the old order. They had not been simply excluded from the old order: on the contrary, they were a kind of negative part of it, a converse of all its values, its anti-image. The society had been Christian, and they had killed Christ. The society preached (whether or not it practised) anti-commercial values, and they had lived by commerce. All this had been psychically acceptable, or at any rate accepted, in an age of more or less closed communities which saw themselves from the inside rather than from the dominant viewpoint; but it became quite unacceptable in a mobile, open society in which individuals on the move see no reason to accept a collective stigma. To identify with a positive collective illusion instead, tied to a shared idiom, then became a most natural aspiration.

The return to the old folk culture was of course an illusion, *whoever* indulged in it: as far as that went, there was not much (if any) real difference between the majority and the minority. The real difference was that the minority had no illusion *of its own* to go back to. It only had the recollection of the ghetto, which by definition was not a self-sufficient community or culture at all, but an unromantically (commercially) specialised sub-community of a wider world within which it was pejoratively defined. Although in fact a literary populist nostalgia for the *shtetl* does exist nevertheless, Jewish populist romanticism is in the end a contradiction in terms. Romanticism proposed a return to a pristine and homogeneous *Gemeinschaft*, within which spontaneous unconstrained communication is possible. By contrast the ghetto was, precisely, an alien even if functional and specialised element in a plural society, incomplete in itself, a forcibly imposed and sustained counter-culture, deliberately made morally discontinuous from the rest of society, and thus precluding *Gemeinschaft* with the self-sufficient social whole. Its very specialism and the necessary but re-sented complementarity with an alien and hostile social environment made it a kind of anti-community.

So the romantic reaction placed the Jews in a dilemma far sharper than the Enlightenment had done. They were largely deprived of the illusion of a possible return to the roots, an illusion indulged by their gentile neighbours with enthusiasm and conviction. Thou shalt not covet thy neighbour's *Gemeinschaft*! But, of course, one does. So what's to be done? The options which were logically open were either to infiltrate the Others' *Gemeinschaft*, or to create a new one of one's own, whether or not there had been any peasants available for the past two millennia, who could define its folk culture. The second solution is known as Zionism, and of course did not appear on the scene till somewhat later. Needless to say, these are just the extreme poles of the spectrum. In between, there was a whole range of intermediate and mixed positions, and no doubt many people vacillated as to just where they stood. But the problem-shift from mere adherence to doctrine, to that of community membership, was summed up by a remark made in 1914, and quoted in the book, to the effect that during the Emancipation period one was asked what one *believed*, whereas now one was asked who one *was*.

The old communities had *Gemeinschaft* but thought of themselves in religious terms. The new wider and anonymous community tried to see itself as a *Gemeinschaft*, and romanticism was the literary and philosophical means used to pursue that end. The old community could use religion to close itself off: even if conversion theoretically made it open, social sanctions made conversion difficult. (Montesquieu commented on the theological oddity and the social logic of the mediaeval rule, which required confiscation of the goods of any Jew converting to Christianity.) In the new setting, religious belief became so lightweight that social sanctions could not even latch on to it. So racial ideas (irrespective of the validity of the biology on which they were based) were obvious candidates for a technique of closing the community, if that was desired – which it often was. It was Heine who foresaw that the anti-semitism of the pagans would be worse than that of the Christians.

It is a considerable merit of Miss Young-Bruehl's biography that she makes very plain this problem base-line from which Hannah Arendt started. The Arendt family had found their place on the spectrum of possible solutions. They remained Jews, but ate pork, and the revelation which guided and dominated their lives was not the Torah, but Goethe and the idea of *Bildung*. This compromise, like many logically incoherent compromises, might have worked well enough, and indeed probably did work tolerably well, but for one thing: the problem was ever self-renewing. It was fed with wave after wave of new entrants. The train line linking Königsberg with Odessa, and the enormous human reservoir to the south-east and east, ensured that *every* decade, there were many for whom *this* was the first generation of Emancipation and Enlightenment. There was, of course, a chasm between the middle-class Jews who had passed through the rite de passage of the Enlightenment, and the working-class Ostjuden who had not. But the perpetual inflow of the latter ensured that the terms of the problem did not change.

So in its way time stood still. This is highlighted by the fact that the one relationship of Hannah Arendt's which comes over more clearly and convincingly than any other in the volume is her friendship with Rahel Varnhagen. She herself described Rahel as 'her greatest friend, though she has been dead for some one hundred years'. Rahel Varnhagen had experienced the dilemma in its full intensity in the first generation in which it had presented itself, and had gone through the cycle of assimilationist aspiration (through trying for a marriage with a member of the Prussian nobility) to an eventual return to her Jewishness. Hannah somehow retraced Rahel's path: the difference was, I suppose, that for Rahel, Goethe was a contemporary solace, and for Hannah he was the very baseline of existence. Hannah was a better-looking Rahel, with the option of Zionism thrown in. A further difference was that the issue eventually became entry not to a salon, but to a gas-chamber.

If the relationship to the long-deceased Rahel is the most illuminating one in the volume, there can be no doubt about which one has recently aroused the greatest interest. It is, of course, the young Hannah's affair with one of her teachers, the celebrated Martin Heidegger, star pupil of the Jew Husserl, and himself later involved with Nazism. The circle begun with Enlightenment in the days of Rahel was now coming close to a full revolution. She herself was to describe him as 'the last ... romantic', and thus to be identified, Miss Young-Bruehl says, with those who had destroyed Rahel's cosmopolitan salon. The wheel was now about to come full circle. The leading romantic of the age, who was to endorse that romanticism's most ruthless implementation, went to bed with one of those for whom German romanticism had created an insoluble problem of identity, and for whom it was shortly to become literally lethal.

Although the disclosure of this relationship has actually aroused great interest, its presentation in the volume is very disappointing. The author treats it with hushed reverence. One had hoped for something like this: 'Martin's left hand was still firmly grasping *Die Phänomenologie des Geistes*, whilst his right hand began gently to unbutton Hannah's blouse...' But no. Instead, Miss Young-Bruehl bursts into her own translations of Hannah Arendt's poetry. Unfortunately she actually mistranslates a crucial passage on which her own interpretation hinges: 'starre Hingegebenheit an ein einziges' cannot really be translated as 'unbending devotion to a single one', because *ein einziges* is neuter, and thus suggests a thing or an abstraction, and cannot signify a person, a single *one*. (Unless the person was a child, which Heidegger was not.) The phrase evidently commends singleminded devotion to an abstraction, an activity, or value, to *something* unique, rather than to a beloved *person*. It might just about mean a relationship, but not an individual. Miss Young-Bruehl does not really seem all that much at home in German. Elsewhere she mis-translates 'Angst vor dem Dasein ueberhaupt' (fear *of* Being in general) as 'anxiety *over* existence in general'; and in another reasonably important passage, because it is significant for an assessment of Arendt's character, she mis-translates 'Schwindel' as 'fib', when in fact it means trickery, deception, cheating. She also describes Hannah's husband as having attended a *Volkeschule*.

Abelard-and-Eloise relationships cannot be uncommon in the universities. As the lawyers say, this can be demonstrated from opportunity and inclination. Within the zone of their professional aura, middle-aged professors can hope for better sexual bargains than they could possibly secure by their own unaided charms on the open market. As for the student, she can expect closer attention in bed than in the seminar, and some professional advantage may be gained. It is understood that the meeting of bodies is an expression of the communion and fertilisation of minds. What, however, marked the Heidegger–Arendt liaison as distinctive is that on this occasion, the high esteem in which the participants held themselves and each other, and the intellectual significance they attributed to the relationship, were actually shared by many other people. Heidegger and Arendt, conscious of the *welthistorische* significance of their relationship, arranged for their mutual correspondence to be deposited in a literary archive in Germany.

The account of the actual relationship is less than vivid. What does come to life are the as it were *Lotte in Weimar* episodes after the war, when the ex-Nazi and his Jewish ex-mistress meet again. It was *then* that he confesses to Hannah that she had been *the* passion of his life and the inspiration of his work.

Here Miss Young-Bruehl is interesting, but a tiny bit disingenuous. The text flatly asserts, in two quite distinct passages, that Heidegger admitted to Hannah that she had been his great passion and inspiration, though it also quotes Hannah as noting that he was notorious for lying about everything, with the implication, however, that now at last he was telling the truth. How many readers, I wonder, will check the voluminous notes and find that the evidence cited for this comes from letters which Hannah Arendt herself wrote to a third party – *not* even to Heidegger himself? How trustworthy is a woman's uncorroborated claim that a man told her that she was the passion and inspiration of his life? It may well be true that this was what he told her, but on an interesting point like this, a biographer's duty is to make plain the unsymmetrical nature of the evidence, and to distinguish between an *ex parte* claim and an established fact.

The important truth is probably the other way round. As will emerge, the central oddity and incoherence of her work make me suspect that this was so. What Martin Heidegger the concrete man actually meant to her is not for me to say. With respect to the original episode, the biography is coy and uninformative (it does not even properly raise the question why Hannah left Marburg); when describing the post-war reunion, it is, perhaps rightly, patronising and condescending to Heidegger. It is all seen very much from Hannah's viewpoint. Ironically, as stated, the one reiterated piece of evidence about the young Hannah is a mis-translation. But what can hardly be doubted is her deep involvement with German romanticism, and that *is* of central importance. Her characterisation of Heidegger as 'the last (we hope) romantic' is probably the most important piece of evidence about his role in her life. This remark, jointly with her identification with Rahel, suggests one conclusion. She loved him, not despite the leanings which eventually led him into the Nazi Party, but because of them. And to damn romanticism would have been to damn *him*. This, it seems, she could not bring herself to do, and the oddity of her most famous work is congruent with this.

The real separation of Arendt and Heidegger was of course ratified by the events of 1933. Heidegger went into the Party, Arendt into exile. She went to live in France. In Paris, just as in Germany earlier and in Manhattan later, she manifested her capacity of being close to many of the leading intellectuals of the day. To be absent from the index of this volume is to be excluded from the mainstream of intellectual history, and is not a fate to be borne lightly. There really ought to be an adaptation of Tom Lehrer's superb song about Alma Mahler-Gropius-Werfel to Hannah Arendt:

> Hannah, tell us,
> How can they help being jealous?

She lived through the fall of France and through the treatment of the refugees as 'scum of the earth', in the phrase Arthur Koestler used for the title of his book describing his own experiences at the time. She and her husband eventually succeeded in leaving Europe via Lisbon and reaching America.

She rapidly entered that legendary hothouse of mainly Jewish intellectuals on Manhattan, the famous 'tribe', and achieved a prominent and respected position within it. This part of the biography should make an excellent scenario for a Woody Allen film. The wealth of personal and intellectual experience she had acquired on the way to it provided her with the material for commenting on the problems which emerged when the war against German romanticism was won. She now became very productive, and acquired world fame.

New York, like Königsberg, is a port; but there the resemblance ends. America is, so to speak, a post-Enlightenment society: it was born modern. Liberalism is its tradition, not its radicalism or self-transformation. All this changes the rules of the game. America has no Goethe, and its intellectuals have no bitter-sweet love affair with the local folk culture, or a nostalgia for its *Gemeinschaft*, whether real or illusory. They tend to hate its guts, and live as close to the Eastern and Western seaboards as is possible without actually falling off. They stay as far away as they can from Middle America. It is true that America has its populism, but the difference is that in America this is a movement of the people themselves, whereas in Europe it is a vicarious sentiment of intellectuals on behalf of the people.

As a matter of fact, Hannah Arendt was very perceptive about the virtues and idiosyncrasies of America. Not for her the mechanical anti-Americanism of, for instance, her French opposite numbers of the time. She notes that American thought is almost uninfluenced by European 'worshippers of history', and that even American Marxists 'theoretically, cannot believe their eyes' when they look at their own country. Americans have the Enlightenment as their birthright, as something inherent in their historical society. Taking it for granted without ambivalence, they need no romantic philosophy of history as a corrective or antidote... She also saw the merits of a political liberalism, co-existing with a social illiberalism, and thought the latter should be challenged whilst the former was sustained. She did not, like Tocqueville, seem to consider the possibility that the latter could be a condition of the former.

Apart from America, she also had to think about newly re-emerging Israel. Here, her reactions were generous rather than profound. She had some kind of federal scheme for Palestine which would have ensured that no one was in a minority anywhere. She later took a naive pride in the Israeli military triumph of 1967, without evidently considering the possibility that it might be a political disaster. Being a Jew is like awareness of death or sex: it is always present, there are no solutions for the problems it engenders, and one can only talk about it in aphorisms. But Hannah Arendt now talked in a confident, non-Existential tone, as if solutions existed. Her romanticism did stay with her, as when she thought she saw a general social solution in the spontaneity of workers' councils in the 1956 Budapest rising.

But it wasn't her reflections on America or Israel which brought her prominence. It was her contribution to the attempt to come to terms with, to understand, what had happened in Europe which made her famous. Her background, her family and personal history, all her previous intellectual involvement, had after all prepared her for this task.

She turned to it, and what she wrote was fully acclaimed. Was the acclaim justified?

Later, ironically, when she wrote about the Eichmann trial, she came to be associated with her phrase 'the banality of evil'. The irony lies in the fact that her central idea, when trying to come to terms with the horrors that had occurred in Europe, was precisely the opposite. The evil was not banal, it was totally alien, unpredictable, daemonic, quite outside the range of what we could expect or comprehend. In a way, this mystical over-dramatisation is in itself very much in the romantic tradition – even if here, ironically, it is used to exculpate romanticism and philosophy from having fathered the allegedly alien evil. She used the language and ideas drawn from the witches' brew of Weimar intellectual life – some of which later became popularised by Marcuse's denunciation of liberal industrial society.

There was, of course, no contradiction between all this and her characterisation of Eichmann. On the contrary, after she had given a kind of account of totalitarianism which was half Kafka's *Trial* and half Wagner, the ordinariness of Eichmann was bound to strike and puzzle her. Would it all have made more sense if he had looked and acted as if he came straight out of *The Cabinet of Dr Caligari*?

Miss Young-Bruehl quotes a 1952 statement of Arendt's which sums up her attitude:

All ... elements [other than Bolshevism] which eventually crystallise into the totalitarian forms of movements can be traced to subterranean currents in Western history which emerged only when and where the traditional social and political framework of Europe broke down... The shocking originality of totalitarianism, the fact that its ideologies and methods of government were totally unprecedented and that its causes defied proper explanation in the usual historical terms, is easily overlooked if one lays too much stress on the only element which has behind it a respectable tradition ... Marxism.

What on earth was she up to? If Marxism is the *only* reputable element in the witches' brew of totalitarian ideas, if all the others had emerged from some unspeakable underworld, then all those themes which *were* present in the intellectual mainstream are thereby given a clean bill of health. This it seems was what she wanted to achieve. She was, with affectionate condescension and some irritation, prepared to see how her ex-lover's ideas had led him to Nazism and personal megalomania, but once she faced the situation in the abstract, she wanted to exonerate the lot!

To put it bluntly, her contribution to our understanding of what it was that had happened to Europe in the 1930s and 1940s seems to me grossly over-rated. Her over-colourful canvas may in a way have brought home the all-too-genuine horrors, but at the same time made them seem unreal, operatic, metaphysical, and above all, comfortingly alien, not really after all very much connected with *us*. And there she was wrong; and given her background, her life-long preoccupation, her error is strange. She was well equipped to understand the evil which had nearly engulfed her, and which had engulfed so many whom she had known, but when it came to comprehending it, she failed.

Let me say first of all that I do not think that Nazism has mainly or primarily intellectual causes. But, contrary to what she tried to argue, it was continuous with, not *all*, of course, but many perfectly recognisable, not subterranean themes and attitudes in European thought. In a number of senses, Hitler was Europe's destiny. First of all, in a military sense: he was only stopped by an off-shore island, and a half-Asian tyranny almost as bad as his own (though much less efficient), and by a transatlantic power. Secondly, very large parts of Europe's middle and working class were quite prepared to accommodate themselves to the New Order. Thirdly – and this is what is most relevant to Hannah Arendt's argument – the ideological cover of the New Order was in fact perfectly compatible with at any rate one significant strand in the European intellectual tradition. Marxism, contrary to what she was saying, was not the only element in totalitarianism with a reputable intellectual ancestry; and demonstrably she knew this, even though she denied it.

Let us return to the story of romanticism, which Hannah Arendt blamed for the destruction of Rahel Varhagen's cosmopolitan salon. It began as the revaluation of idiosyncratic, folk *cultures*, against universalistic, cosmopolitan Reason. But in the nineteenth century, Culture, in its fight with barren Reason, found a powerful ally – *Nature*. The ally was all the more significant in that it could outflank Reason. Reason had itself taught, in its Enlightenment form, that man was part of Nature, should revere that lady, and should not seek any exemption from Nature. So reason legitimated nature, and nature in turn legitimated un-reason. Unfortunately, in the nineteenth century, Darwin had also popularised the fact that Nature had a lot of nasty habits, notably ruthlessness, willingness to eliminate the unfit, and to be very wasteful with life whilst in the pursuit of excellence.

It also became widely recognised that if we are parts of nature, then we are animals, and if we are animals, then we obtain our true, our deepest, our most life-enhancing, genuinely fulfilling satisfactions, not from abstract aims or universal brotherhood, but in more earthy,

brutal and exclusive ways. This can be named the call of the Dark
Gods, Blood and Earth, etc. Now as a matter of fact, romanticism had
already been susceptible to earlier and pre-Darwinian versions of
such ideas, ever since the *Sturm und Drang*. It had always been rather
keen on *das Daemonische*, which titivates in a way that Reason cannot.
As Hannah Arendt noted in connection with her ex-lover, this element led talented individuals working within this tradition after a certain time to take themselves far too seriously. So when Nature red in
tooth and claw came to reinforce Culture, the tradition of romantic
claims for Culture against Reason was well prepared to incorporate
this new ally in the struggle with cerebral coldness.

The problem of the Enlightenment had been: why are the self-
evident truths of Reason so little respected, so difficult to implement?
Hegel and Marxism had one answer: History has its dance of seven
veils and will only reveal the naked truth after a sequence of social
forms and beliefs, each with its temporary illusions, has been passed
through. Romanticism proper had another answer: both cultural togetherness and natural instincts entail that we only get our true satisfactions in a way quite different from the false and abstract ideals of
the Enlightenment. If natural instincts include the call of the kin
group, as was often held to be the case, then the two criticisms co-
alesce.

When Nature and its corollaries, competition and natural selection,
came to be invoked against conscious Reason – in the name of both
excellence and health and true human satisfaction and its honest recognition – this could be done in two ways, either individualistically or
collectively. The former, which is shorn of the more colourful romantic elements, is what may be called the Austro-Chicago way (with
side-glances to Glasgow and Manchester). Nature had progressed by
competition in the jungle, and can do so again in the market (though it
then rather awkwardly needs a peace-keeping state, with a somewhat
extra-natural status). The problem is only the *Gemeinschaft*, that awful
inclination to excessive cooperativeness which we had picked up in
the tribal-band period of human history. *This* vision does not yearn for
the *Gemeinschaft*, it wants to get rid of it, and quick, for *it* is the root of
totalitarianism. (Neither Hayek or Popper occur in the very extensive
index. Nor does J. L. Talmon, who worked out a far more precise
theory of the origins of totalitarianism in terms of its intellectual antecedents. This suggests that neither Hannah Arendt nor her biographer is all that interested in advancing the question of the origins of
totalitarianism by considering rival views. Here I cannot resist a little
vulgar-Marxist sociology of knowledge. Could this Viennese theory of

the origins of totalitarian leanings have its source in the reaction of the liberal, individualistic Viennese bourgeoisie, to the terrible spectacle of hordes of mutually supportive cousins descending on Vienna from the *shtetl*, not to mention *zadruga*-loads of Balkan peasants?)

But in Königsberg, Marburg, and similar places, the Viennese, individualistic-naturalistic reaction was not the dominant one. The communal-naturalistic one prevailed. Nature's imperatives of ruthlessness, excellence, and instinctual fulfilment were superimposed on the romantic stress on cultural *communities*, a line of thought which had been present ever since the first reaction to the Enlightenment. Some people romanticise their real or supposed ancestral community, and at the same time oppose ethnic prejudice and wish to be fair to everyone. But you can't really have it both ways. The cosy old community *was* ethnocentric, and if you wish to love and perpetuate it as it truly was, prejudice against outsiders must be part of the romantic package-deal. The trouble about the Nazis was that they were only too consistent on this point.

The resulting mix of community-romanticism and naturalism, though perhaps never formally and elegantly codified, was precisely the ideology of Nazism. If Hitler had won, there would without any doubt whatsoever have been a major philosophical industry on the Continent explaining why the victory was a culmination, a completion of a necessary and philosophically appropriate development. We may also assume that Heidegger would not have confessed that Hannah Arendt had been his great passion and inspiration, letters would have been destroyed and not placed in any archive, and the aptly named Elfriede Heidegger's feelings would have been spared.

Hannah Arendt must have been incomparably more familiar with the details of this part of intellectual history than I am. All this being so, why on earth did she go out of her way to try and exonerate European thought in the way she did? Whilst privately castigating her ex-lover for his tendency to personal megalomania and its roots in his intellectual tradition, was she still nevertheless eager to exculpate his ideas and the tradition itself? But we shan't come to terms with what happened if we pretend it was all totally alien to us.

Hannah Arendt must have known this. Miss Young-Bruehl herself, summing up a proposed work of Arendt's, says:

She would have stressed the central difference between Nazism and Bolshevism, the difference between the ideology of Nature and the ideology of History...

Nature is as important a bolthole from Reason as is History in the

European philosophy of the past two centuries, and Hannah Arendt knew it. So why did she have to pretend that it all had nothing to do with European thought, that it had all crawled out from beneath the stones? Was she trying to cover up for her youth or her lover, or both?

Having declined to carry out an account of the horrors in terms of their intellectual antecedents, she had to do it sociologically instead, for which she was, in various ways, ill equipped. Her theory seems to boil down to some kind of release of subterranean forces by the breakdown of European order, atomisation, masses, the mob, a system which can dispense with men. What all this means is much less than clear, and quite neglects the fact that Hitler's New Order was indeed an Order, which as long as it was victorious, was acceptable to many, without the sanction of terror, and which could be justified in terms of themes that had long been present – albeit implemented with a consistency and thoroughness which were tragic for those who were now wholly excluded where before they had only been half-included.

The verbosity, logical untidiness, impressionism and imprecision of her style make her contribution of dubious value. Not for her the attempt to reconstruct, with as much accuracy as possible, the actual constraints operating in a given social situation. The phenomenological method of her intellectual mentors Husserl and Heidegger of course encouraged her in this style. Here is another line connecting her to the Enlightenment and to the reaction to it.

The Enlightenment, apart from its Rationalism and cosmopolitanism, had also devalued the ordinary world we live in (quite apart from whether it is linked to some concrete community). The 'lived world' was doomed to become a kind of limbo between the sensory empirical data-base on the one hand and the realm of abstract scientific explanatory concepts on the other. It loses all standing, becoming a kind of habitation-of-convenience, but without any genuine cognitive significance. The phenomenological movement in philosophy, led by Husserl, gave it a name (*Lebenswelt*), and restored dignity to it, by making its study, 'bracketed' (i.e. disconnected from the explanatory concepts and questions of validity, evidence and origin), into the main business of philosophy. Phenomenology tends to be a rather dull business of describing our own daily concepts, and only acquires sex-appeal when it turns to the very personal part of the *Lebenswelt*, to the human condition, to our phenomenological private parts, to the way in which we are 'thrown into the world' and so on, which is where Heidegger came in.

Now the phenomenological method makes some sense when applied to established concepts which had long helped to organise our

world, and which presumably have a well-defined use. A phenomenological exploration in such a case can presumably lead to a kind of
enhancement of our conceptual self-knowledge. But what sense does
it make when applied to a new phenomenon and a new idea such as
totalitarianism? It then has a kind of inherent and inescapable arbi-
trariness: whatever you put into the bag, you can then also pull out. . .

Hannah Arendt had lived through it all, and it was an interesting
and symptomatic life, and it is well and readably recorded. But when
dusk came, the owl of Minerva failed to take off into flight. 'Loyalty is
the sign of Truth', proclaims one of Miss Young-Bruehl's chapter
headings, questionably (*Meine Ehre ist Treue* was the SS motto). But
Hannah Arendt seemed, in the end, more loyal to her lover than to
truth.

6 The social roots of egalitarianism

Lord Acton saw history as the story of liberty. Tocqueville, on the other hand, saw it – though he did not put it that way – as the story of equality. It was the equalisation of conditions which provided the underlying plot of social development. If indeed it does so, the plot is a curious one, as is documented in an admirably thorough historical survey by Gerhard Lenski.[1]

The pattern of human history, when plotted against the axis of equality, displays a steady progression towards increasing *in*equality, up to a certain mysterious point in time, at which the trend goes into reverse, and we then witness that equalisation of conditions which preoccupied Tocqueville. What on earth impelled history to change its direction? Lenski invokes ideology: modern society is egalitarian because it wills itself to be such, because it was somehow converted to the egalitarian ideal.

I find it difficult to accept this theory of collective conversion, and I feel the same about the supposition that ideals are quite so effective socially. At any rate, before we fall back on this kind of intellectualist explanation, with its hint of the *Allmacht des Gedankens*, it may be as well to explore other, more concrete, tangible, visibly constraining factors which may have impelled us all in the direction of equality. The psychological appeals of equality, and of its opposite, are no doubt complex and murky. The appeal of equality, whether as a corollary of fairness, as a manner of avoiding intolerably humiliating inequality, or as a precondition of fraternal affection, seems obvious, at any rate in our age; but there is a danger that we may credit the human heart with a tendency which is merely the pervasive spirit of our age.

The psychic appeal of inequality may be as deep and important, and *not* merely to the beneficiaries of unequal status. Somewhere in the works of the late Cyril Connolly there is a passage in which he observes that it gives him deep satisfaction to remember that there are houses in England whose portals will for ever remain closed to him.

[1] *Power and Privilege*, New York, 1966.

There is glamour in the existence of socially unclimbed and unclimbable peaks; and a wholly conquered or easily conquerable mountain range, devoid of the inaccessible, loses its appeal. The soul-transforming glamour of great privilege is conveyed in the celebrated exchange between Scott Fitzgerald and Ernest Hemingway. 'Ernest', said Fitzgerald, 'the rich are different from us.' 'Yes', replied Hemingway, 'they have more money.'

Egalitarians react to this story by feeling that Hemingway won, and that he scored off the socially over-awed Fitzgerald. But there are many who feel differently about this, and who value inequality, not simply as an unavoidable means towards other social ends, or as an incentive, or a way of providing the leisure required for progress, or a concession – but as good and above all a thrill in itself. I remember reading a defence of the snobbery of the superb novelist Evelyn Waugh by his friend Mr Christopher Sykes, in which the argument went roughly as follows: Waugh accepted inequality because he was clear-sighted enough to see that modern egalitarian political movements will merely result in new forms of inequality, as harsh eventually and crass and perhaps worse than those which they replace. In brief, Waugh's inegalitarianism is turned into a corollary of his social perceptiveness, a resigned acceptance of a necessary evil. This seems to me a total misrepresentation of the spirit of Waugh's novels, and unfair to their literary merit. He may well of course also have held the belief about the consequences of egalitarian reform with which Sykes credits him: in all probability he did. But to invoke that as the explanation of his inegalitarianism is to imply, absurdly, that he was a *regretful* inegalitarian – that, if only equality were socially feasible, he would have embraced it with alacrity. But in fact one of the merits of his work is the convincing manner in which he captures and portrays the deep positive *passion* for inequality, even, or especially, as felt by the *less* privileged. Paul Potts does not merely recognise the hard social fact that one law applies to him and quite another to Margot Metroland: he loves her for it. Waugh, like Connolly, conveys that positively sexual frisson, the skin-tingling titivation engendered by radical inequality, by the brazen and confident denial of the equality of man which profoundly excites both the active and the passive partner, the higher and the lower, so to speak, in the ecstatic union of inequality. It is perfectly obvious that either of these authors would have loathed to be deprived of it.

I mention these complications merely in order to stress that the psychic appeal of equality and its absence are complex, probably tortuous, and certainly many-sided. There are men who love inequality, like the Admirable Crichton; and though the complications cannot be ignored, they may perhaps usefully be laid aside until after we have explored the historically more specific *social* roots of the manifest current trend towards egalitarianism. I shall offer a list, no doubt incomplete, of the factors which are liable to impel us in this direction.

1 Mobility

Modern industrial society is egalitarian and mobile. But it is egalitarian *because* it is mobile, rather than mobile because egalitarian. We can assume this, because we can see why it is *obliged* to be mobile, and why in turn mobility is bound to engender egalitarianism. If this argument is correct we are spared the double embarrassment of treating conversion to an ideal as a prime social mover, and of assuming it to be socially effective.

Modern society depends for its existence on technological innovation. It is the first society ever to secure, over quite a considerable period, sustained increase in wealth. Notoriously, its political organisation hinges on this: it has relied on this sustained growth of the total cake for buying off the discontent of the less privileged, and the general softening of manners, and the reduction in the severity of social sanctions, is presumably connected with this continuous bribery. The recent crisis in the West is of course connected with the failure, presumed to be temporary, to maintain this growth of wealth at the rate to which we have become accustomed.

What concerns us in connection with equality is certain obvious implications of sustained technical and economic innovation. It means that changes in economic organisation, in the nature and distribution of jobs, are not occasional, but permanent and constant. They do not occur, as they might in some agrarian society, merely as the occasional consequences of a natural disaster, of the introduction of a new crop, or some other relatively extraneous change; they occur perpetually as part of the normal working of the system, and they occur even if the external environment (however defined) is stable, which in any case it is *not*. The instability of the economic roles is built into the system, and is self-generated.

A corollary of this inherent and inescapable occupational mobility is what I wish to call Lady Montdore's Principle. Lady Montdore is a character in some of the novels of Nancy Mitford, and she expressed and applied a certain principle of behaviour, which ran as follows: Always be polite to the girls, for you do not know whom they will marry.

Within her social circle, the young marriageable girls formed a fairly undifferentiated pool of potential brides, and some of them – but there was no safe way of telling in advance *which ones* – would eventually marry men of position, importance and wealth. It was obviously impolite and unwise to offend and antagonise those particular girls who were going to end up as wives of men of importance. But – there's the rub – there was no way of identifying this sub-class in advance. Were it possible, obviously one could and would adjust one's behaviour to any individual girl in accordance with whether she was a member of this important sub-class, or whether she fell into the residue. But it was *not* possible; and this being so, the only sensible policy, which Lady Montdore duly adopted, was to be polite to them *all*.

It is an occupationally very mobile society, it is not merely the pool of upper-class brides, but virtually the whole population which benefits from Lady Montdore's Principle. (There is one supremely important exception to this. Members of underprivileged sub-groups which are easily identifiable – by pigmentational, deeply engrained cultural, or other near-indelible traits – actually suffer *additional* disadvantages in this situation. The statistical improbability of social ascension which attaches to such a group as a whole is more or less forcibly applied, by a kind of social anticipation, even to individuals who would otherwise rise to more attractive positions. The bitterness of 'racial' tensions in otherwise mobile societies is of course connected with this.)

But to leave aside identifiable and systematically disadvantaged groups, and concentrate on the relatively homogeneous majority, the Principle militates powerfully against the attribution of permanent, profound, deeply engrained status distinctions. In a relatively stable society, it is possible – and very common – to establish legally, ritually or otherwise enforced and highlighted status distinctions, which turn people into basically different *kinds of men*. Radical, conceptually internalised inequality is feasible, and is frequently practised.[2] But even

---

[2] Louis Dumont has consciously attempted to perpetuate the Tocquevillian tradition and to analyse both egalitarian and inegalitarian societies, and to separate the issues of hierarchy and holism. See his *Homo Hierarchicus* and his *Homo Aequalis* (translated into English as *From Mandeville to Marx*, Chicago, 1977). Both his account of Indian and of Western societies – treated as paradigms of hierarchical and non-hierarchical organisation – are open to the suspicion that he overstresses the role of ideology, and does not sufficiently explore non-ideological factors.

Dumont's insistence on separating the issue of egalitarianism and holism (Indian society being for him the paradigm of a society both hierarchical and holistic) receives a kind of confirmation from Alan Macfarlane's recent *Origins of English Individualism*, Oxford, 1978, with its striking and powerfully argued claim that English society was individualistic since at least the later Middle Ages. It would be hard to claim that it was also egalitarian.

such traditional, relatively stable societies are frequently obliged to 'cheat'. Roles ascribed by heredity and those actually available to be filled do not converge. Demographic accidents, or other causes, lead to the overproduction of hereditary occupants of one kind of socio-economic role, and the underproduction of the occupants of others; and, so as to keep going, the society fills its roles, and has its essential tasks carried out in a manner which, more or less covertly, violates its own principles of the hereditary or otherwise rigid ascription of status. But, given the relative economic stability or stagnation of such societies, this kind of cheating is nevertheless kept within bounds.

But in the occupationally high mobile industrial society, the cheating would have to be on such a scale as to become intolerable and absurd. The most eloquent testimony to mobility is precisely the fact that when it fails to occur – because of ineradicable 'racial' or otherwise engrained traits – such a society experiences its most intolerable tensions. In fact, of course, modern industrial society cheats in the opposite direction. As egalitarian left-wing critics frequently point out, the mobility and equality of opportunity which is credited to liberal society is not quite as great as it is painted. This is indeed so: life-chances are unequal, and the extent to which this is so varies in diverse occupations, countries and so on. But at the same time, mobility is real and frequent enough to impose formal equality as a kind of external norm. Hereditary rank and status, so common and widely acceptable elsewhere, would be in collision with actual role so very frequently as to lead to intolerable friction. Formal equality – the intolerable nature, in modern conditions, of dividing men into different *kinds* of being – however much sinned against by substantive inequalities, is not merely the compliment of hierarchical vice to egalitarian virtue, it is also the recognition of the genuine reality of occupational mobility, and hence of the non-viability of any serious system of rank which would prejudge status independently of occupational position. Where occupational position is both crucial and unpredictable, the only workable system of hereditary rank is one which confers the same rank on all – in other words, egalitarianism.

Note that a complex division of labour joined to occupational mobility is imposed internationally. There are no autarchic economies, and all national economies are obliged to run if they are even to stay in the same place. If they lag behind relatively, they eventually suffer absolutely. Thus innovation and its corollary, occupational mobility, are imposed on all cultures.

2 The nature of our work life

J.-P. Sartre observed somewhere that the working class was predisposed towards materialism because its work experience brought home to it the constraints imposed on us by *things*, whereas the middle class tended towards idealism because its work situation consisted largely of the manipulation of words, ideas and people. If this so to speak materialist, or at any rate sociological, explanation of why people embrace materialism or idealism is correct, then the future prospects for materialism would seem distinctly poor: the proportion of jobs at the coal face, so to speak, involving the direct handling of extra-human, extra-social, physical reality by human hand is rapidly diminishing. On the whole, we deal with *choses* only, as you might say, *par personnes interposées*, and these *personnes* diminish in number. The tools by means of which brute things are handled are themselves sophisticated, and their controls require the recognition of conventional meanings, in other words of ideas, rather than the application of brute force.

A very large part of the working life of a very large, growing and probably majoritarian proportion of men consists of encounters and interaction with a large number of other men, in varied, unpredictable and anonymous contexts. If this is so, this underscores once again the impracticality of rigid and visible social ranking. Inequality is viable when the ranking is agreed, more or less, by both parties: if superior A and inferior B both accept their relative ranking, they can cooperate peacefully. B may or may not resent the situation, and he may or may not look forward to its modification; but for the time being they can communicate. Not every ranker respects every officer, but for the time being, the clearly defined and identified difference in their respective ranks enables them to communicate in their work situation without constant and immediate friction. But if people are constantly encountering, communicating with and temporarily cooperating with men of unidentified rank, in a multiplicity of different organisations whose respective rankings may not be easily inter-translatable, then to insist on the recognition of rank is to ask for constant trouble. It would be an encouragement to both parties to impose their own vision of their own standing, on each occasion.[3]

[3] It is arguable that this in fact does happen; that the high valuation of a kind of aggressive 'personality' in middle America is connected with an egalitarianism which denies that a man can bring previous rank to a new encounter. He is expected to establish his standing by his manner, but not allowed to appeal to his previous history and position. If so the cult of restraint which is so characteristic of much of English culture (and which Weber considered to be one of the conse-

Complex, intricate social organisation, with all the consequences this has for the nature of human encounters, does not *on its own* generate egalitarianism. There are ample historical examples which prove this. But in conjunction with occupational mobility, the complexity, anonymity, brevity of human encounters all provide a powerful impulsion towards egalitarianism. A society which was simply occupationally mobile, but in which each person carried out his work without numerous and unpredictable contacts with many other people, would find it easier to combine its mobility with *in*egalitarianism. The so to speak gregarious-mercurial nature of our professional life, jointly with mobility, makes egalitarianism hard to escape – because *deep* ranking would be endlessly friction-engenderng. Where ranking is superimposed on such a society, by the symbiosis of 'racially', religiously, culturally distinguishable sub-communities with differing prestige, it does notoriously lead to intolerable friction.

3 Our home life

For the great majority of members of advanced industrial society, work life on the one hand, and home or community life (or lives) on the other, are clearly and distinctly separate. There are exceptions to this, but they are relatively rare. For an Israeli kibbutznik, the work,

---

quences of Protestantism) could be attributed to a valuation of rank and status, which frees its carrier from a vulgar need to insist loudly on his standing. He *is*, he doesn't need to *do*. This provides a useful and discouraging hurdle for the would-be climber, who is faced with a fork: if he conducts himself with restraint, he will remain unnoticed and outside, for as yet he *is* not, but if he makes a noise, he will display his vulgarity and damn himself. (In practice, many have, however, surmounted this fork.) Tocqueville attributed English reserve not to rank as such, but to the fluidity and ambiguity of ranking, which makes it dangerous to establish a connection with a stranger whose standing is as yet necessarily obscure.

If my argument about the connection between egalitarianism and the multiplicity of organisations is correct, one might expect egalitarianism to be less marked in socialist industrial countries, given the fact that socialist economic organisation approaches more closely the unification of production in one single organisation whose sub-parts employ the same idiom and can have mutually translatable, equivalent rank-systems. This tendency, if it obtains, may perhaps be compensated by the greater overt commitment of socialist societies to egalitarianism.

It is also possible that the whole argument is empirically contradicted by the case of Japan which combines a notoriously successful industrial society with, apparently, great rigidity of and sensitivity to rank, at least within any single one organisation. One would like to know whether ranking is ignored with a polite egalitarianism, in encounters between men of different organisations. Cf. R. P. Dore, *British Factory – Japanese Factory*, London, 1973.

social, and military unit are all identical or overlapping; a Head of an Oxford College is performing one of his duties when he dines; and there are still, here and there, servants who are also full-time retainers. But all this is manifestly exceptional and atypical. A normal existence, or *Existenz*, notoriously involves travel from home to place of work. (Living over the shop is a privilege or burden given to few.) This means more than a merely physical move: it means a shift from one set of persons to another, from one authority and hierarchy to another, from one idiom and moral climate to another. This separation is, notoriously, one part of what Marx meant by 'alienation', and which constituted a part of the indictment of capitalism.

No doubt this separation has an inhuman aspect. It enables men to purchase the labour of another, and treat it, as Marxism stressed, as a mere commodity, without assuming any of the other responsibilities (however inegalitarian) which had been characteristic of more *personal*, pre-capitalist forms of domination. It was this aspect of the impersonality of labour relations which first struck observers of industrial society.

But, interestingly, the separation of home life and work life also has other implications, relevant to egalitarianism and favourable to it. The relative amount of 'labour as a commodity' has diminished, though it still exists: the condition of foreign labour migrants, providing brawn, and morally non-incorporated in the society in which they work, approximates to that of the 'classical' working class observed by Engels. But a large part of the skilled working class is in quite a different condition. But at this point, I am not concerned with the transformation (by skills, etc.) of their working situation, but rather with the long-term implications of the *continuing* separation of work and life.

This means that work relations are not carried over into home life, and there are no radical obstacles in the way of a homogeneous, or at least continuous, home and leisure culture. The authority structure of work is in no way transferred into the home. A serf was a full-time serf; even a servant, for the duration of his service, was full time. He did not escape from his condition into a private world. In the modern world, the inequality of the working condition is restricted to working hours. The inequality between those who give orders and those who execute them, where it obtains, does *not* carry over into the (ever lengthening) leisure periods, and is not deeply internalised, or perhaps not internalised at all.

There is an enormous difference between a full-time and a part-time servile role. Service roles which are circumscribed in time and specific in function, such as waiting in a restaurant, are not felt to be demeaning, and occupations of that kind do not seem to have any difficulty in recruiting personnel. By contrast, so to speak 'real' servants, living-in as unequal members of a household, are notoriously difficult to obtain. *Au pair* girls in the West, though performing some of the functions of a maid – easing the wife's work load, baby-minding, providing sexual temptation for male members of the household – have to be treated as equals, and this is of the essence of the situation. Gracious living, which is conditional on personal service and dependence, survives only in a very restricted and make-believe measure, and is available to ordinary members of even the prosperous middle and professional classes only if they succeed in joining certain Consumer Cooperatives for Gracious Living, such as Oxbridge colleges or West End clubs. Here, by sharing the expense involved, it is possible to recreate the illusion of hierarchy and dependence. It is, however, largely an illusion: just as the consumers in these places do not generally enjoy the services full time but only intermittently (returning for the rest of the time to their suburban houses and helping with the washing-up), so similarly the 'servants' *take turns* in assuming this servile status, and shed it when off duty, to adopt in their leisure time a life style not differing from non-servile members of the working class or indeed differing all that much from those of their 'masters'. Certain ritual symbolisms are still observed: West End clubs are one of the few places left where it is still possible to have one's status confirmed by having one's shoes polished by human labour. Elsewhere it has become impossible, as I realised when I left my shoes outside the door of a New York hotel in the 1960s, and the hotel staff, quite misinterpreting my intention, simply threw the shoes away. Hotels nowadays provide shoe-polishing machines as their own distinctive contribution to the equalisation of conditions.

4 The new cultural division of labour and the mass media

Whether the human heart as such is egalitarian, or only the human heart as formed by our kind of society, is an open question; but it is a fact that 'real' (full-time retainer) servants are very difficult to obtain. This has certain consequences for the possibilities of creating differential life styles. You can live your leisure in any style you wish – if your environment is liberal and allows you to do so – but, on the whole, only within the limits of your own labour resources and those of your household who are your equals. In other words for all but a very small minority, activities dependent on a tail of retainers and dependants are *out*. This fact contributes more powerfully to the relative homogenisation of life styles than anything else, whether one calls it the embourgeoisement of the working class (which seems to be a fact, notwithstanding its contestation by some sociologists) or the impoverishment of the middle classes.

If leisure activities are, on the whole, restricted to such as do not presuppose retainers, the options available to affluent industrial man are: either to join leisure consumer cooperatives, clubs of diverse kinds, or to accept the highly specialised and professional entertainment services provided by the mass media. By and large, it would seem that these services, enjoying as they do the advantages of selection, professionalism, and resources, prevail, and constitute the main and inevitably rather standardised culture-forming influence.

No doubt there are great differences in the manner of consuming these available services, and cultural differentiation persists, and may even have great prestige and overrule economic differentiation; this seems liable to happen, for instance, in socialist societies.[4] Nevertheless, and notwithstanding this qualification, it is reasonable to suppose that the restriction of the availability of human resources in leisure time, and the cheap availability of television, music, paperback, and the like must militate against culturally enforced inequality. If money can no longer buy you *people*, and a basic minimum living standard is widely assured, can it still buy you cultural diacritical marks? The answer is that it can, but not nearly as much or as convincingly as it could in the past. We shall return to this topic in connection with the meaning of wealth under conditions of industrial affluence.

5 Diminished vulnerability

Inequality (like equality, and perhaps like most things) depends for its systematic implementation on enforcement. The coming of industrial affluence has significantly diminished the vulnerability of men to some forms of pressure and intimidation at least. It has certainly not freed all men from such pressure, even in the privileged set of developed industrial societies: there are notorious and important exceptions. There are those who combine poverty with isolation and some kind of personal (for instance medical) disablement or inadequacy; and there are ethnic or religious or other minorities which are not properly incorporated in the moral community and do not effectively share in the citizenship of the society. But for the big bulk of the population, benefiting from the welfare infra-structure which is now common to developed societies, and from the benefits of the right of

[4] See Pavel Machonín a kolektiv, *Československá Společnost*, Bratislava, 1969.

association and so forth, vulnerability at any rate to economic pressure has decreased very significantly. The sexual revolution has also contributed to this trend, by greatly diminishing one important motive for seeking control over people. Sex is now more easily available even to those not occupying positions of power or influence.

Inequality has thus lost one at least of its important sanctions. It is presumably this diminished vulnerability which at least helps to account for the marked decrease in willingness to occupy servile positions. It seems that this diminished willingness to be servile is not accompanied by a strong need for independence: insecurely remunerated work (notably independent peasant agriculture) has also lost appeal, and people leave it when they can. The dominant ideal seems to be employment which is secure (wage or salary arriving independently of vagaries of weather), but where the work is clearly circumscribed in time and the work-time authority relations in no way extend into home and private time.

This ideal is widely attained in the developed societies, and the welfare provisions and governmental assumption of responsibility for full or high employment (or tolerable conditions for the unemployed), all of which has become part of the shared political norms, jointly ensures that almost no one need cringe and kiss feet so as to avoid destitution. This was not always so, but it is so now. Servility amongst the lower orders is only encountered as an occasional survival. I remember reading a novel in which a character used to take visitors by a roundabout way through a village because this increased the chance of meeting an old man who sometimes called him 'sir'. This entirely catches the spirit of our present situation.

6 Uniform training and socialisation

Private control over quite extensive leisure time, plus the mass media, facilitate a common culture, not markedly diversified over social strata. But in all probability, the most powerful factor contributing towards this end is uniformity of training and socialisation. Once again, this is not (as is often supposed) a consequence of egalitarian ideology; it is rooted in general features of our social organisation, and egalitarianism reflects rather than causes it.

It is the most strikingly paradoxical feature of advanced industrialism that this society, the most highly specialised society *ever*, should have (at least when compared with other complex societies) the *least* specialised educational or training system. Is this a paradox? Does our education system go against the grain of our form of economic organisation, is it a strange, ideologically inspired defiance of it? Should a society which has pushed the division of labour to a length and refinement never previously dreamt of similarly refine and differentiate the educational experiences to which it subjects its young, instead of imposing on them, as in fact it does, a strikingly similar pattern?

No. There is no paradox. On the contrary, the diversification of socio-economic roles, and the simultaneous standardisation of educational experience, far from being in disharmony, dovetail with each other perfectly. As stressed, the diversity of occupational roles is not static but *mobile*. People must be retrainable. It simply isn't feasible for them to attain their professional skills in a seven years' apprenticeship with a Master and then, when they change jobs, to go for another seven years to a new one. Instead, they spend seven or more years at the start in *generic* training, which provides them (ideally) with enough literacy, numeracy, and technical and social sophistication to make them retrainable fairly quickly. Moreover, the division of labour is not merely mobile, but also presupposes frequent interaction and effective communication between members of diverse occupations.

The high prestige of unspecialised education (even if the centre of gravity of prestige has shifted from literacy to numeracy) is not (or only in very small measure) some kind of Veblenesque survival of a high valuation of uselessness or futility as an index of high status. (Specialised schooling, such as is offered by medical or law schools, only has prestige when it follows a good dose of generic training.) On the contrary, it reflects and reinforces our egalitarianism. If training must needs be similar – and indeed it must – then a deep sense of inequality cannot easily be inculcated in the young, in those undergoing the process of education. Education standardises and unifies – not because this aim is part of public policy, which is also often the case, as in the United States it is part of assimilation of immigrants, or in Britain as a consequence of Labour Party egalitarianism – but, more significantly and reliably, as a consequence of the kind of education which needs to be imposed. This educational aim, the establishment of a shared and broad basis for quick specific retraining, is imposed on the educational system by deep requirements of the wider economy, and thus is not at the mercy of minor ideological fads.

7 The nature of wealth in affluent industrial society

The very meaning of wealth and ownership has changed under modern conditions – though this fact has not been widely recognised. In agrarian society (or early industrial society, of course), the difference between wealth and its absence is, above all, the difference between having and not having enough to eat. The poor are periodically hungry, and some starve when periodic famine hits the land. Quite late in the history of industrial society, the poor ate more bread during lean years than during prosperous ones, because they were obliged to shift expenditure towards the cheapest nourishment so as to avoid actual hunger. Notoriously, they did not eat enough for full physical development: in various near-affluent societies, the older generations are still markedly smaller than the present younger generations.

But in the highly developed societies, literal hunger is fast receding beyond the historical horizon. And if we exclude the 'submerged minority', the handicapped, isolated, or members of groups subject to racial or political discrimination, a certain significant minimum is also coming to be taken for granted by very wide strata (though not by all). This wider minimum includes not merely freedom from hunger, but also access to currently accepted standards of medical attention, housing, and culture (education, literacy, a degree of leisure).

What are the implications of this situation, in which very broad strata are approaching a *confident* possession of this minimum? One must add, of course, that access to *more* than this minimum is very unevenly, very unequally spread out. A big majority are in seeming possession of this minimum, but within this majority, the *extra* is distributed unevenly.

How we assess the consequences of this situation depends very much on our philosophical anthropology, our general vision of man. If we suppose that man's needs are boundless or open-ended, we shall conclude that the inequality of extras is very important. If, on the other hand, we believe that above a certain minimum, man's material needs are definitely limited, we shall assess the importance of inequality-in-extras differently, and treat it as much less important. May I say right away that I belong to the second school. In other words, the difference between a man who is in secure and assured possession of access to adequate nourishment, medical care, shelter and leisure, and a man whose 'means' enable him to purchase this minimum many times over, is not very great. The difference is simply not comparable to the difference which once existed between having access to these goods, and not having it or only having it intermittently and precariously.

But of course, there still *is* a difference. But it consists not in genuine additional consumption, but in prestige, power and influence. A man cannot sit in more than one car at once, and leaving out relatively

marginal considerations (there may be some benefit in owning different kinds of car), the only thing he attains by owning $n+1$ cars is an
unofficial status of superiority over an unfortunate possessor of
merely n cars. In capitalist societies, he can of course also put his
wealth, not into symbolic prestige possessions, but into ownership or,
much more commonly, part-share ownership of the means of production, which theoretically gives him a voice in economic decisions.
These two options open to him – prestige and economic power – need
to be considered separately.

The very fact that extra wealth can only go into prestige, the minimum being so widely satisfied, also means that relatively little can in
turn be attained through prestige. Servility simply does not seem
easily attainable, at least by economic as opposed to political means.
As indicated, vulnerability has declined, and people are no longer
willing to crawl, or not much, or only when scared politically. Moreover, prestige is also attainable by means other than wealth, and these
means often seem to be preferred. This will be discussed under the
very next heading, and the use of economic power, in section 9.

8 The work ethic

Most forms of prestige attainable by wealth are now also attainable by
occupancy of appropriate positions, usually bureaucratic ranks within
organisations. Interesting travel, good hotels, encounters with interesting people under agreeable and *soignée* circumstances with
attentive service – these can of course still be purchased by money,
but they are also the natural and recognised perks of professional success. Though a rich man can buy these things, it is my impression that
he will often do so apologetically; but those who are granted them on
merit and on expense account, as inherent in their *position*, enjoy them
with *pride*. Has the work ethic become so pervasive that people enjoy
the perks of their professional position more than they do the fruits of
mere wealth? Or is it rather that the work ethic has become so pervasive in the middle and upper strata of industrial society, because it
reflects a kind of universal mamluk-isation, a form of organisation and
ethos in which privilege honourably attaches only to achieved status? I
think the latter.

9 The nature of power

In agrarian society, power is visible, concrete and immediate in its
effects. The major form of wealth is agricultural produce. Power consists of the possession of the means of physical constraint, by means of

which a significant part of the produce is channelled towards those who wield power in the society in question. Power is manifested in the capacity to compel people to work and to determine the distribution of the fruit of labour. Neither the coercion and its agents, nor the labour and its fruits, are so to speak distant: they can be *perceived*, they need not be *conceived*.

Developed industrial society, with its enormously complex division of labour, is quite different. Visible physical constraint, known as terror, is not part of its normal working order, and only occurs in a-typical situations (civil war, coup d'état) when a new political authority imposes itself, or even imposes a new social order, by killing or threatening to kill those who oppose it. It may be said that this violence is ever-latent and inhibits those who would change the social order as such. This may well be so; but the fact remains that within its normal working, power and physical coercion are not normally conspicuous.

The division of labour is intricate and the social machine exceedingly complex. The power of a feudal lord of the manor is continuous and simple, and manifests itself in similar and repetitive situations: he makes sure that the peasants work, and that in due course they deliver the required proportion of produce. But 'power' in a complex industrial society is not visible in this kind of monotone manner. Power consists in having one's hand on the crucial lever of the total machine at a moment when an option arises for the system which will be decided primarily by the position of that very lever. Crucial decisions occur here and there at diverse and irregular times. Power is not continuous but intermittent.

If this fact is taken in conjunction with the previously stressed point about the inherent and inevitable occupational mobility of advanced industrial society, we end once again with a powerful factor favouring equality. Power being volatile, intermittent and tied to special positions, or rather the combination of a position and an alternative-generating crisis, it follows that there is no clear and demarcated class of power-holders, and that it is necessary to treat a wide class of persons with respect and as equals, because they may on occasion find themselves at an important lever.

As against this, it can of course be argued that, notoriously, industrial society possesses vastly superior means of centralisation and communication, and if it is organised in an authoritarian manner, can control all appointments and most decisions from one single centre – so that, despite the complexity and mobility inherent in its economic organisation, a systematic inequality of power can be imposed. It is possible to ensure that all decisions are referred upwards, and also to ensure that all occupants of intermittently crucial and hence powerful posts are only recruited from a special sub-class of people. This argument is also weighty, and militates against the egalitarian one which was cited first.

10 Deliberate equalisation from above

The anti-egalitarian tendency in authoritarianism (which is made possible, though not necessarily engendered by, industrial organisation), can however be countered by another consideration.

The mamluk-isation of men seems to me inherent in our condition: it is natural that we should derive our standing from our achieved position rather than from inherited wealth or kin connection. But over and above this (and irrespective of whether in fact it is natural under industrial conditions), it may also be the consequence of deliberate policy on the part of authoritarian government. The essence of a mamluk is that he is powerful, but at the same time he is legally a slave: his property, his life, can be revoked arbitrarily from above. As we say in the university, he has no tenure. Now the vesting of status and power in revocable, non-tenure positions only, the preventing of wealth- or kin-based power bases, makes everyone dependent on the single centre of authority. As Marx pointed out, Bonapartism rested on the equality of small landholders. So authoritarian centralism, whilst capable of generating inequality in one way, does further equality in another.

11 Egalitarianism as camouflage

The above is a well-known right-wing argument, purporting to show that the equalisation of conditions leads to tyranny, and that tyranny can only be avoided by allowing or encouraging state-independent power bases, of wealth or of association, and hence inequality.

In the interests of symmetry and of the semblance of impartiality it is also well worth citing a left-wing argument, which also has some substance behind it. The argument is very simple: modern society is egalitarian in ethos because it is unequal in fact. Ideology inverts and hides reality. The superficial egalitarianism, the myth of mobility, the apparent diminution of social distance, simply serve to hide the astonishing and often unperceived inequalities in wealth, power and life-chances which persist or even increase.[5]

[5] Cf. John Westergaard and H. Resler, *Class in Capitalist Society*, Harmondsworth, 1977, or P. Bourdieu and J.-C. Passeron, *Les Héritiers*, Paris, 1964 (translated as *The Inheritors*, Chicago, 1979).

I do not myself believe mobility to be a myth, nor do I hold the diminution of social distance to be something merely superficial. It is important in itself. At the same time, the persistence or augmentation of material inequality, and the camouflage of this inequality by a relative congruence of life styles, are also realities.

12 Talent-specificity of many posts

Imagine a society (there must have been many such) in which no senior position really requires exceptional inborn talents. One suspects that any fool could be a feudal lord, or even a mediaeval bishop. The lord had to be taught to ride and fight from an early age, and the bishop had to learn to read; but, given training, these accomplishments seem to be within the reach of most men. Hence the society could fill these positions by any random method if it chose, as long as it picked the incumbents young enough to ensure that they be duly trained. The Athenians recognised this by drawing lots for the selection of occupants of some public offices. A society could, as the Tibetans have done until recently, select appointees by the *time* of their birth; or it could, as is more common, select them by their paternity. (This, of course, has the advantage that the domestic unit can also provide initial training and familiarity with the job.)

Modern society is interesting in that it contains a high proportion of posts in which the standard expected is so high that the posts simply cannot be filled at random. The level expected of concert pianists is so high that it simply would not be feasible to recruit such pianists from a pianist clan, in the way in which musicians often are recruited in tribal societies. They now need not merely training but also genuine inborn talent, which is beyond the reach of social manipulation or ascription. The same is true of professors of physics. It is not quite so obviously true of professors of philosophy, and it is possible that the standard in this field would not be very different if they were selected, say, by horoscope. It is said that when the University of Durham was founded early in the nineteenth century, the Bishop simply instructed the personnel at his disposal to mug up various subjects and thereafter to become professors in them.

The precise limits of talent-specificity in modern society are obscure, but it does seem obvious that it does obtain in some measure, and in far greater measure than in earlier societies. A society bound by occupational mobility to provide roughly the same generic training for all, and at the same time bound by the fact of talent-specificity to seek out and to reward independently existing and unpredictable talent which is not under its own control, is thereby certainly impelled in the direction of egalitarianism.

13 Ideological impoverishment

Developed industrial society tends to lack firmness and vigour of conviction (perhaps for a good reason – possibly no convictions deserve firm adherence, and the merits of scepticism should not be ruled out). Whether this lack of conviction is well based does not concern us here. What does concern us is certain of the implications of this state of affairs, if indeed it obtains.

Agrarian societies, by contrast, tended to be both hierarchical and dogmatic. The dogmas which they upheld with firmness and sanctioned with severity at the same time provided warrants and legitimation for the inequalities which prevailed within them. But what happens when this dogmatic underpinning of a system of ranks and inequalities is withdrawn?

As far as I can see, egalitarianism then inherits the earth as a kind of residual legatee, for lack of any others. If there are no good reasons for assigning men to ranks (because there are no good, independent, transcendent reasons for *anything*), then we might as well all be equal. It seems that equality requires fewer reasons than inequality, and as reasons or premises for a specific vision of a social order are now in short supply, well, that makes us into egalitarians by default. This is certainly not a formally cogent argument, but it has a certain plausibility and may well play a part, though probably a minor part, in helping to explain the modern trend towards equality.

The complex interdependence of a modern economy means that there are many areas within which workers are crucial for all the rest; if not physically or otherwise restrained, they can blackmail the rest of society to accept their terms. This of course became specially conspicuous during the troubles connected with the attempts to fight inflation and the consequences of the energy crisis. When it is hard to defy segments of the work force occupying strategic positions – for example the miners – one can only appeal to their restraint, which the authorities did, somewhat pathetically. What moral principle, however, can the authorities invoke? In practice, it tends to be, inevitably, an egalitarianism mitigated by some reward for extra discomfort, risk and so on.

Liberal societies refrain from using force against the occupants of strategic heights in the economy. But when they use persuasion instead, there appears to be very little in the ideological armoury other than egalitarianism which could be invoked, even if there were the will to do so.

The consequence, in liberal and advanced societies, tends to be the following: an egalitarian trend towards the convergence of middle-class and working-class remuneration, with extra privileges then attaching to posts rather than to persons (the mamluk has perks, not wealth, and perks escape tax), whilst surviving personal-wealth-based advantage tends to be discreet and somewhat shamefaced. The major difference between contemporary and Edwardian England seems to me to be that the gentlemanly proscription of ostentation now really is enforced. The rich are always with us, but are now seldom conspicuous. Conspicuous display is practised mainly by pop stars, footballers, pools winners – but the point about *them* is that they show it could happen to *anyone*. They are not different. Hemingway clearly would be right about them. They only have more money. They illustrate rather than defy egalitarianism.

14 Positive philosophical endorsement of equality

A modern economy does not depend only on an intricate division of labour and occupational mobility; it notoriously also depends on a powerful technology, which in turn depends on science.

But it is plausible to hold that science in turn can only function on the basis of certain background assumptions about the nature of things, assumptions which are not self-evident and which, in fact, are very difficult to establish without circularity of reasoning. Perhaps the most important amongst these background assumptions are what might be called the Symmetry Assumption, the supposition that the world is an orderly system which does not allow of exceptions, which ignores the sacred or the privileged, so to speak. This assumption is of course intimately connected with the philosophical issues involving ideas such as the Regularity of Nature, the Principle of Causation (or of Sufficient Reason), and so on.

The philosophic merit or even the precise formulation of the symmetry assumption do not here directly concern us. What does concern us, once again, is its implications for equality. It confers a certain equality on facts, and it confers a similar obligatory equality on knowers. It requires explanation which does not respect status, and this lack of deference is infectious. Theories, ontologies, cannot be defended, given the terms of reference imposed by the Symmetry Assumption, by claims such as that certain facts or certain occasions or certain ideas or personal sources of ideas are exempt from scrutiny or contradiction by their extreme holiness. Belief-systems of agrarian societies frequently contained symmetry-defying elements of this very kind, but science and the Symmetry Assumption tend to erode them.

This in itself is a kind of encouragement to egalitarianism, a kind of Demonstration Effect. But there is more to come. The Symmetry Assumption tends to engender a certain philosophical anthropology, most significantly exemplified by Kantianism. The central notion in Kantian ethics is symmetry or parity of treatment. But joined to this is a vision of man in which our real identity is tied to something identical in all of us – our rationality – whereas the great empirical and social differentiae between us are relegated to a morally inferior realm. What makes us men is the same in all of us and real; what differentiates us lies in the realm of appearance.

A human ontology which strips us of our rank (along with many other things) may reflect a Protestant equality of believers, it may also reflect an emerging society in which professional status is supremely important and not hereditary, and it dovetails with a symmetrical vision of nature. In turn, it makes its contribution – perhaps just a rather minor one – to our pervasive egalitarianism.

Those who are imbued with the egalitarian ideal are naturally and properly preoccupied with the failures to implement it (which do occur in the various forms of industrial society). Yet in a broader context, what seems to me most striking is not these failures, but the seriousness and pervasiveness of the egalitarian ideal, and its partial implementation, which make industrial society so very eccentric amongst complex and literate societies. It seems to me important to try to understand why we have this passion and tendency (to the extent we do indeed have it, and it is not my view that there are no other and contrary trends). Arguments about equality, fairness, and justice, which tend to take egalitarianism for granted and make few attempts to seek its social roots, seem to me doomed to a certain superficiality. Hence I have attempted to see where its roots are to be sought.

7 Recollection in anxiety:
Thought and Change revisited

Despite everything, the decades between 1945 and the oil crisis will in retrospect be seen as a new *belle époque*. The basic features of our social and ideological landscape have not changed since, yet somehow the sky has become darker, lowering and menacing. There is a sense of civilisation, liberty, decency being in a state of siege, more deeply precarious than before, more fragile, and also more rotten and betrayed from within.

Why, all in all, had things seemed so good? Indeed, we had never had it so good, in a variety of senses. Now it feels as if we were going to pay for it.

The Second World War had ended in victory. Unlike the First World War, which in retrospect seems sheer madness, the second was one which could not be avoided and which allowed of little doubt about the merit of the two sides. It was followed not by a return to the depression of the 1930s, but by sustained and better diffused prosperity. Within the developed world there was greater equality; and the same seemed due for repetition on a global scale when, by the early 1960s, decolonisation was more or less completed, and seemed destined in due course to repeat the same kind of equalisation-of-dignity process between entire national communities. Within developed societies a mixed economy and the Keynesian formula seemed to allow both growth and the striving towards social justice and liberty, all at once, so that it seemed that no major value need be painfully sacrificed. The precise mix of these ingredients might be open to debate – but that was a good thing anyway, for were we not liberals? – and the optimal solution might vary from place to place; but that clearly was no ground for deep anxiety.

There were of course problems. The most obvious one was precisely the diffusion of this blissful, and cosy, fusion of affluence and freedom to the rest of the world, which as yet had neither. There was no point in pretending to oneself, or anyone else for that matter, that this Great Transition to developed Industrial Society could be anything other than painful, and often brutal. But one accepted this suffering of others with a vicarious stoicism which may, no doubt rightly, seem complacent and comic. But then, what help would it have been to anyone if one had become hysterical? The state of perpetual moral outrage, occasioned indifferently by good causes and bad (and seldom with enough knowledge to know just *which* it is) and used simultaneously to titivate oneself, to justify a shriller complacency, a meddling and demanding interference with others and a suspension of rules of propriety, is a habitual stance of the Far Left, and one which is in the end self-defeating and repellent. Cheap moral indignation drives out good. In any case, one was aware of the tragic situation of the rest of humanity, and if one's attention turned towards the Third World, it was precisely because, within the limits of one's particular capacities, one wished to help alleviate the agony. All the same there clearly was an element of patronising complacency in it all.

That was the problem, and if it was a grave one, at the same time it provided an intellectual fascination which the consensual, apparently post-ideological politics of a developed society could no longer give. That was a field which no longer provided interesting questions, and it could safely be left to TV commentators and their like. Within the world which mattered, a world undergoing the fundamental transformation which was to fix its political character for a long time and to be its social contract, the crucial issue was being decided: would any given country 'develop' in a manner which would leave it with free institutions, or not? That 'development' would take place at all, that industrial affluence would eventually be reached by most societies, seemed to me reasonably certain (with certain provisos), and I have not really changed my mind on that point. But if the two sovereign masters in my philosophy (though not in that of others) were affluence and liberty, and if affluence – in the long run – was not seriously in doubt, then the crucial question for our time was that of liberty, not poverty; liberty was the precarious element. What mattered was its preservation or establishment, above all at that fateful moment when the turbulence of industrialisation calmed down, and when social orders were liable to set, to congeal, under the political order and ideology which had presided over the rough passage. Or so I thought.

There was no undue complacency or facility in contemplating this issue. There were obvious powerful forces making for an unfavourable outcome: the authoritarian traditions of most pre-industrial societies, the acute miseries of what might be called the middle passage to the shores of affluence, the consequent escalation of the political struggle in the course of it and hence the premium on blinkered single-mindedness and ruthlessness – all these were loading the dice against the desired outcome. All the same, liberalism or pluralism had a fighting chance; there were factors weighting the scales in its favour too; and if it prevailed in some places at least, it might eventually become more general, simply through its demonstration effect. If successful development was indeed possible without tyranny, then tyranny would eventually be seen to be redundant.

There were other problems. The possibility of nuclear holocaust is a *sui generis* matter, and like other highly idiosyncratic problems is consequently not easily amenable to rational consideration. Blaise Pascal provided cogent reasons for accepting the existence of God in terms of probability theory, but the unique nature of the hypothesis always made this treatment rather bizarre and unconvincing (the oddity is perhaps its point) and the same seemed true to me of the nuclear issue. (Strangely, Bertrand Russell was accused of inconsistency for having advocated both a preventive war in the days of American nuclear monopoly and unilateral disarmament when that monopoly was lost. Far from being incompatible, both these recommendations follow cogently from the premiss that collective nuclear suicide is worse than anything else whatever, and there is not the slightest contradiction between them.) But I refrained from making any wager on that one, just as I cannot follow Pascal about God.

But I did not avert my gaze from other problems. Nationalism and ethnic hatreds of diverse kinds, are plainly a major force in the modern world, yet do not on the surface seem reducible to the problem of the social quantum-jump from agrarian poverty to industrial wealth. But appearances are deceptive. It seems to me obvious that modern nationalism has nothing whatever to do with the reassertion of atavistic loyalties (other than invoking or inventing them for its convenience); it has nothing to do with the *Blut und Boden* to which it appeals but is, on the contrary, an inescapable consequence of the atomised, mobile and universally literate modern society.

The need for cultural homogeneity follows from the requirements of rapid, easy and precise communication, of the possibility of slotting people rapidly into new economic roles, of a complex, sophisticated, and quickly changing division of labour. In such circumstances, cultural discontinuity – tolerable and often positively functional in stable agrarian societies – becomes unacceptable, and when it correlates with the persisting inequalities of industrial society, explosive. The stratification of industrial society as such is not acutely conflict-engendering, but it rapidly becomes such whenever the inequalities can, so to speak, seize upon cultural differentiae and use them as their symbols. As we cannot beat this force, we should do our best to accommodate ourselves to it with least pain. All this I believed then and continue to believe now. The emergence, in the meantime, of new regional nationalisms, not always fed by any genuine cultural differentiation, has on occasion made me think my theory may be incomplete – but this remains an open question. This in outline was the kind of stocktaking, a general overview of our collective social situation which I attempted in *Thought and Change* (1964) and which was intended to capture the underlying, effectively operating premises of the period. Have recent developments made it necessary to reassess the picture? Has the world changed fundamentally since that *belle époque?*

Take that complacency and condescension which were, alas, inherent in the very manner in which the question was formulated – can we help *them* to become as free as we are, in the process becoming more or less as rich as we are, and preferably also helping them speed up the process of enrichment? Of course, even then lip service was paid to the need to preserve cultural diversity, and their *nationalist* doctrines proclaimed that they did not wish to be like us; but that was rhetoric, verbiage, harmless as far as it went, to be encouraged if it made them feel good, and one must after all make some little sacrifices in the interest of helping others maintain their self-esteem. The social life of nations as of men must be oiled by a little illusion: there's no harm in that. It is thanks to the illusion by which everyone gives himself top ranking that life is not a mere Zero Sum game...

Since those days, the inclination towards divergent values on the part of the new nations has acquired bite. The balance of political and economic power has shifted in their favour. Whether or not we have surmounted condescension, whether or not we were guilty of it, the opportunity to indulge in it has drastically diminished. To be honest, the most important single factor in this shift of power is the nuclear balance of terror between the two super powers, which prevents either of them from too blatantly and directly imposing its will on the neutral Third World, where they can only use coercion by proxy or by local invitation. This enables new nations to defy the super powers. I suspect that were it not for the Soviet Union, OPEC would long ago have announced that in the interest of helping the world avoid a bad recession, oil prices would be lowered ... for without such sweet reasonableness, OPEC countries might well have anticipated that outraged oil consumer countries, without even indulging in any direct and outright invasion, would rapidly and ruthlessly manipulate local conflicts so as to undermine over-exorbitant producers. But the Soviet Union does exist, and so the consumers grinned and bore the price rises. To this extent, the Soviet Union is of course right in claiming to be the protector of the ex-colonial world, though of course it is just as true that the West similarly saves the Third World from a far more total Soviet 'protection', a form of assistance which would become more intimate and complete than its beneficiaries would wish.

But the nuclear stalemate, and the leeway and protection it offers the developing world, are not the whole story. In the post-war world the terms of trade went against the raw-material producing countries. Since then, the very success of 'development' has dramatically reversed that situation. And one must add the military political achievements of some of the Third World powers. In historical perspective, the Vietnam war may yet rank as more important than the Russo-Japanese war; in the war of 1905, all that happened was that the most advanced of the backward countries beat the most backward of the advanced ones (as it then was). In Vietnam, an *ordinary* backward country, without much hardware, beat the greatest of the technologically powerful societies. The Ramadan/Yom Kippur war pointed in a similar way; it did not merely make possible the Egyptian/Israeli peace, by conferring pride and thereby elbow-room for manoeuvre on Sadat; it also helped to make possible the oil price rises, by destroying the illusion that there was only one effective army in the Middle East which could, in an extremity, be let loose against the oil Arabs without directly involving any super power. There is an irony in the reflection concerning how many Egyptian fellaheen in uniform had to die so that the accidental beneficiaries of oil price rises should reap enormous profits and install themselves in the West End of London. The paths of history are strange. Thus the nuclear stalemate, plus a shift in economic, political and military clout, has caused the question to be reformulated. Above all, its tone has changed. Once we were (though we tried not to be) compassionate and patronising; now we are scared.

What is it that we have cause to fear, in the manner in which a humanity, newly and but partially freed from the servitude of agrarian life, uses its partial and emergent freedom, its acquisition of a measure of control over its own destiny? The liberal hope had been that industrial society would opt for the instrumental state, that the centralised power-wielding agency in society would be seen as a mere tool for the carrying out of certain limited functions (their precise delimitation being of course a matter for debate), functions which would help ensure that men had adequate access to the preconditions of the good life – whilst leaving the identification and pursuit of the good life to individuals or to voluntary associations. As in some small rural town, human fulfilment and the relationship to the absolute would be one thing, and the maintenance of drains, sewerage, and the municipal car park quite another. One does not go to the local mayor or town clerk for a sacrament or to pronounce on the contents of the school syllabus; at most, he may ceremonially open the new stand at the local football ground. The desacralisation, the instrumentalisation of power has gone as far as can be desired.

The question now is – can mankind at large live without such a sacralisation? Is there not a deep psychic or perhaps organisational need for what one might call, in contrast to the instrumental state, the 'moralistic state', which does not merely manage drains but also incarnates and protects the values of society, which as the Muslims say, promotes good and suppresses evil, and which is firmly assigned this role? Societies at present no doubt possess authoritarian regimes for a diversity of reasons, including simple coercion, whether imposed by extraneous or internal forces. But if one abstracts from the various local and more or less historically accidental factors which have contributed to the emergence and maintenance of tyrannies, one is in the end left with a special, generally operative, factor: ideocracy, to use Raymond Aron's term, a regime identified with a dogmatically imposed and seriously enforced belief system, is more to the political taste of at any rate many men (who is to say whether they are a majority?) than is its desacralised, instrumental alternative.

We always knew that societies undergoing the acutely painful transition to industrial organisation might need strong ideological meat to see them through; it was precisely our detachment from that need which had that somewhat offensively patronising air about it. This, however, does not save us from being somewhat surprised, pained and frightened when we see them indulging this taste with such zest, and in a manner which does not suggest that, after a while, this enthusiasm will abate and become routinised. Perhaps it will: but just now it takes a lot of nerve or optimism to expect such an outcome with any confidence. Could it be that the psychic taste for, or the social need of, the moralistic state is there for keeps, rather than as a temporary palliative for the suffering of the transitional period? No one knows the answer, but it is hard not to feel uneasy.

The moralistic state in which the demanding morality is formulated in Marxist idiom is of course old hat. (In fact, it is in this area that the world has actually improved since the early part of the *belle époque*: for then it looked as if rigid Stalinism were due to perpetuate itself for a long time in the regions in which it had been imposed.) At present, it looks as if one may be facing a new species of it. The Iranian revolution was, in its way, an astonishing achievement, more remarkable than the Russian and Chinese revolutions. Of these two, the former had only succeeded in toppling a regime savagely battered by a lost war; the latter was accomplished from a long-established, carefully nurtured power-base, against a rotten regime. The Iranian equivalent toppled a fully equipped, powerful regime, and did it from no material power-base whatever. The consequence, however, is foreseeable: a good proportion of aspiring revolutionaries will probably now emulate not Lenin or Castro, but the Ayatollah. If they prevail, and some presumably will, we can also expect similar sequels.

Not all developing societies, of course, are playing out the once anticipated struggle between moralistic/oppressive and ultimately liberal development. There is also what might be called the non-ideological, opportunist fringe, usually in smaller countries, often endowed with military rulers. It is as if the colonial period had left behind a state machine too powerful for the society it surveys, so that politics becomes the most paying business, or at worst, the *only* paying one. This is perhaps a repeat of what happened to parts of Latin America earlier, and is not an unduly cheering alternative either.

But whatever internal mechanics and forces within the developing world impel it in an illiberal direction receive a kind of confirmation from the internal demoralisation of the developed world. Only the future can tell, of course, whether the British crisis is idiosyncratic or a harbinger of a general disease. But many of the elements which contribute to it seem generic rather than specific. Consider some of them. An industrial society cannot function on barter, cowrie shells or gold. Its credit system, not being 'natural', must be politically controlled. Moreover, an expanding economy requires an expanding money supply. Keynes deduced this need for an extra expansion from the tendency of the middle classes to save even at times when investment opportunities did not compensate for this, but it is difficult to believe that there are not some deeper underlying reasons for it. In any case, once this practice becomes institutionalised and hallowed, as conspicuously became the case in the Keynesian state, it becomes impossible to refuse any claim on the mere ground that it is financially 'impossible'; financial impossibility, at any rate in the short run, ceases to exist. At the same time, the capital-intensiveness of the economy, the intricate, complex, fragile and ever-growing interdependence of its elements, increases the extent to which the totality is at the mercy of any of its parts which chooses to go on strike, which they will do if the right to an improving standard of life is threatened. Welfare provisions ensure that the parts can, if determined to do so, exercise pressure without any undue painful cost. Their demands cannot be refused as illegitimate, in part because they actually follow from the only available political philosophy – Legitimation by Affluence, interpreted as turning growth or, at the very worst, no diminution, of real income into a civic right – but also because no per-suasive legitimating theory, which would underwrite such a demand, happens to be available.

There is, as far as I can see, only one major reason why these forces have operated with special vigour in Britain: it is the only major devel-oped country in Europe which has no folk memory of a real national disaster, a memory which would inspire restraint. The United States, which shares this good fortune, is not pervaded by an ideology which delegitimises capitalism, and is also in some measure protected by its size from the power which complex interdependence confers on parts of the economy.

This is the serious crisis, that of the 1970s, which brought the oldest industrial society to the verge of collapse and may do so again. It is in part the consequence of the internal mechanics of a society which is all at once liberal, plural, affluent, mixed/Keynesian, and endowed with a welfare state and conscience. The ideological ele-ment in the crisis is in the main (though not exclusively) negative: one cannot shore up the system by moral appeal, for there is no available moral/political theory with a hold over those who need to be per-suaded. One party does not believe that the system should be shored up by *moral* appeals, but that it should work through (legitimate) pri-vate interest; the other side does not morally endorse the system at all. Without being eager to destroy the social order, these participants feel no debt to it; and, not having any sense of its fragility either, they do not link its survival to that of their own comforts. (Some are also eager to destroy it, but they are in a minority.) The particular combination of circumstances which makes this a self-perpetuating stalemate may be locally specific. But a social order which possesses neither sanctions nor a sustaining conviction may well be the shared fate of many liberal-affluent societies.

This grave crisis, in which the ideological element plays but a minor part, was preceded in the 1960s by another and predominantly ideolo-gical crisis. *That* crisis was not serious; but it was instructive. It con-sisted of the histrionic repudiation by a major part of the more leisured youth of the legitimacy of the wider society. It was accompanied by a flamboyant challenge to the established order, that it should show cause why such a withdrawal of deference should not be made. The established order was hard put to it to say anything whatever. Of course, if the deepest and hardest questions had easily credible, clear and demonstrable answers, we philosophers should quickly be out of business. But they don't have such answers. A viable culture consists of ways of evading the questions, of inhibiting an insistent inquiry into them, for there are no answers. The counter-culture had no better ones – the dissidence of youth was not accompanied by any worthwhile intellectual rationale – but that did not worry its followers much, they were happy to make do with a cover-all relativism which justified their own position amongst others, or which *was* their position.

But all this was instructive. The real crisis shows the difficulties of legitimation in affluence; the protest movement showed the difficulties of using affluence as legitimation. If 10 per cent of beneficiaries of affluence could turn against it, and against the rationality which had engendered it, so soon, how many may not turn against it again later, if/when people feel secure? Contentment with a full stomach and a washing machine does not last long. Marx said that events repeated themselves in history, coming the first time as tragedy, the second time as farce. The irrationalist repudiation of civilisation may yet reverse that order. It certainly came as farce the first time; it may yet return as tragedy.

Given the feebleness of the ideological resources of developed societies, societies forging ahead elsewhere along new paths may have little desire to emulate their values and belief. The effect produced by superior technological and economic power has gone; there may even be something like an inverse halo effect. When we consider our own ideological predicament, we are of course acting under a double set of constraints. When we look at others, we are only interested in whether their beliefs effectively sustain them; the question whether those beliefs are also true is not of great relevance. But when it comes to ourselves, we want *truth* as well as moral support. How credible are the visions, the general orientations current at present in developed society?

The answer seems to me to be – *not much*. The two major inherited creeds of industrial society are of course economic liberalism and Marxism. They have closely related roots and to some extent similar, to some extent complementary, faults. This was so during the *belle époque* and it is so now; if anything has changed, it is that there has been a certain weakening in the middle ground between them. It is sometimes claimed that there are no believing Marxists left in the communist world. This I hold to be an exaggeration, though it may approximate to the truth in some of the satellites, and there has also been a kind of routinisation elsewhere. But what of the West?

There has been a shift towards a kind of formalistic, a-historical liberalism, in political philosophy, general philosophy and in economics; and I cannot bring myself to believe that this is salutary. In philosophy, the acme of complacency, the once so enthusiastically heralded view that our conceptual custom is self-justifying and hence all ideological crises must be *maladies imaginaires*, a view accompanied by the offer of what in truth was a *thérapie imaginaire*, has been replaced by a return to an arid and suspect technicism. In economics, the tautologies of the quantity theory of money reappear as serious explanations of the crisis, with all the in-built moral bias of the atomistic picture of social life on which it is based. (In the tangled world of social affairs, the seemingly neutral selection of the cause of a phenomenon is generally also a moral position. The thing to be explained has countless necessary conditions: its 'cause' is that one amongst the conditions which is held to be both accessible to our manipulation and to be *legitimately* manipulable. And our views of that depend on our morally saturated background picture.) In political philosophy, there is a parallel occurrence: for instance the most influential volume of recent years reintroduces the Social Contract idea, on the bizarre assumption that our social order can be legitimated by being the object of a hypothetical choice of pre-social individuals. Whilst endless petty difficulties of this view are examined with scholastic attention to detail, the fundamental difficulty, arising from the complete circularity of the whole procedure, is not seriously faced at all. The values which actually inspire the choice commended, in the popular version of this approach, are perfectly acceptable, being in fact blatant projections of the erstwhile middle-ground consensus of the *belle époque*; but the idea that men of other cultures with different visions, let alone hypothetical pre-social men, would all oblige us by choosing just this set of values, and very specific background assumptions, is absurd. The hardening of conceptual arteries by this kind of abstract, formalistic liberalism in the West, in fact the vogue of an abstracted formalism in many spheres of thought, will, one can only hope, prove a temporary aberration. Its a-historicism is as misleading as the dated historicism of its Marxist rivals.

It used to be said that the Social Contract is absurd if treated as a historical reality, but that it is a useful fiction. The very reverse is true. When treated as a useful fiction, it turns out to be an absurd device for feeding back to us our own values, endowed with a perfectly spurious air of impartiality and human universality. But if you see the Social Contract as a historical reality, embodied in a concrete process which sets the limits to our option, and which we endorse by our acceptance of that process, it becomes the correct approach to political philosophy. The process in question is industrialisation, the establishment of scientific/affluent society. Those who sign this contract do not always know what they do but the Cunning of Reason is there to ensure that they do sign.

The shared weakness of the two great ideologies inherited from the nineteenth century is a misguided conception of the relationship of the economy to the polity and to the wider aspects of the culture, a notion born of some unusual circumstances obtaining in the age in which industrialisation was engendered. *Laissez-faire* or formalist liberalism thinks it possible to have a minimal state, leaving the rest to a politically untainted realm which will be both more efficient and automatically fair, legitimate. (Under the real conditions of the modern world, this delegation of responsibility is bound to be spurious. The trouble with the programme is not simply that it will not work, but that, constituting as it does a logical absurdity, it does not correspond to any possible state of affairs.) In its utopian final state, which also provides it with its justification, Marxism of course goes further and dispenses with the state altogether. The trouble with the ultimate eschatology of Marxism is not that it is illiberal but that it is absurdly over-liberal... It is an ironic fact that, under the new relatively milder ground rules of theoretical discussions in the contemporary Soviet Union, in which various themes within Marxism are open for discussion, the one doctrine which continues to be rigidly upheld is the linking of the existence of the state, any state, to pre-existing class conflict.

The facts of the case seem to me manifestly different. The power of modern technology and its side-effects (man no longer struggles with nature, but with the side-effects of man's conquest of nature), the intricacy of the interdependence engendered by the ever-increasing division of labour, the interdependence of coercion, belief and production, require us to rethink the relation between power and wealth, indeed the very meanings of those terms under modern conditions, rather than indulge in fantasies (as they inescapably are) about their separation or the conjuring-away of one of them, here and now, or in some eschatological terminal condition. It is of course comic to see so many converts to anti-consumerism and anti-'materialism'. Now that economic growth has become so difficult, this sounds like making a virtue of necessity. But it is more than that: the nature of satisfaction and of social contract, of the maintenance of order and minimal harmony, needs rethinking *anyway*. The models available in the inherited ideologies are of precious little use or relevance. The nineteenth-century visions which we have inherited are sometimes castigated for being 'grand' theories. Their fault lay not in their grandeur but in their faulty formulation. Neither the a-historicism of economic neo-liberalism nor the dated, evolutionist historicism of Marxism is now usable. The time is ripe for a basic reformulation of our problem.

So, looking back at our *belle époque*, I would say that in basic outline, our situation has not changed so very much; but the new balance of power and demoralisation have made it much more frightening. As for the proper understanding of our situation, my feeling is that overall there has even been, if anything, a certain retrogression, which I can only hope is temporary.

8 The captive Hamlet of Europe

Agrarian societies have existed for nearly ten millennia, but we still do not know to what extent the species of agrarian society which *actually* emerged exhausted the range of all *possible* agrarian social forms. Industrial societies have only been in existence for a short time, and we certainly cannot suppose that the types which we have witnessed even remotely exhaust the range of possibility.

All the same, we have by now seen a certain range of models of this amazing product, industrial society. The earliest, spontaneous and accidental version of it notoriously maintained social order within itself through economic constraint. But the continued reliance primarily on *economic* constraints enabled this society to remain politically liberal, indeed to expand and develop its political liberalism which, according to its critics at least, was spurious.

The successor of the first such society now looks unviable and doomed. A system has been developed in which the rational and perfectly legitimate pursuit of special interests ensures eventual collective disaster. Private virtues and private vices *both* become public vices. The satisfaction of individual aims guarantees the frustration of the aims of all.

It is interesting to compare this familiar form of malaise or *misère* with its opposite number on the other side of the hill, in the alternative form of industrial society, in the socialist world. Socialism of course also had its celebrated, sharply outlined early form: an ideocracy, a caesaro–papism in which total fusion of state and church, known as party, made possible an overwhelming reliance on political and ideological coercion.

But in most places, this early version of the socialist social order based on unbounded police terror plus imposed total faith is happily on the way out. Real old Stalinism used terror in an overkill manner (rather literally); and there now exists a precision-tooled, moderate version, which kills minimally, if at all. Socialism, even illiberal socialism (as contrasted with socialist societies which deliberately strive for some measure of liberalisation), now also has its own distinctive Mark II, with its own new inner rules and conventions and logic.

It is the sad fate of Czechoslovakia to exemplify an unusually pure model, perhaps an ideal type, of this kind of social formation. The sharp outline with which its features are displayed it presumably owes to the fact that the system had to be imposed with fair speed and political deliberation, after the suppression of the Prague spring in 1968 – thus simultaneously maintaining less continuity with a proper Stalinoid past, but also being able to afford fewer liberal concessions and compromises than do more fortunate neighbouring lands.

Milan Šimečka's *Obnovení Pořádku* (*The Restoration of Order*), published by Index (5 Köln 41, Postfach 410511, 1979, 207 pp.), is a very serious, perceptive, intelligent and coherent attempt to fill this gap. Šimečka is a dissident who continues to live in Czechoslovakia, harassed by the police; a Czech who happens to live among Slovaks, in Bratislava; and an erstwhile member of the Communist Party, a member of the generation who joined it after the war and who will, I imagine, remain for ever marked by the memory of the fact that they endorsed the series of bizarre, unspeakably vicious political murders in the early 1950s.

The present book was written between 1975 and 1977, during spare time whilst the author was (and is), like so many intellectuals in his country, compulsorily employed in menial work. The Czech intelligentsia is the captive Hamlet of Europe: ironically, the sloppy, inefficient and ill-disciplined industrial economy of contemporary Czechoslovakia (for communism has reduced one of the most work-addicted nations on earth to just such a condition), which has made its writers, teachers and thinkers into its hewers of wood and drawers of water, is also so lax as to give them, evidently, a fair amount of time to think, and even to write. There are some – like J. Sládeček, whose book will also be commented on – who believe that they have benefited from this forcibly imposed and constrained self-examination to acquire a previously lacking self-knowledge and understanding.

But the interest of Šimečka's book emphatically does not lie in the Czech anguish which, inevitably, emanates from time to time from its pages. He at any rate is not a new Dalibor to enchant us with a plaintive violin from a prison-tower of Hradčany castle. It would be a great mistake to read this book simply as a check-list of the various forms of chicanery employed by the Czechoslovak Socialist Republic to suborn its own citizens. The book is that as well, of course; but its central aim, and in any case its achievement, is to give a cool, in the main rather dry, clinical, profound and well-rounded, and needless to say deeply felt and experienced, account of a profoundly repellent, but alas perfectly viable and perhaps quite permanent and stable social form, and one which consequently has a great claim on our attention. That it *may* be stable and permanent is a repugnant thought, but one which must needs be faced. Šimečka's book should be read alongside Vladimir Kusín's excellent *From Dubček to Charter '77* (Edinburgh, 1978) and J. Sládeček's important, as yet untranslated *Osmašedesátý – Pokus o Kritické porozumění historickým souvislostem* (1968: an essay at a critical understanding of historical connections), which appeared in Prague in Samizdat in 1979. (Kusín is in exile, while Sládeček is another dissident who remained inside the country.)

But Šimečka's book differs from these other volumes. Kusín admirably documents the story of opposition; Sládeček's book is a truly remarkable attempt to place the disaster of 1968 in the wider context of Czech history and society and to come to terms with the situation of his own communist generation, initially true believers, then reformists in 1968, then expelled and reduced to impotence. Sládeček's book also contains some interesting and I think valid reflections on the manner in which the Communist Party has effected a deep split in an otherwise and previously rather consensual and not very stratified nation – a split between those who are or were in it and those not contaminated by it. I have heard deep-felt comments on this new chasm from either side of the great divide. But Šimečka's account is, in the best sense of the word, sociology: it gives us a model of *how* it was done, how it *is* being done.

What, then, are the principles of this new 'realistic socialism', as Šimečka calls it? After some reflections and reminiscences, the author gets down to brass tacks in chapter 2, and with total lucidity and firmness singles out what he calls the crucial link in the entire chain. 'The functioning of the entire system absolutely requires a party, which ensures a unitary proceeding at every step in the guidance of the state, complete control over the manifestations of public life, total obedience of lower institutions towards the centre... That is the main element, all else is secondary.'

The party must govern, and it must govern alone. Whether it continues to follow the official Moscow line does not matter nearly so much; deviations are tolerated, but abdication of power is not. The party means its inner centre, of course. And here Šimečka digresses into the specific events and failure which aided the 'restoration of order' in Czechoslovakia. Why did virtually the whole Prague Spring leadership cooperate in their own destruction and of everything they then stood for? (In fact, I was told in the spring of 1980 that the grave of František Kriegel, who died of natural causes, the only member of the 1968 government who *refused* to sign the Moscow agreement after the occupation and the kidnapping of the Cabinet, and who consequently was the first of the reformers to be eliminated from a position of authority, is now permanently covered with flowers.)

Smrkovský, one of the main figures of the Spring, apparently claims in his memoirs that he was seduced by the hope of at least saving something from the ruins. Šimečka is sceptical about this ex post explanation, and suggests that communist leaders never resign, that there is a disastrous tradition of clinging on and never refusing to carry on, on principle. This is part of the game. The slow-motion destruction of the then leaders, with their own bizarre cooperation, has left many Czechs with a deep and permanent conviction of the filthiness and uselessness of politics and participation.

It led them to what Šimečka admirably and correctly sums up as the standard attitude of the contemporary Czech citizen: 'the choice of a politically disengaged pursuit of private welfare, purchased by a formal loyalty vis-à-vis power, and the illusion of decency within the limits of a private existence'. This splendid summary is indeed the motto of that inner emigration which is now the standard human condition in Prague. There is a little variety in it: people live along a kind of spectrum, such that anyone to one side of one's own position has compromised a little too much, and anyone on the other side lacks a sense of reality. Wherever you happen to be along this spectrum, it always looks just like that. The revolting spectacle on the public stage drives people into their internal forum (symbolised by the country cottage).

Here Šimečka indulges in some reflections on the ruler of 'normalised' Czechoslovakia, Dr Husák. Husák attained his present position in part thanks to his previous good record, that of, as Šimečka says, a persecuted, brave, intelligent and broadminded man, with many years in prison behind him; a man who only escaped execution in the early fifties thanks to a series of accidents. During the re-establishment of order, Husák gave the impression that his solution was always the optimal one, given the narrow constraints of a harsh reality, and he continues to maintain this still. Although Šimečka does not add this reflection in so many words, the claim is by no means absurd. *Lest worse befall* is a central motto of this form of government.

In the spring of 1980, for instance, the rumour of a forthcoming complete incorporation of Czechoslovakia in the Soviet Union persistently circulated in Prague. The rumour has little if any inherent probability. One can only suppose that either such a rumour is deliberately encouraged from above, or it is engendered from below on the principle that the fear is father to the thought. Husák protects the Czech citizen from such a fate, and who is he to hamper him in this achievement by rocking the boat? And if a few excessively eager souls are confined to prison...? A small matter. Šimečka observes, repeatedly, that Husák's personal experience makes him disinclined to take mere prison as a great tragedy: it is a politician's professional risk, and to allow losers to survive at all is a great achievement in his world.

The principle that the party must rule and retain a dominant position was in fact upheld by many reformers even in the heady days of the liberalisation of 1967–8: it was part of the contract they were so naively offering the Russians – namely, that two principles, the dominance of the party and the adherence of the country to the Warsaw pact, would remain inviolate. As Šimečka observes, what seemed most incongruous and disturbing to the Russians was precisely the spectacle of a party which for once, under Dubček, evoked genuine popular enthusiasm.

As far as I know, there is no definite statement in the Leninist canon which actually requires the vanguard of the proletariat to be *detested* by those whom it leads, but in practice, everyone concerned now knows that something very fishy must be afoot if the party general secretary is actually liked... When replaced by Husák, and when the principle of an exclusively governing party was effectively reaffirmed, the next and crucial step was its self-purification.

The general formula was simple. The party membership was divided into three categories – the healthy kernel, the representatives of reaction (destined for dismissal), and the large middle mass of those who had been beguiled and misled, and who had to be re-examined. This categorisation from above, it must be understood, was applied to a people which had in fact been very nearly unanimous in support of liberalisation and 'socialism with a human face'... It is sad to report Šimečka's observation that he knows of *no one* among those, more or less arbitrarily selected to constitute the 'healthy kernel' and hence to sit in judgement in the purification of the others, who actually had the courage and integrity to refuse this unsavoury honour. The selection of the healthy kernel was not done on a person's actual record but by psychological type, Šimečka insists, and his account is convincing. You had to have the *Gestalt* of a reliable conformist, without the smell of anything bolshie about you.

The party rules, and rules alone. It selects its own membership, by unstated and obscure principles which in practice select for conformity and mediocrity. Šimečka quotes Brecht's joke that when things go wrong in a democracy one changes the government, and in a popu-

lar democracy one changes the people. In fact, the (slightly) en-
franchised part of the people are the party members, and they are
literally replaced to suit requirements from above. The vanguard of
the working class ensures that substantially progressive considerations prevail above mere formal considerations. But as there seems
virtually no doctrinal substance left, and the human content of the
party is itself variable, we are left with substantivism without substance ... It is all a splendid new application of Leninism. The proletariat now does not merely have a vanguard, but has a *disposable
vanguard*, which can be replaced by a new one with perfect ease whenever necessary. This is perfectly logical: you need a different
vanguard according to where you want to go.

This achieved, there is the restoration of a homogeneous, self-
censoring, vacuous press, and of course the same holds for the mass
media generally. Šimečka has some interesting observations about
the period of liberty in 1968: whilst people delighted to read revel-
ations about the regime and at the time queued up to be able to do so,
there were many who felt ill at ease at the sudden plurality and diversity of viewpoints, which destroyed the previous simplicity and
uniqueness of social norms. The short-lived freedom of the press did
not, he says, strike deep cords in the population, and indeed when the
débâcle came there was a certain feeling that it was all the fault of
journalists, which also facilitated the subsequent persecution of writers and journalists. Šimečka is a professional philosopher and sees
the irony of university philosophers, who earnestly explain to their
students how subjectivism and idealism can be overcome, and truth
attained, by *praxis* – and who then go home and switch on the television and patiently listen to some Kingsize fib. Šimečka, like the
now-exiled Moscow dissident Valentin Turchin (*The Inertia of
Fear*, Columbia 1981), notes how the socialist world engenders
sound appreciation of the seriousness of the problem of truth and
knowledge.

The control of the press and mass media is attained without censorship. Šimečka is not the only author to note that under this type of
regime, the abolition of censorship is actually a misfortune for freedom. As long as it exists, individual journalists deploy their ingenuity
to outwit it, and so find some measure of security in the awareness
that if something displeasing to authority gets through, the censor
takes the rap and they can invoke his endorsement in self-defence.
But if no such excuse exists and all censorship is self-censorship, all
limits are removed from the zeal for conformity and safety ... But all
this being so, how is the rest of the population, outside the party,
suborned?

Here Šimečka makes a sad claim for his country's priority in world history: the scale on which economic pressure (deprivation of *appropriate* employment) was used on this occasion was quite unprecedented in the history of *accomplished* socialism (a phrase which seems to concede that it was rivalled in early stages of the edification of socialism, either in his own country or elsewhere). He goes on to say that the striving of the Czechoslovak nation for a more democratic form of life was not crushed by the tanks and infantrymen of the fraternal socialist countries, but was crushed by the bureaucratic cadres at all levels, by means of dismissals of all kinds, and without much protest ... and also, he stresses, without much inhumanity, in a sense.

The victims were not to face hunger. They were only deprived of meaningful work, of the possibility of self-expression in their labour. As this – N.B. *not* tanks or bayonets, let alone gallows – is *the* crucial means of social control, one can say that this mature and realistic socialism can only work with a large reserve army of unemployed intellectuals.

Šimečka knows and has the honesty to admit that this fate of his generation closely parallels that which they themselves helped to provide for the victims of the initial establishment of socialism after 1948. But there is a difference, which Šimečka records: the new persecution is carried out without phrases and illusions. Virtually no one endorses it in the name of the better distant future. It is done for the sake of a current present political prophylaxis (Šimečka's phrase), and that is that. And it works. The large-scale use of this means of persuasion, available to a state which is in fact the only employer, has never previously been used to the full and constitutes Czechoslovakia's contribution to the practice of power... But it is effective against intellectuals, who can be hurt by being deprived of meaningful work. Hence it is only effective overall if the rest of the population, which in any case has a highly instrumental attitude to work, can be bought off by at least relative affluence by consumerism. Fear of alienation from meaningful work for some, incremental consumption for the rest.

An entire chapter of the book is devoted to the civilised nature of the violence employed in this war against the intelligentsia. It *was* directed against the intellectuals: Šimečka tells us that even before the invasion, Soviet propaganda was directed far more against those who forged the ideas which inspired the Prague Spring than against its political leaders. And why does he insist so much that the violence was indeed civilised? It did not use crude force. Police investigations are carried out during working hours; no one is woken at 4 a.m. Political prisoners are treated in accordance with the rules. The police obey rules, and according to Šimečka behave better even than they did in the 1960s, let alone of course during the terror-dominated 1950s...

The picture is completed with the other well-known institutional and cultural traits of realistic Czechoslovak socialism: police harassment rather than terror, a judiciary devoid of independence, and the sustained and systematic use of children as hostages, the insistence on the principle that higher education is the reward of conformity of parents, and the generalisation and acceptance of corruption (it is impossible to secure services, spare parts, etc., without reciprocated exchanges of benefits). The early perfection of this method is, like most of the realities of life in the building and maintenance of socialism in Czechoslovakia, brilliantly described in Škvorecký's remarkable novel *Mirak'l* (Toronto, 1979), which is a splendid literary counterpoint to Kusín's, Šimečka's and Sládeček's analyses.

His observations about the economy are interesting: far from this being an authoritarian society, it is a society deprived of half its economic effectiveness by a complete collapse of authority in productive life. The workers may indeed be totally impotent in political and trade union life (this is not Poland) and contemptuously ignore its manipulations; but on the shop floor, they have eroded discipline and have ample and ingenious means of doing as they please; and, as long as they do not try to subvert the political order, there is no one who tries to gainsay them.

So? Šimečka comes close to formulating a Czech version of the End of Ideology. The socialist world is now emptied of ideology. Stalin was the last to discuss the transition to communism, and the XXth Congress of the CPSU(b) was the last to attempt some general orientation.

Under the new Stalinism with a human face it is the intellectuals who suffer. But at the same time their number grows with increasing technological sophistication: and the party hacks are eager to send their offspring to the universities, and the complexity of the productive and administrative technology does require at least some people with genuine intellectual aptitude and training. But people like that, in turn, have a taste for competence, genuine performance, and sometimes for irony and wit, and some at least amongst them will occasionally struggle for the right to indulge these tastes.

This, in substance, would seem to be the social base of the dissident movement in Eastern Europe and the USSR; and the indispensability of the social stratum which engenders this dissent makes it difficult to extirpate it. In Prague intellectuals of this kind would, in fact, be quite willing to leave the party hacks in power and in possession of their advantages (to be fair, the inequalities and perks of power are not so very outstanding, and are probably much less than the perks of wealth in the West); nor would they insist on taking Czechoslovakia out of the Soviet empire and defence system. Would that not be a solution?

Alas no. The party is right to fight the intellectuals. If they were granted liberty of speech, the thing would inevitably snowball; the cultural change would totally subvert any respect for the authorities – it did in 1967–8 – and culminate, under whatever name, in a *de facto* pluralism in politics. The Russians in turn, facing the same problem at home, need an ideological cordon sanitaire – an idea once, long ago, developed against them – far more than they need a military one, let alone the dubious advantages of the adherence of the Czechoslovak army to the Warsaw Pact.

So, by an ironic series of interdependencies, a class of hacks *has* to suppress one of the potentially richest cultural ferments of Europe, so as to maintain itself. The communists like to point out that Czech Catholicism, imposed outwardly and forcibly by the Counter-Reformation, is largely a lukewarm shell. They have succeeded in reproducing the same phenomenon.

No doubt Šimečka's book should be read jointly with Kusín's and Sládeček's. Kusín's careful record of the suppression of the Prague Spring inspires not only horror at the ineptness of its leaders (providing the Russians with maximum provocation and minimum deterrent), but also a sad admiration for the elegance and economy of the Soviet operation.

Sládeček's as yet unpublished book sets the current reality of Prague against the backcloth not of the destiny of Europe, but of Czech history. Some facts of that history deserve recapitulation. As an effective political and cultural unit, the Czech nation disappeared after the Thirty Years War and in the course of the Counter-Reformation. In the nineteenth century, the nation managed to effect a veritable resurrection, reviving its language as a cultural instrument ·(as opposed to being merely the speech of peasants). But this left its mark: as the nineteenth-century struggle was primarily a cultural one, it provided insufficient training in the realities of politics. 'We thought of politics simply as a slightly more daring form of culture' – so runs a brilliant aphorism of Sládeček's.

National liberation came in effect as a gift from Versailles, and was attained under the leadership of a philosopher-king, or philosopher-president, who believed in the West and its official values, in the superiority of the West's moral and physical strength. The national motto, *Truth Prevails*, was operationally interpreted as meaning that those great nations in the West are: (a) democratic, and (b) invincible; ergo, if we emulate their values, the (invincible) West, appreciative of our imitation as the sincerest form of flattery, will make quite sure we are all right. Munich was a trauma which destroyed one half of this illusion, and the second half was destroyed by the fall of France. The generation of Sládeček and Šimečka experienced all this at best as children. But their own traumata were still to come. The early 1950s were not a trauma for them at the time, but they are or ought to be in retrospect; any decent man who endorsed the murderous mendacity of the Slanský series of trials should be marked by it for life. The year 1968 has a different meaning for this generation, or rather, a different set of variable meanings; it is far more of a political projection test. This great failure leads Sládeček to ask above all 'What is wrong with us Czechs, and in particular what is wrong with us reforming communists?' Šimečka asks instead 'How does this *type* of society, which we have alas pioneered, actually work?' Both questions are worth asking.

An outside observer may be tempted by some comparisons. Britain is a free, mixed-economy society, half-haunted by the guilt of capitalism. Czechoslovakia is a Stalinoid society haunted by the sins of Stalinism. De-legitimated capitalism faces de-legitimated socialism... Britain was the first industrial society, and the Czech lands were the first industrial area in central Europe. So there are many parallels. Both societies are ailing. What are the contrasts?

They share, as Šimečka says, the attempt to buy off discontent by consumerism. In Britain, the sins of capitalism were to be atoned for and remedied by the welfare state and Keynesianism; growth and affluence were to soften conflict, the economic disfranchisement of unemployment was to be controlled and minimised, the reserve army of unemployed was henceforth to be not very large, and its precise scale at any given time was finally to be adjusted according to need; Keynes's euthanasia of the rentier would eliminate privilege without causing disturbance or excessively sudden pain; and the instrument was to be, as the now ironic-sounding phrase has it, economic fine-tuning.

It is also now known not to work, partly for the curious reason that the supposedly pragmatic British have retained ideology, and ignored the trumpet which announced the end of ideology. Because a significant section of the population continues to consider the system to be inherently illegitimate, they refuse to give it the help it needs in a crisis. They do not dislike it enough to favour a revolution, but quite enough not to succour it. Though possibly willing to moderate their claims under threat of unemployment, they will not heed persuasion.

Czechoslovakia on the other hand committed the sins of Stalinism in full and ample measure, and with nauseating and sycophantic zeal, and those who took part in them are deeply marked by this shame. It endeavoured to correct these sins in an over-exuberant, unrestrained, politically inept manner, and was forcibly – and alas successfully – restrained and corrected. It now presents a picture of reformed Stalinism – control through access to meaningful work and to education, but not through absolute terror, or through the threat of indigence.

Relatively few political prisoners, no executions... The ideology must be outwardly honoured, but that is all. There are a few slogans (in Warsaw there are none), but no more. Opportunists in power, inner emigration in the middle, consumerism at the bottom. And the result? The economy is unimpressive, but as long as beer does not go up in price, as Šimečka notes, this does not matter too much in an unfree society.

Before we generalise from these two societies to the general destinies of reformed-capitalism and reformed-Stalinism, we must by way of precaution note their idiosyncratic features, which may undermine the reliability of any generalisations. Britain, alone of the great European nations, has no living memory of disaster. Every other major European nation has known either foreign occupation, terror or disintegration of civil authority, total inflation, civil war, acute economic collapse – and usually, some combination or sequence of these.

Britain has not: and the fact that disaster is consequently not imaginable may now be a severe handicap in trying to avert it. The Czechs, by contrast, whether in victory or defeat – 1918, 1938, 1948, 1968 – have received sustained and eventually self-fulfilling lessons in national impotence. Independence came as a gift from the West, and what the West gave it took away; the second liberation came from the East, and the bill was presented soon after; and the inability to control one's fate seems to be habit-forming. Though the Czechs like to quote Comenius's prophecy to the effect that the mastery of their fate will return into their own hands, they don't appear capable of believing that this could really be so. These points must be borne in mind before we conclude too easily that the same could happen elsewhere. Too little fear or too much may make reformed capitalism *un*workable, and reformed Stalinism workable, in a single country each, alas.

9 Waiting for Imam or
The political and hygienic theology of
Khomeini or
Government not by Imams but by
lawyers

During evacuation, one must not squat facing the sun or the moon, unless one's genitals are covered.

... it is recommended that one keep his head covered while evacuating, and have the weight of his body carried by the left foot.

Every part of the body of a non-Muslim individual is impure, even the hair on his hand or his body hair, his nails, and all the secretions of his body.

During sexual intercourse, if the penis enters a woman's vagina or a man's anus, fully or only as far as the circumcision ring, both partners become impure ... they must consequently perform their ablutions.

If a man – God protect him from it! – fornicates with an animal and ejaculates, ablution is necessary.

If one commits an act of sodomy with a cow, a ewe, or a camel, their urine and their excrements become impure, and even their milk may no longer be consumed.

We see today that the Jews – may God bring them down! – have manipulated the editions of the Koran published in their occupied zones. We have to protest, to make everyone understand that these Jews are bent upon the destruction of Islam and the establishment of a universal Jewish government.

Women of the lineage of the Prophet are menopausal at the age of sixty; others, once they are over fifty.

The Islamic movement met its first saboteur in the Jewish people, who are at the source of all the anti-Islamic libels and intrigues current today.

It is absolutely forbidden to dissect the corpse of a Moslem, but the dissection of non-Moslem corpses is permitted.

It is not strictly forbidden for Moslems to work for a concern managed by a Moslem which also employs Jews, provided the work does not serve Israel in any manner whatsoever. However, it is shameful to do one's work under the orders of a Jewish foreman.

Misdeeds must be punished by the law of retaliation: cut off the hands of the thief; kill the murderer instead of putting him in prison; flog the adulterous woman or man ... any judge fulfilling the seven requirements (that he have reached puberty, be a believer, know the Koranic laws perfectly, be just, and not be affected by amnesia, or be a bastard, or be of the female sex) is quali-ﬁed to dispense justice...

These quotations come from *Sayings of the Ayatollah Khomeini.*[1] Though they are evidently the products of a two-stage translation, via the French, the substantial accuracy of these renderings has not, as far as I know, been challenged. The primary purpose of this particular 'Little Green Book', as it describes itself, is not scholarly; rather, it is to supply the public with a sample of the extraordinary range and nature (by contemporary Western standards) of Khomeini's ideas, and in this it succeeds. But apart from the theo-porn and the coarse savagery and the visceral anti-semitism, it does also contain material which illuminates the central intuitions, inspirations and tensions of Khomeini's thought. A reader puzzled by why a theologian should pontificate about the precise fate reserved for a sodomised camel, the significance of the depth of penetration or the disposal of a believer's weight between his two feet while urinating, will also be led to the theocratic, or more precisely, divine-nomocratic nature of this system:

Islam has precepts for everything which concerns man and society. There is no subject upon which Islam has not expressed its judgement.

The type of casuistry practised by Khomeini is not idiosyncratic, but part of the duties traditionally expected of the members of the clerisy to which he belongs. This is a routine exercise, not required to be original. The reader will note the distinctive separation of powers inherent in Islam, the reservation of the legislature for the deity:

In this democracy ... the laws are not made by the will of the people, but only by the Koran and the Tradition of the Prophet.

Or,

The Sacred Legislation of Islam is the sole legislative power. No one has the right to legislate and no law may be executed except the law of the Divine Legislation.

> (*Islam and Revolution: Writings and Declarations of Imam Khomeini*, translated by Hamid Algar, Berkeley, 1981)

Or, again,

Islamic government is ... constitutional. It is not constitutional in the current

[1] New York, 1980.

sense of the word, i.e. based on the approval of laws in accordance with the opinion of the majority. It is constitutional in the sense that the rulers are subject to ... the Noble Qur'an and the Sunna of the Most Noble Messenger ... The Sacred Legislation of Islam is the sole legislative power.

(Islam and Revolution, p. 55)

He might also, if perceptive, note some hints of the important inner tensions which pervade Shi'ism: between the attribution of legitimate power to the Imams *only*, to distinct beings 'infinitely gifted and by birth and nature superior to other men' – so much so that even the Archangel Gabriel conceded that were he to approach them too closely he would be burned – and its attribution to scholars selected merely for learning, piety and zeal; and between insisting that power be exclusively in the hands of the latter (when the Imams are absent, which in Shi'a belief they generally are), and a grudging recognition of secular rulers, who may exist independently of the clerics, as long as they respect the bounds of the Law.

But these deep and enormously significant tensions are only sketchily present in the *Little Green Book*. Anyone wishing to explore this fascinating theme more thoroughly and in depth must turn to the much more weighty *Islam and Revolution: Writings and Declarations of Imam Khomeini*. This volume constitutes a far more serious scholarly enterprise and provides more copious and thorough documentation; but, *but* ... though edited and directly translated by a reputable scholar, it is, by the nature of that editing and selection, somewhat misleading and distorting.

The editor is a convert to Islam and an enthusiastic admirer of the man he calls *Imam* Khomeini. One must suppose that what attracts Algar to Khomeini is the man and his ideology in its entirety – one feels like saying, in all its enormity. There can be no doubt but that Algar is fully conversant with all the aspects of Khomeini's thought and practice, including those which are deeply repugnant and/or tragically comic to post-Enlightenment eyes. Bluntly, valuable and interesting though Algar's edition of Khomeini is, it is open to the serious charge of distortion by omission and relative emphasis, and on occasion, a little more than omission. Consider this: Khomeini accuses the Israelis of burning and destroying (*sic*) the al Aqsa mosque in Jerusalem, and Algar's accompanying footnote fails to point out that the *unsuccessful* act of arson was the work of a non-Israeli and a non-Jew; Khomeini candidly endorses the imposition of extra taxes on non-Muslims, whilst Algar's footnote most misleadingly softens this and suggests that these extra obligations, forcibly imposed on non-Muslims, are set up by some sort of freely accepted contract...

Or again, Dr Algar's Foreword explains the sense in which Khomeini is referred to as *Imam*. The term has two meanings, so utterly disparate in their potency that one should really in all logic use subscripts and refer to $Imam_1$ and $Imam_2$. $Imam_1$ is a Shi'ite notion of a being whose 'spiritual status ... far transcends human comprehension', who existed before the creation of the world in the form of a light beneath the divine throne, and who differs from the other men even in the sperm from which he grew. $Imam_2$, in the 'common lexical meaning of the word', is simply 'leader' or 'guide'.

In a passage which reads as if butter wouldn't melt in his mouth, the editor admits that the term has been applied to Khomeini 'in recent years', in recognition of the fact that 'his role has been unique among the religious scholars of Iran and has exceeded what is implied in the title "Ayatollah"', but assures us that what is intended is $Imam_2$. It is really just a matter of homonyms, he seems to say. You must learn to note these differences. But given the fact that, on his own admission, the appellation has been conferred on Khomeini *in recognition of his uniqueness*, does he really expect us to believe that the average Iranian Shi'ite is, in his inward semantics, aware and respectful of the invisible subscripts, and that he does not, at the very least, extend the resonance of $Imam_1$ to $Imam_2$? Contemporary Iranians may not have explicitly claimed the Hidden Imamate for Khomeini, but the ambiguity is an essential part of the situation, and Dr Algar's hair-splitting at this point is not harmless, but obscures the true situation.

But the most important charge against Algar's editing is that, though the book does indeed give us marvellous material for the understanding of deep currents and stresses of Khomeini's thought, it refrains from telling the whole truth, and gives us a cleaned-up, expurgated, bowdlerised Khomeini, and thus a distorted one. From this book one would not get the full feel for the heart and mind of the man who warmly endorses the liquidation of entire tribes if it furthers the welfare of the Muslim community (in modern conditions, tribes would clearly be replaced by nations), who favours the flogging of adulterers and summary rapid justice, and who gives so much loving thought to the varieties of sweat, excrement and penetration. Strangely enough, though a convert and enthusiast, Algar retains enough familiarity with (and respect for?) Western values to select the elements of his portrait of Khomeini in such a way as to diminish his offensiveness to the Western reader.

In a curious kind of way, I find this editing somewhat insulting to Khomeini himself: whether or not one finds him appealling, there is something coherent, sincere and elemental about him. It is not by accident that he brought off a staggering revolution against enormous material odds. To understand him, we need to see him as he is. In taking him as he is, we show him more respect than if we present his works in a way which makes them almost acceptable as family entertainment. The brutal moralism and the hair-splitting scholasticism, but almost tenderly careful handling of sodomy, sweat and excrement are all part and parcel of the man's mind. To change the stress almost furtively is to insult both the reader and the subject of the book. The reader is advised to use Algar's important volume, but also to keep the *Little Green Book* close to hand as an absolutely essential complement of it.

From its very inception, three main principles of legitimacy have co-existed (not always peaceably) within Islam: scripturalism, sacred leadership, and consensus of the Community, with special weighting for its own learned members. The political conflicts of the very first generations of Muslims in effect concerned the priority or emphasis accorded to each of these principles – to the Revelation of the Divine Word, to the divine selection of the Messenger and subsequently of his Deputy, and the inspired agreement of the illuminated community, or at least of its learned and literate leaders. Roughly speaking, the partisans of divine selection become Shi'ites, the adherents of Consensus become Kharejites, and Sunnism represents a compromise blend, stressing scripturalism and learned consensus, but in practice accommodating itself to some recognition of a special status to the Prophet's progeny. Those early conflicts are copiously documented, and vividly present in the minds of educated Muslims, and later theo-political conflicts are generally seen in terms of them. Non-educated Muslims also tend to be very familiar with these conflicts, and in the case of Shi'ites, relive them annually in the form of rituals and passion plays.

Those early struggles eventually engendered (or at any rate provided the idiom for) the main sectarian fissures within Islam. Shi'ism is defined, basically, in terms of giving priority to Sacred Leadership, certainly over consensus, and in some cases (though this certainly does not apply to Khomeini) even over Scripture. Further conspicuous features of Shi'ism include stress on martyrdom (at least one of the early divinely chosen rulers was killed by his enemies), on the bloody avenging of martyrdom, and on the legitimacy of dissimulation whilst living under invalid albeit Muslim rulers. Whilst illegitimate rulers continue to govern, true authority appertains to Imams endowed with absolute status and mystical properties, but who are mostly in hiding, incognito, in a state of 'Occultation'. Sub-segments of Shi'ism are differentiated partly in terms of *when* or *whether* the Occultation took place. Diverse sub-sects differ concerning the precise generation at which the Imam went into hiding or hived off from the main Muslim community. One extreme variant holds that it did not occur at all and that the divine incarnation is concretely present amongst us. This lineage now boasts a Harvard degree as well as divinity.

Shi'ism began as a religion of oppressed or disadvantaged segments of the community, revering a martyred and defeated ruler, and in most places in which it is to be found, it continues to be the religion of the underprivileged. Even more than early Christianity, it is, in its ideas, a religion of the politically dispossessed. Hence it faces theoretical difficulties when it attains power, though Shi'ites are not averse to acquiring it, any more than Christians. One way of handling the use of power is crypto-Sunnism in the Khomeini style: the attribution of political authority to divine law alone. In the absence of the Divine Imam, the law is to be implemented by scholars. In the past, the scholars never had such power, for political authority depended on tribal leadership, and the scholars had to accommodate themselves to it. Hierocracy was not feasible. In our age, for the first time, they could gain power themselves, unbeholden to tribal leaders for support. To wield power, they need almost no one else; to attain it, they needed the martyrdom hysteria which is ever latent in Shi'ism, kept close to the boil by rituals and passion plays.

Iran is an exception in the Shi'a world. Since the sixteenth century, Shi'ism has become not merely the official, but the so to speak defining religion of the Persians. A non-Shi'a Persian, like a non-Catholic Pole or a non-Catholic Croat or a non-Orthodox Serb, is something of a contradiction. It is tempting to speculate whether Shi'ism, with its tendency to see the true fount of legitimacy as hidden and suspended, and the visible political order as evil and illegitimate, does not appeal to some deep dualistic strain in the Iranian soul, a kind of revival in Muslim terms of the Manichean, dualistic faiths so conspicuous in pre-Muslim Persian history. Such a speculation would of course have to explain why this strain had remained submerged for so many centuries.

What concerns us now, however, is not the origins, but the implications of the Shi'a vision. These implications are deeply, inescapably and persistently ambiguous, indeed ambivalent. Various scholars, such as Nicki Keddie, Yann Richard, Said Arjomand, Shabrough

Akhari, A. H. Hairi and others have explored this. At the heart of Shi'ism there lies what can only be called a political mysticism and absolutism. The usual Muslim nomocracy is fused with a Messianism, and complicated by the fact that the divine Messiah is in hiding.

Under the old order, when at best tribal uprisings, but not urban frondes, could overturn a government, the martyrdom cult in cities could provide an escape for the oppressed, but it was not political dynamite. Revolutions needed a tribal base, and the scholars who legitimated a rising had to content themselves with the role of counsellors to tribal leaders. But under conditions of modernisation, the martyrdom cult, fuelled by the resentment of lesser beneficiaries of economic progress against the major ones, does acquire explosive revolutionary potential. The major beneficiaries of oil wealth flaunted it in ways which were inevitably counter-Islamic, and envy could easily present itself as piety and rectitude.

Khomeini profited from all this. The Shi'a martyrdom cult, unlike the Christian one, is quite free of any pacifism; and unlike the Marxist one, the martyr is a concrete person, not an abstract class. All this makes the symbol far more potent. (The cult of the martyr-Imam Hussein resembles a kind of inverse Mariolatry. Amongst underprivileged Shi'a women, its rituals become hysterical and overtly sexual.) If Islam in general is spread-eagled between Doctor and Saint, the Shi'ism in particular is caught between Martyr and Lawyer. The martyrs, and the recollection of martyrs, have at long last propelled the lawyers to the summit of power. There they preach the Sovereignty of Law, and the martyrs, though greatly revered, are, logically speaking, pensioned off. This is a government not of Imams, but of lawyers.

Like the rest of Islam, Shi'ism sees the faith as inherently concerned with the regulation of all social life; but unlike the rest of Islam, it strives for the implementation of the divinely imposed social order not ultimately by the hands of ordinary men, selected merely for zeal and knowledge, but by the hands of (in effect) quasi-divine beings:

In fact, according to the traditions that have been handed down to us, the Most Noble Messenger and the Imams existed before the creation of the world in the form of lights situated beneath the divine throne; they were superior to other men even in the sperm from which they grew and in their physical composition.

(Islam and Revolution, p. 64)

This would lead to a crystal-clear political situation, if only these

Imams were present and identifiable. All power to the Imams, you might then say, and there could then be no disputed legitimacy. But alas, the Imams may be and often are in hiding, and are known to have suffered even worse indignities:

For we know that our Imams were sometimes subject to conditions which prevented them from pronouncing a true ordinance; they were exposed to tyrannical and oppressive rulers who imposed *taqiya* (dissimulation) and fear upon them.

(Islam and Revolution, p. 71)

A radiance too bright for the Archangel Gabriel and liable to scorch him if he came too close was not bright enough to overawe the tyrants of this world. They seem to be made of harder steel than Gabriel. In these conditions, what's to be done? As Khomeini puts it:

Now that no particular individual has been appointed by God ... to assume the functions of government in the time of Occulation, what must be done? Are we to abandon Islam? Do we no longer need it? Was Islam valid for only two hundred years? Or is it that Islam has clarified our duties in other respects but not with respect to government?

(Islam and Revolution, p. 61)

There are a number of possibilities:

(1)   Total passivity and withdrawal from an evil and illegitimate social order, whilst waiting for the return of the legitimate order.

Moslems are forbidden to seek redress of their grievances from the executive or judiciary of improperly constituted governments. They are forbidden to have legal recourse to kings or other despotic administrations ... even if they have the legal rights to defend.

(Little Green Book, p. 29)

(2)   Grudging cooperation with the temporal power provided it does not violate the divine order.

(3)   Active support for the Shi'ite ruler, even though he is not *the* Imam.

(4)   A formal and uncompromising affirmation of exclusive political guardianship for the religious scholars, during the persisting occultation of the Imam, and a firm insistence on their duty to be politically active in bringing about a situation in which this guardianship is granted to them. This reduces any remaining political or military agencies into simple executors of the will of the legitimate clerisy, and declares any other form of government to be illegitimate. As Dr Algar puts it in a footnote (p. 154):

> ... in the absence of the Imam or an individual deputy named by him ... the task [of government] devolves upon the *Fuqaha* [clerics] as a class.

The essence of Khomeini's position is that the inner ambivalences and tensions of Shi'ite theology, in the context of recent social and political development in Iran, have come in the end to propel Khomeini into an uncompromising version of (4) and to put him in a situation in which he can actually put it into effect. There is no question of Muslims, Shi'ites or Iranians, or indeed Khomeini himself, having *always* been permanent adherents of this position. They were not, most of the time. Not only the history of Islam, but also the history of Shi'ism when not occupying an underdog position, is overwhelmingly monarchical. Khomeini has in effect developed a new position, which combines Sunni law-worship and this-worldliness with Shi'a intransigence and absolutism, but without the Shi'a tendency to abjure the present political world. The end result: a republic of the lawyer clerics.

Ironically, it was the Shi'ite clerisy itself which pushed the late Shah's father to establish a monarchy, for fear of the alternative, namely a Kemal-type republic. It is only now that Khomeini has become unambiguously fundamentalist/republican, and declares monarchy to be non-Islamic. To what extent Khomeini passed through the other positions, and in what spirit he did so throughout the course of his intellectual and political development, is something which one hopes Dr Algar's forthcoming biography of the Imam will establish and document with accuracy.

In the present collection, for instance, Algar includes a speech which was actually delivered in a teaching centre in Qum in 1963. It was indeed an unbelievably brave speech. But, defiant and insolent though it was vis-à-vis the Shah, the interesting thing about it is that it asks him only *to mend his ways* ('I don't want you to become like your father. Listen to my advice, listen to the scholars of Islam ... don't listen to Israel ...'); it does *not* suggest that he should abandon his position and dismantle the monarchy itself. Given the fact that the tone of the speech is such that it was bound to get him into trouble anyway, as in fact it did, he might just as well have declared monarchy as such to be illegitimate, had he already at that time believed it to be such. You might as well be hanged for abstract republicanism as for calling the Shah a 'miserable wretch' (which he is quoted as having done). It is very hard to imagine that Savak made any fine distinctions between virulent abuse of the King of Kings on the one hand, and abstract anti-monarchical political theory on the other.

Later, some of Khomeini's remarks made after the Revolution about popular validation of government did have a touch of Rousseau about them (p. 255), reminiscent of what Jean-Jacques says about the suspension of popular sovereignty in England between elections, but of course the sovereign for Khomeini really is the Divine rather than the General Will. The General Will can choose the executive, but it cannot make commitments for the future or permanently delegate authority. It would seem to need to be in permanent session. And it can never legislate, that function being pre-empted for the deity.

The basic moral intuition of mainstream Sunni Islam is the divinity of Law: unique, eternal, the uncreated Word of God. The obverse of this is the impermissibility, the sinfulness of revering anything in this world as divine: anthropolatry as well as idolatry are *out*. Orthodox Sunnism does admittedly make certain mild concessions in the direction of bestowing fiscal and political privileges on the (very numerous, putatively) progeny of the Prophet, but these relatively modest expressions of respect remain well this side of divinisation. Shi'ism, by contrast, endows certain personalities with quasi-divine status. The emotive aspect of this is strengthened because some of these personalities are also martyrs, and the political implications of this become profoundly ambiguous – for most Shi'ite sub-segments, these sacred Leaders are and remain in hiding, with no clear indications as to when the Occultation will terminate.

Within the folk versions of both Sunni and Shi'a Islam, sacredness has been widely diffused by its attribution to many petty saints, dead and alive. Within both traditions, this old proliferation or inflation of the sacred has been severely combated and reduced of late, under the impact of a Reform movement which benefits from changed social circumstances: the autonomous rural communities which used and needed their petty saints as arbitrators or leaders have themselves been much weakened by the greatly strengthened modern state.

But within Shi'ism, anthropolatry has nevertheless remained *at the centre*, applied to the key martyr figures, and sanctioned by the High Theology of the sect. So where Sunni Islam absolutises Law, Shi'a Islam contains an apotheosis of *both* Law *and* certain Persons. It is thus a doubly Absolutist faith. The essence of Khomeini's position is that the absolutisation of Law has been stressed and emphasised to a point at which the sacred Imams, whilst by no means denied, become logically redundant. When Law acquires this kind of status, the obvious political corollary is a divine nomocracy, administered by lawyer-theologians. Sunnism is anomalous when Muslims are deprived of political power; Shi'ism becomes anomalous when Shi'ites do attain power, because they ought to hand it over to the

Absolute. Its continual occultation is an embarrassment. Khomeini has found a way out of the anomaly, not in the old way (accepting monarchy pro tem), but by stressing the Sunni elements of the theology and reserving power for the clerisy, whilst *waiting for the Imam*.

Sunni *ulama*, however, have not been able to secure a position implied by their theology, and are in practice content to be watchdogs of the orthodoxy of a distinct political authority, whom they are not reluctant to serve in clerical, administrative and judicial capacities. (In Iran, as Said Arjomand has shown, there was a certain polarisation between populist and bureaucratic ulama.) This is as true in modern times, in the countries where fundamentalism has prevailed, as it was in the past. Shi'ites by contrast can accommodate themselves to hostile power-holders and possess doctrinal tools for explaining such an accommodation: after all, the only valid ruler, the Imam, is away in hiding. But when they attain power and the Imam is *still* in hiding, they face a quandary.

Ironically, it is the Shi'a *ulama* who have now at long last attained the great power which Law-worship should rightly confer on legal scholars – even though they, given that for them only Hidden Imams have a real and absolute legitimacy, logically have rather less claim to it... In terms of logic, they can and do claim that power only as Caretakers, as long as the Imam does remain in hiding. (Or they may slide close to the blasphemy of claiming the Imamate for one of their own number.) Concretely, they were able to seize the power just because the martyrdom myths associated with the Imams turned out to be outstandingly effective, mobilising masses for the ultimate sacrifice and on a massive scale, thereby making revolution possible. But when the revolution prevails, martyrs must give way to lawyers. A further irony lies in the fact that the Shi'ite ulama were only able to do this just when the content of their theology was moving towards Sunnism, when Divine Law was receiving rather more stress than the Divine Persons. The paradox is easily explained: the surviving Shi'a elements were crucial for revolutionary ardour and sacrifice, whereas the Sunni strain provides them with legitimation and content once power has been attained, and was well adapted *both* to the absence of the Imam *and* to various distinctively modern traits of its own world.

Amongst the pre-industrial world religions, Islam stands out as the one which has retained a unique political hold over both masses and elites. This is true of Islam in general, and not only of Shi'ism. But the Iranian revolution cannot simply be explained as one further example of this remarkable power. There are two very closely related paradoxes in the Iranian situation. The first of them is this: the persistent or increasing power of Islam is due to features which are *least* conspicuously present in Shi'ism. So why should Shi'ism bring off the most spectacular revolution of all, one in which a militarily and financially intact, indeed opulent, government is brought down by rioters, who by means of willingness to endure a massive megamartyrdom overcome an undefeated, extremely large, well-drilled and well-equipped army?

The other paradox is: in other places in which fundamentalism is influential, its power is indirect, and springs from the moral hold which clerics have over those who wield coercive power. The powerholders are either descendants of tribal conquerors who emerged in pre-modern conditions, admittedly with religious inspiration and blessing – the offspring of the Wahabis of central Arabia, or of the Fulani followers of Osman dan Fodio in northern Nigeria – or alternatively, technocrats and soldiers, successful Muslim Decembrists, who know how to operate a coup or run a revolutionary war, as in Libya or Algeria. The followers of the fundamentalist revivalist Ben Badis in Algeria, for instance, did indeed make the Algerian revolution possible by preparing the moral climate, but the revolution itself was not led or made by clerics. Successful direct clerical leadership seems unique to Iran, and it is strange that it should have occurred within Shi'ism, which in many ways is furthest removed from the spirit of the Islamic Reformation of the past hundred years. How did this come about?

The reason why reformed Islam is so influential of late is that it has certain conspicuous traits – strict unitarianism, sobriety, orderliness, scripturalism, egalitarianism – which are consonant with the organisational and ideological requirements of an industrialising age. Faced with the predicament of backwardness, Muslims are not forced, as others are, into the painful dilemma of either emulating the colonialist enemy and thereby disavowing their own tradition and identity, or on the other hand inventing a populist counter-tradition. Instead, they can turn to an old local tradition, the High Culture of Islam, and thus define and reform themselves in the name of a genuinely indigenous and quasi-modern set of beliefs and values, not visibly indebted to the West, whilst at the same time disavowing a large part of customary low culture. But Shi'ism, in which the cult of personality is proportionately stronger, and the cult of divine nomocracy correspondingly weaker, fits this model much less well than does mainstream, Sunni Islam. Why did it then, in the end, perform so brilliantly, as a catalyst and mobilising agent?

The explanation falls into two parts. One relates to Shi'ism as such, and the other, to the form of it represented and eventually led by Khomeini. The cult of personality and martyrdom inherent in Shi'ism causes its scholars, or some of them, to retain more effective links with the unregenerate masses than Sunni clerics are able to do. Shi'ite *ulama* are not merely experts on the Law, on how to dispose of a sodomised camel, and on precisely what degree of penetration requires an ablution; they are also, and in equal measure, expertly professional and eternally evocative biographers of the Founder Martyr, remembrancers of a highly personal and righteous-indignation-arousing model. They speak not only through words and texts but also through vivid and intense annual passion plays, through a symbolism of an ancient bloody injustice which is easily linked to current resentment.

In other words, they speak in an idiom far more rousing and moving than mere preoccupations with the niceties of the law can ever be, even when related to intimate physiological functions. Moreover, the ever-reactivated memory of Martyrdom is accompanied by an equally vivid and quite unambiguous, emphatic message, that the Martyrdom ought and must be bloodily avenged, and that the tyrant may well himself be a Muslim. The great ambivalence vis-à-vis the temporal power, which is stronger and deeper in Shi'ism than in Sunnism, makes it more logical for Shi'a scholars to be cast and to cast themselves for the role of revolutionary leadership.

That is one part of the answer. The other is to be sought in the particular development represented by Khomeini, and very well documented by Algar's collection of his writing. It has already been said that Khomeini is the most Sunni of Shi'ite theologians; one may go further and say that he is a positively Kharejite Shi'ite. This was sometime a paradox, but now time has given it proof. The egalitarianism-republicanism, the scripturalist nomocracy, is in the end pushed very far indeed by Khomeini. In modal Shi'ism, the nomocracy or hierocracy is merely a kind of Provisional Government, at best an interim caretaker authority, legitimate whilst mankind awaits the end of Occultation and the return of the Hidden Imam. But not for Khomeini: the Law must be upheld *at all times*, and in identical form, style and with undiminished severity, Occultation or no Occultation. Let justice be done though the heavens fall. Or rather, let justice be done, without worrying about whether the Imam be present or absent. And justice means implementing an unchanging Law.

The Law has not been dead
Though it hath slept.

If the Imam chooses to return from Occultation, or hasn't yet departed for it, well then he simply doubles up as mystical and absolute Imam *and* Scholar-Law-Enforcer; but it is all a kind of contingent personal union, a merely historical superimposition of one role upon another. The two roles have no inherent or necessary connection with each other.

The authority that the Prophet and the Imam had in establishing a government ... exists also for the *faqih* [lawyer/theologian].
The Imam does indeed possess certain spiritual dimensions *that are unconnected with his function as a ruler.*

(*Islam and Revolution*, p. 64, my italics)

The replacement of the basic political intuition of Shi'ism – sacred, quasi-divine personal ruler – by that of the other ideological pole within Islam, the orderly imposition of an Eternal Divine Law by *anyone*, whether quasi-divine or merely learned and pious, could hardly be clearer or more explicit. Government, the implementation of eternal divine Law, is what it is and not another thing. Should it happen to coincide with another thing, a near-divine incarnation, well then that is a conflation of two distinct things, but it does not really modify the essence of either. So Sunnism is hidden under the Shi'a cloak. In one sense, government is devalued by this argument. Government is a necessary chore, and not to be valued in itself:

Rule and command, then, are in themselves only a means...

Some people, whose eyes have been dazzled by the things of this world, imagine that leadership and government represented in themselves dignity and high station for the Imams...

It is the duty of the Imams and the just *fuqaha* to use government institutions to execute divine law ... Government in itself represents nothing but pain and trouble for them, but what are they to do?

(*Islam and Revolution*, pp. 65, 66)

If there is anyone still foolish enough to believe that there is an inherent connection between the special mystical state of the Imams and government, let them be disabused:

Fatima also possessed these states, even though she was not a ruler, a judge, or a governor.

(*Ibid.*, p. 65)

The mystical status of the Prophet's daughter is not in dispute: but obviously no one in his senses could ever suppose that a woman might rule. This proof of the analytic separability of political authority and mystical standing, so close to each other in traditional Shi'ite sentiment, could hardly be more conclusive.

In other words, Khomeini's theology, though Shi'ite in name and in some of its substance, nevertheless does *not* constitute a counter-example to the general trend observable in the Islam of the past hundred years, the overall shift towards a symmetrical, egalitarian, rule-oriented, scripturalist, anti-mediationist and anti-ecstatic pole of the faith.

This aspect of his thought, the attack on the old religious brokers, the divine patronage networks (an onslaught so central to recent Muslim reformism), is well represented in this volume. Khomeini tells us how he had spoken to his followers (p. 142):

Before anything else, you must decide what to do with these pseudo-saints. As long as they are there, our situation is like that of a person who is attacked by an enemy whilst someone else keeps his hands bound behind him.

Here the usual accusation is implied. That the 'saints' are agents, witting or unwitting, of the imperialist foe.

we must advise these pseudo-saints and try to awaken them. . .

If our pseudo-saints do not wake up . . . after repeated admonition . . . it will be obvious that the cause . . . is not ignorance, but something else. Then, of course, we will adopt a different attitude towards them.

(pp. 142 and 143)

The saints must be corrected and made to mend their ways; the Imams are to be revered, but as far as the activity of government is concerned, they are a kind of optional and almost irrelevant extra. (In any case, as they are in hiding, the issue is a bit hypothetical.) So – only the clerisy remain as the sole residual legatee of rightful authority, and secular agents must obey them. This is the essence of Khomeini's political philosophy.

At the end of Algar's volume there is also a set of Khomeini's philosophical/mystical writings, as distinct from his political ones. (One ought not to call them theological, in so far as in this system theology embraces politics and philosophy equally.) These are of very considerable interest and merit. They show us another aspect of Khomeini, as coherent and passionate as the man devoted to the maintenance of severe and undiminished punishment – Imam or no Imam – or deeply preoccupied with the minute governance of physiological functions. Here we find a philosopher/mystic of very considerable force, within whose thought rational and trans-rational appeals are fused in a convincing, profoundly felt and powerfully expressed whole.

There are echoes of St Anselm and of Descartes and of neo-Platonism in Khomeini's proofs of the existence of God. Both the ontological and the cosmological proofs of the existence of God are invoked. Presumably the former reached Khomeini from Avicenna, who had formulated a version of it.[2] Consider a passage such as the following:

God is a being that is infinite, that possesses the attributes of perfection to an infinite degree, and that is subject to no limitation. A being that is unlimited in this manner cannot be contingent... If there is no limitation in the existence of a thing, then, reason dictates that it cannot be other than the absolute and necessary being...

(p. 368)

This is combined with a negative or deficiency theory of evil (and thus a solution of the problem of evil) which is reminiscent of Spinoza.

all things that exist have two aspects: an aspect of existence and an aspect of deficiency. The aspect of existence is light: it is free from all deficiency and pertains to God. The other aspect, the negative aspect or that of deficiency, pertains to us. Now no one can praise the negative; it is only the affirmative – existence and perfection – that can be praised. There is only one perfection in the world and that is God, and there is only one beauty and that is God. We must understand this, and understand it with our heart.

(p. 373)

From this, Khomeini quite legitimately, and explicitly, derives the doctrine that God possesses the monopoly of all legitimate praise:

You imagine that you are praising someone's handwriting, but in reality you are praising God.

(p. 380)

It is hard not to reflect that, if only one combines Khomeini's theodicy with his politics, it is easy to establish a cogent proof of the non-existence of both Israel and of the USA. Here the wish would seem to be the father of the logic, though there can also be no doubt but that the Imam would also enforce those non-existencies in a more concrete and empirical sense, had he but the power.

But the rationalistic elements are integrally fused with a kind of characteristically Muslim semantic mysticism:

[2] See Roy Mottahedeh, *The Mantle of the Prophet*, London, 1986, p. 87.

A name is a sign. Names are given to people and assigned to things in order to provide them with a sign by which they can be recognised... The names of God are also signs, signs of His Sacred Essence; and it is only His names that are knowable to man. The Essence Itself is something that lies totally beyond the reach of man, and even the Seal of the Prophets, the most knowledgeable and noble of men, was unable to attain the knowledge of the Essence. The Sacred Essence is unknown to all but Itself. It is the names of God that are accessible to man.

The whole world is a name of God, for a name is a sign, and all the creatures that exist in the world are signs of the Sacred Essence of God Almighty. Here some people may reach a profound understanding of what is meant by 'signs', while others may grasp only the general meaning that no creature comes into existence by itself.

(p. 367)

What is interesting about this theology and mysticism is that it contains a deep tension which is strikingly parallel to a strain which also pervades the concrete social life of Islam. The firm insistence on the absolute transcendence of the deity makes it unutterably blasphemous to claim identification with God, and on at least one famous occasion, a great mystic paid for such blasphemy with his life. But at the very same time, the absolutist claims made for the deity inescapably tend, as these passages illustrate, to turn everything in the world into 'signs', emanations, aspects of the deity. Thus the severe uncompromising transcendentalism is liable to flip over into a kind of pantheism, which at the same time is abhorred by the faith.

The concrete socio-religious life of Muslim communities was traditionally pervaded by a similar conflict between a severe scripturalist transcendentalism, sustained by the literate scholars, and a pursuit of divine refractions or emanations *in* the world, represented characteristically by the 'saints', the dervishes and the marabouts. The need for these refractions was not simply a consequence of the ambivalence inherent in the theology: it also had more mundane bases. Ill-governed communities needed leaders and mediators, and in the tribal worlds in particular, there was no room for scholarship, but a great need for living, ecstatic saints, who mediated between social groups in the name of mediating between men and God.

Yet reverence for anything other than God constitutes the sin of *shirk*. (Though if Khomeini's argument about automatic divine monopoly of all praise is correct, it becomes impossible to commit *shirk*, however hard one tries: one's praise automatically rises up to God, even if misguidedly directed elsewhere.) At the very heart of the great Reformation which Islam has undergone in the last hundred years, there is a sustained attack on *shirk* and on the religious brokers. Khomeini clearly is part of this movement, notwithstanding his Shi'ism:

The social environment created by ... *shirk* invariably brings about corruption such as you can now observe in Iran, the corruption termed 'corruption on earth'. This corruption must be swept away, and its instigators punished for their deeds.

(p. 48)

Yet ironically the Shi'ite themes which, at least to an outsider, seem most tainted by *shirk*, the anthropolatrous attitude to the Imams and martyrs, were precisely what helped Khomeini to bring about that staggering revolution, which now nevertheless endeavours to extirpate *shirk*. The deep tension is there, both in the vision and in the social order.

In the end, it seems clear that the theological revolutionary, the ruthlessly brutal moralist and politician, the scholastic Solon of bathroom etiquette, and the forceful mystic and thinker, are one and the same coherent person. He reflects the deepest currents and strains of the society which has engendered him, and which he now dominates.

10 The Rubber Cage: Disenchantment with Disenchantment

The Iron Cage

There is the celebrated story about the Scots boy who was asked what the preacher had talked about in his sermon. He talked about sin, was the reply. What did he say about it? *He was agin it.*

When it was agreed by the *kolektiv* which was planning this conference that I should prepare a paper about Disenchantment, I had a curious after-feeling that I was expected to be *agin* it. Now I do not wish to be misunderstood: I am not suggesting for one moment that I was given a brief, a commission, that in some sort of informal way I was told 'Gellner my boy, you have a certain name for writing abusive prose though for not much else; now we expect you to do your stuff on Disenchantment.'

There wasn't anything like that, even in the most tacit form. But all the same, I do have a sense of atmosphere which seems to say that it is high time we gave the Disenchantment thesis a good critical going over. We are not disenchanted, we do not wish to be disenchanted, and there are no good reasons for being disenchanted. The German version of the title – 'Entaeuschung mit Entzauberung' – seems to illustrate this line of thought. *Entzauberung* out: we are *entaeuscht mit Entzauberung.*

One might say that, like the influence of the Crown under George III, Disenchantment has increased, is increasing, and ought to be diminished. Or perhaps it would convey the underlying idea more accurately to say that Disenchantment has increased, is now diminishing, and ought to be diminished further.

The Disenchantment thesis can be broken up into two parts: (1) Mankind is becoming disenchanted, and (2) rightly so.

Now I agree with the critics of the Disenchantment Thesis in so far as they insist that (1) needs reconsideration – perhaps even radical revision. It is (2) that I am inclined to uphold. Perhaps we are not disenchanted, or not nearly as much as consistently as we once supposed or anticipated; but perhaps we certainly *ought to be.*

Let us restate the Disenchantment thesis in the starkest possible way:

The modern world is organised in a rational way. This means that clearly specified goals are pursued by a calculated allocation of means; the means include not only tools but also human activity and men themselves. These things are treated instrumentally and not as ends in themselves. Effectiveness and evidence are kings. The procedures are also rational in the sense of being orderly and rule-bound: like cases are treated alike. It is not only the procedures of organisations which are in this sense 'bureaucratised'; the same also happens to our vision of nature, of the external world. Its comprehensibility and manipulability are purchased by means of subsuming its events under orderly, symmetrical, precisely articulated generalisations and explanatory models. *This* is Disenchantment: the Faustian purchase of cognitive, technological and administrative power, by the surrender of our previous meaningful, humanly suffused, humanly responsive, if often also menacing or capricious world. *That* is abandoned for a more predictable, more amenable, but coldly indifferent and uncosy world. The Iron Cage is not merely one of bureaucratic organisation: it is also a conceptual one. It places constraints not merely on our conduct, but also on our vision.

This is the thesis. In Max Weber, it is combined with a theory about how we came to acquire this vision, but that theory does not concern us here.

It has of late been noticed that the factual component of the thesis is not fully borne out by contemporary evidence: the contemporary vision of the world favoured by much popular culture, especially by youth culture, let alone by the counter-culture (which is not so much *counter*, as an exaggerated version of traits pervasive even in non-dissident society), is *not* marked by discipline, orderliness, abstention from affect, and preference for the implementation of clear rules. Such features, which on any simple interpretation of the Disenchantment thesis ought to be prevalent, have in fact been far from conspicuous of late. The current seems to be running in a different direction.

Some, like Daniel Bell, have concluded from this that we are witnessing a contradiction between the organisational requirements of industrial society on one hand, and its culture on the other. To adopt this view is to accept one part of the old Disenchantment thesis – to the effect that massive technological production does indeed require the Iron Cage spirit – and, noting that the Iron Cage spirit is in decline, to conclude that a tension or incompatibility is at the very heart of contemporary society.

My own suspicion is that, on the contrary, the two elements which on the Daniel Bell view are in conflict are actually in harmony. So, as an alternative to the Iron Cage thesis (whose applicability to the *emergence* of industrial society I do not wish to dispute), I should like to propose the Rubber Cage thesis, which is meant to apply to a later or fully developed stage of industrialism.

The Rubber Cage

The icy intellectual discipline of rationality applies in the first instance to *design* and in the second instance to the *production* of the industrial artefacts. The modus operandi, the style and spirit of the individuals and organisations responsible for these two crucial aspects of our society, must exemplify that responsible and orderly *Geist* in which Max Weber discerned the progenitor of our world, and which is displayed by the free entrepreneur and by the bureaucrat alike.

But: with the growth of affluence and automation, the number of workers and of man-hours devoted to design and to actual production goes down, above all in proportion to the total. The working week shrinks, leisure expands; evenings, weekends, and the period of 'education' all grow larger. Education itself is markedly unrigorous and lacking in discipline. Within working hours and within the working population the tertiary, service sectors expand, and the proportion of people actually engaged in production goes down. Leisure, work in the tertiary sector, and a good proportion of labour in the productive sector as well have a certain feature in common: they all consist of using or serving machines, the control of which becomes increasingly more simple and *intuitive*. By an 'intuitive' control I mean one whose operation seems more or less self-evident, if not to any human being whatever, then at any rate to one brought up in the ambience of industrial gadgets.

Consider that hackneyed but appropriate symbol of the modern human condition, the motor car. To design a new model requires, no doubt, a fair amount of Cartesian thought; so, in some measure and a different way, does the supervision of its production, or its repair. But the *use* of it does not. The principle involved in using a steering wheel, an acceleration pedal, and a braking pedal, are so simple and obvious that even to spell them out seems pedantic. But the point is that the number of people involved in designing or producing motor cars is small and possibly shrinking. The amount of repair work involving thought – the elimination of possibilities which is involved in locating and correcting a fault – is probably also going down, given the tendency to replace entire units rather than repair them. But whilst the number of car users continues to augment, what follows? The activities requiring Cartesian thought are diminishing (both as a proportion of the population and as a proportion of the time of individuals), whilst the activities calling only for easy, intuitive, near-self-evident responses are increasing.

If this is a valid generalisation – and I find it hard to have serious doubts about its truth – it would be odd indeed if the state of affairs it describes were not also reflected in our cosmology.

This of course is precisely what we do find. The interesting feature of the contemporary scene is not so much whether it is religious, revolutionary, conservative, etc. It is, at different times and in different places, all these things. What is interesting, and to a large measure shared throughout, is the kind or style of religion, protest, conservatism and so on which we encounter. A certain similarity of spirit pervades otherwise quite diverse movements, and ranges from the abstract heights of formal philosophy to the earthy immediacy of youth culture and pop stars. One can hardly substantiate so wide-ranging a generalisation, but one can illustrate it. My choice of examples is of course governed by what I happen to be more or less familiar with, and it does not claim to be more than illustrative.

1 *Pragmatism*

This is generally held to be both the most distinctively American philosophy, and to be expressive of the American spirit. Its most distinguished contemporary representative is probably the famous Harvard logician-philosopher Quine. In his hands, however, the doctrines of Peirce, James and Dewey have undergone a subtle transformation which very much illustrates my thesis. Quine himself is, in terms of my previous analogy, very much a car designer rather than user: he happens to be a virtuoso in what is recognised to be an extremely rigorous, abstract and demanding part of higher mathematics. But the sustained effort which must have gone into our collective acquisition of these abstract structures, and equally into individual internalisation by men such as Quine, is not at all reflected in the philosophical precepts found within his doctrine. That is a great paradox: the most Cartesian–Weberian minds may preach and endorse the Rubber rather than the Iron Cage. Perhaps this is even a natural corollary of our contemporary division of labour: to the best minds, everything seems easy, intuitively obvious, because they have internalised the rigorous Cartesian rules of thought so completely; whereas the rest of us all blithely use the fruits and conclusions of the arduous and rigorous endeavours without any longer being aware that they had been required...

The precepts of Quinian pragmatism amount to a confident ('robust' is the word), happy-go-lucky optimism, quite free of the old Cartesian anxiety that every step must be made quite secure before the next one is attempted ('if the first button is wrongly done up, all the others will also be wrong'), and proudly conscious of its insouciance. Our knowledge faces the world not as the lone entrepreneur, liable in most cases to make the supreme sacrifice on the altar of progress by natural selection; on the contrary, big corporations of propositions face reality in the confident expectation that such errors as may and will occur can be corrected by tinkering with some part or other of the large and safe cognitive corpus. The overall happy outcome is guaranteed by a tacitly presiding spirit called scientific method, who is continuous with, or descended from, the older *Geist* of biological adaptation. The sheer size of these cognitive corporations ensures that the price of individual mistakes will not be too great, in general; their reserves are such that they can carry the strain...

The ethos preached (N.B.: *not* exemplified) by Quine is interestingly similar to that noted a couple of decades ago by W. H. Whyte in *The Organisation Man*. It is un-Cartesian and un-Weberian. It is hostile to any excessive preoccupation with safe foundations and rigid, security-conferring rules. Pliable adjustment, safety-in-numbers, willingness to tinker at any point and a corresponding reluctance to absolutise anything, all these are the order of the day. And in effect, this pragmatism opposes other forms of empiricism, precisely because they contain Cartesian residues (attempts to absolutise either sense data or formal logical axioms or both as cognitive bedrocks), and it does so by claiming that such absolute foundations are not merely not available, but also not necessary. To say that they are not needed is, of course, to say that we are very much at home in this world, that all in all our intuitions are sound and trustworthy and need not be checked and corrected by some philosophically established independent criterion.

Just that is my point: that is precisely how the world feels to a man surrounded by intuitively manipulable, easy machines.

2 *Wittgensteinianism*

This is still, deservedly or not, the greatest single success story within academic philosophy. A movement which, less than fifty years ago, consisted of a Cambridge clique with an esoteric, jealously

guarded and unintelligible doctrine, communicated only in dark sayings and secretly circulated manuscripts, has become a major academic industry and a household word at any rate in university-educated
households . . . Bertrand Russell, who held it in total, unremitting and
justified contempt, noted very soon that its secret lay in making
sustained, difficult thought quite redundant, and in replacing it by
something that was, above all, *easy* and, in the present sense, intuitive.

The particular manner in which this rather special facility came to
be launched on the world is interesting. It equates philosophic truth
precisely with what is intuitively obvious in our handling of language,
what we intuitively know *how-to-do*.

It was Chomsky's achievement to show just how problematic
human competence is. For Wittgensteinianism, what we know how to
do institutes our terminal explanation, not a problem. Its general
philosophic programme is to replace explanations which refer to
realms of reality by explanations which refer to linguistic competence.
This is then taken to be self-explanatory and philosophically terminal.

This truth is easy and close to hand (it is this doctrine which ap-
palled Russell), if only we look to what we know and what is built into
our already-available language-using skill. The only reason why it
ever eludes us is either that we do not properly attend to what we are
really doing when we use words, or, worse still, that we are led into
positive misdescriptions of it by mistaken theories of language.
Linguistic philosophy takes us back to our real custom; it equates,
very significantly, philosophy with conceptual table-manners.

How did this doctrine arise? It began as a mistaken diagnosis of all
other philosophy. It supposed that all other philosophic theorising
arose from the expectation that all language-use is one kind of thing,
and in particular from the assumption of one or another of the 'echo'
theories of language. There are two main rival echo theories, Platonism and empiricism. The former holds that words have meaning in
virtue of being names of abstract entities; the latter holds that words
or groups of words have meaning in virtue of being linked, by human
convention, with actual or possible configurations of concrete events,
experience. Curiously, these two theories were very much in the air at
the time this movement crystallised. A form of Platonism had a revival
thanks to certain developments in mathematical logic, where a new
notation seemed to mirror reality better than natural language; whereas in the philosophy of natural science, empiricism continued to be
influential. Either programme, however, called for an intellectually
strenuous reinterpretation of what we normally think we know. Under
either programme, philosophy remained strenuous.

But no! claimed the 'later' Wittgenstein. Language does not echo the world; in fact it does not do any one thing. It is functional, and consists of a large number of quite diverse functions, of what people *do* with words. All those difficult and inconclusive old philosophic theories were only by-products of the contrary supposition, which were in effect a mistaken theory of language. They were answers to questions which need not and should not ever have been asked. If you want them answered at all – and you will be disappointed by the answer – just look to how *you* used words. The truth of morality lies in how you use moral language; the truth in epistemology lies in how you use cognitive terms; and so on.

In fact, all this was quite wrong. People had not asked philosophic questions because they had made a mistake about language. They asked them because they are unavoidable: they imposed themselves by the very nature of our situation. Men did not turn to theories such as Platonism or empiricism because they supposed these to be accounts of how language was in fact used, but because these doctrines have a certain plausibility as accounts of how we may *legitimately* use it. But all that is another story. What matters here is this: if you accept the Wittgensteinian diagnosis – and I have given the gist of it, minus the sales patter, insurance, camouflage, etc., which normally accompany it – an amazing *facility* results. Scales fall off our eyes: we can see the solution of the problem of freedom in the rules governing our use of words such as 'free', of the problem of probability by observing our use of words such as 'likely', and so on.

This amazing facility can operate either at a piecemeal level, by examining the words connected with this or that problem – as when the mind/body problem was 'solved' by examining our use of terms describing mental competence – or at a general level, when the underlying idea of this 'method' is made explicit and applied. It then runs as follows: every language has its own norms, and these are quite self-sufficient within it. Our ideas are based on our verbal custom – on no more than that, but on no less! It had been most misguided ever to seek external warrant for our norms, in any field. Now that we understand that language (alias culture) is self-sufficient, we have surmounted that temptation, and we rest secure in our world. 'Philosophy leaves everything as it is.'

Thus the facility operates not only at the level of providing an easy pre-fabricated solution for all philosophical problem ('examine the actual employment of the words from which the problem arose') but also as a ready-made carte blanche for the validation of any belief-system or any culture and its norms and convictions. Wittgensteinian philosophy has in fact come to be used in this way, as an incredibly facile ratification of what one wishes to believe. Contemporary pragmatism fused the self-reliant confidence of the frontiersman with the deep internalisation by an expert logician of the operations of his craft, and ended with a new doctrine which underwrites the unsystematic adjustments of a technical structure (cognitive or organisational) as *the* proper way to conduct. In the case of linguistic philosophy, the elements which went into the combination were different. It was born in a non-technical milieu in which privileged intellectuals possessed few skills other than a very high level of literacy and sensitivity to the behaviour of words. It told them that philosophy was about verbal table-manners. This delighted them, for they were great experts at this and at nothing much else. It secured their position and made their skills important, by making philosophy into a therapy which consisted of accurately describing the conduct of words. All this happened at a time when an eager throng of entrants were only too keen to come to the finishing schools and learn table-manners, verbal or others, before they discovered that their own entry spoilt the market for them. But in the wider society, there was still much demand both for a defence against technicism and for a vindication of faith. This philosophy provided it all, and with such ease too.

3 *Modernist religion*

One of the beneficiaries of the preceding line of argument was modernist religion. The argument ran: religious language is as legitimate and self-justifying as any other kind. Its rules and norms must be elicited by observing its proper functioning (have we not learned that this was the only correct procedure in philosophy?) and then judging it only by its own terms, rather than absurdly imposing preconceived extraneous criteria on it. And when judged by its own criteria, it is found (not surprisingly) to be as sound as a bell. Religious language is in use. Meaning is use. The criteria of meaning are only found in use. By the criteria elicited from its actual use, this employment of speech is in order. Hence its concepts are meaningful and valid. Hence God exists.

But though this linguo-philosophic device of confirming the validity of faith from the mere fact of faith-language was available, religion did not need to wait for Wittgenstein for its salvation. Many other devices were available, and I could not enumerate them all. All one can do instead is to indicate their generically shared traits. These traits are of course often intertwined. They are found in the linguo-philosophic approach to religion, but they are also found far beyond it, in many other approaches. The main traits are

(1)   Autofunctionalism and Double Citizenship, and
(2)   Decognitivisation.

Autofunctionalism consists, as the name implies, of a kind of turning in upon oneself of the functionalist insight. The functionalist looks at strange beliefs and institutions and notices that, notwithstanding their surface oddity or even absurdity, they are in their context highly functional, or even ideal. He concludes that their surface absurdity should be disregarded and that they should be accorded a kind of functional validity, a validity in virtue of function (rather than in virtue of overt message, which would not warrant it). He says, in effect, that it is not exactly true but it is very useful; and he is often tempted to take the next step, and say that truth is a kind of usefulness, or the other way round, or both, and end up by endorsing, in its context, the belief in question. Linguistic philosophy, with its 'meaning is use' approach, was one example of this. Use (function) guaranteed meaning; the meaningfulness of a whole category of discourse (e.g. 'religious discourse') amounts to the claim of truth for what that whole category presupposes. Q.E.D.

Autofunctionalism does the same, only this time the 'context' is one's own society. The major premiss is a meta-theory linking usefulness or functionality with truth. The minor premiss is a more specific theory concerning the functional role of one's beliefs in one's own context. The conclusion is readily available.

The practitioner of this ideological ploy is at the same time claiming a kind of Double Citizenship, in so far as the major premiss is only articulable in some inter-contextual (inter-cultural) stratosphere, for what it says is true about all cultures, all meaning-contexts, and is not itself necessarily or perhaps not even possibly part of any one of them; the minor premiss is about one of them; and the final conclusion is articulated *inside* the idiom of one of them...

Decognitivisation is also linked to functionalist interpretation, but in a somewhat different way. Instead of linking use and truth, the ploy consists of subtracting the cognitive or doctrinal element from the significance of pronouncements, so as to allow them to be valid by some other criterion. The rest of the operation is similar, and results, once again, in the practice of Double Citizenship. To take some examples: it is asserted that the real significance of a religious pronouncement is to express a commitment, or to celebrate the cohesion of a social group. If so, and if that is all there is to it, it is of course a terrible solecism to treat these expressions of commitment or cohesion or whatever as cognitive pronouncements, to be subjected to the same tests and so forth. They are valid by other criteria (which do not seem to be too demanding – indeed they often seem to be non-existent). The conclusion is then used *inside* the cultural language as if it were cognitively valid. One slogan which used to convey this attitude used to be that religion was a matter of 'believing in', not 'believing that'. (In fact, of course, 'believing in *X*' is a matter of believing *that* certain propositions are true, namely that *X* existed, that he was what he claimed to be, and that the statements he made were true.)

Existentialism, in the days when it was fashionable, was often used in this manner, and might have provided a further separate specimen for our collection. There is a certain irony in this, for it went quite contrary to the intentions of the founder of this movement, Kierkegaard, who had wanted to make things *harder*, not easier, not facile. He was opposed to the facile aspects of Hegelian functionalism, which had made faith that had lost its credibility acceptable again by holding it to be but a coded version of a more acceptable philosophic truth, and justifying it in terms of its alleged role in a socio-historic development. In combating this facility, he unwittingly invented a new one. By stressing the cognitive difficulty of paradoxical faith, which made commitment, like some painful rite de passage, an arduous and hence significant step, he made that awkwardness part of its essence. But if so, it ceases to be awkward. Henceforth, the difficulty is no longer difficult. A paradoxical faith is only difficult as long as it is (as traditionally it was) measured by the same yardsticks as ordinary cognitive assertions. If it is *meant* to be paradoxical, difficulty evaporates. All becomes easy – which is my general theme.

4 *Modernist Marxism*

The amusing thing about recently fashionable forms of Carnaby Street Marxism is how they resemble modernist theology. They are much given to anti-functionalism and Double Citizenship, and even to decognitivisation. This was particularly true, of course, of the forms most prevalent in the 1960s. The scientistic pretensions of earlier Marxism were forgotten or openly disavowed. The whole operation is accompanied by a facility-encouraging epistemology. Alienation was not merely an obscure concept but also a self-identifying one, and an automatic warrant for dissent. If pragmatism combined the modern facility with rugged frontiersman self-reliance, and Wittgensteinianism with the intuitive mastery of etymology by word-specialists, then modern Marxism seems to have taken over the torch of nonconformity. The Protestant idea that every individual can, by an unaided consultation of his inner light, decide about and repudiate the legitimacy of the outer order, was conspicuously present in the spirit of the dissent of that decade.

But a kind of autofunctionalism is also present in the even more recent forms of Marxism which have emerged in reaction to the cult of the young Hegelian Marx. The tortuous scholasticism of the Althusserian school seems pervaded by a self-conscious epistemological sophistication: like the man who could hardly watch the play for watching his reactions to it, these men seem to theorise not so much about society and reality as about their own theorising about society. They have discovered that theorising is one further mode of practice, and it is this practice – their own theorising – which they are most interested in. Moreover, they have learned from epistemology that knowledge is not a simple echoing of facts, of confrontation with reality; theory has a legitimate life of its own and is never simply at the mercy of any one fact (or, one suspects, any number of them). The end result is a kind of selective or sliding-scale decognitivisation. Their Marxism comes to be largely about itself. They do indeed tend to talk about Marxism, not as *a* theory about history and society, competing with others, but as a discipline or subject of its own, and hence with its own inner norms...

One could no doubt add to my list of examples. Likewise one could argue about whether I have interpreted these examples correctly, and whether they do indeed exemplify the general tendency which is my main concern. I can only repeat that I do not for one moment suppose that these examples establish the truth of the generalisation; they are meant to illustrate what my generalisation is driving at.

If there is some truth in it, what should be our attitude to the situation described? To allow it to be true is to admit that the Disenchantment thesis fails, at least as a descriptive account of what is currently happening. We are not disenchanted, or at least very many of us are not. On the contrary, many live within a meaningful world, and one, moreover, they manipulate with some ease to make it so. The Rubber Cage has replaced the Iron Cage. But that does not necessarily mean that we should welcome this development. I have already confessed that I have my misgivings about it. But my mind is not clear about the issue, and perhaps it would be best to sketch out the possible alternative attitudes, as I see them. Perhaps one could do it best by beginning with an analogy – with modern constitutional monarchy.

It is an oft-noted paradox of the contemporary world that whilst the typical form and constitutional idiom of backward countries – inevitably inegalitarian in fact, authoritarian etc. – is republican if not Marxist, stable monarchies characteristically survive in developed, profoundly embourgeoised polities. Ideologically, it is a paradox. Monarchy stands for personal rule, for the use of the principle of heredity or accident of birth for the filling of the highest office in the state, for a religious if not sacred view of authority. In other words, it is an outright defiance of the egalitarianism and secularism which otherwise pervades these societies. How is this possible?

An explanation or justification, or rather an explanation which is also a justification, is not far to seek, and is very familiar. Modern monarchy, in developed industrial societies, is not merely constitutional, but is above all *symbolic*. 'Symbolic', in this context, means *not for real*. (This is also standard usage in social anthropology, where if a native says something sensible it is primitive technology, but if it sounds very odd, then it is symbolic.)

It is symbolic because it is not really continuous with those mediaeval or baroque monarchs who really had a great deal of power. It is useful precisely because it is symbolic. Not being responsible for difficult and perilous decisions, it is not tainted by the failure of policies. But by 'symbolising' the continuity of the state or of the nation, it helps to prevent these elective leaders, who are responsible for decisions and policies, from acquiring too much magic. It is a way of helping ensure that real power is not sacred.

This argument has a great deal of force when applied to the case of monarchy. The question is whether the argument can be transferred to the sphere of belief or ideology, as opposed to the sphere of politics. I shall content myself with describing the case *for* and *against*, without even attempting to decide finally between them.

The case *for* would stress the applicability of the political arguments to belief. One could argue as follows: just as the very power and pervasiveness of modern government make it dangerous to sacralise it to any degree, so the very potency of modern knowledge, *and* its rapid growth and consequent instability, make it unsuitable and unsafe as the foundation of one's moral, social, human vision. It is subject to dramatic transformations. The great discovery of today becomes the fallacy of tomorrow. The precise boundaries of what is included within respectable cognition and what is excluded from it are hard to draw. Spurious fashions sometimes succeed in masquerading in the garb of respectable science. Genuine scientific advances are sometimes accompanied by or inextricably mixed up with most dubious philosophic background theories, which temporarily gain a questionable authority thereby. Moreover, it is difficult for a layman to judge in these fields, in which the most strategic choices or implications may also be the most technical ones, and at the same time, there is no clear way of delegating decisions. The problem of identifying those who could assume vicarious responsibility is even more difficult than shouldering it oneself.

All these considerations – and they could be expanded, no doubt – seem to point in one direction. Why not have a further refinement in the Separation of Powers, imitate the sphere of politics, and have two kinds of sovereign in the sphere of cognition and faith – one for substance, and another for symbolism? Let us leave real cognition in the Iron Cage: it can be icy, impersonal, abstract, technical, devoid of warmth and magic, impermanent, inaccessible, and unintelligible. For our human life, our conceptualisation of ourselves and our relationship with our fellows, let us have something personal, warm, human, intelligible. Quite apart from the obvious attractions of this, it will also defuse the danger inherent in taking the other kind of knowledge too seriously. Let the Iron Cage apply to a perhaps shrinking realm of professional, specialised and manipulative knowledge; our expanding leisure time can be spent in a happily Re-enchanted world, even if we don't take it too seriously when facing grave decisions involving the real world.

Some reasoning like this is in effect influential, I believe. It probably isn't articulated openly – perhaps for the very good reason that to do so might prove self-defeating. And that brings us to the argument *against* it. In substance: how useful is half-serious belief?

In the sphere of politics, the knowledge, however conscious and explicit, that loyalty to a personal monarch is merely symbolic, not literal, and is loyally implemented because it is known to be functional, because it is conducive to the ends of stability and liberty, does not undermine that loyalty. On the contrary, it may give it a reliable underpinning.

Would that be so in the sphere of faith?

It is plausible to suspect that we owe the remarkable knowledge which is the foundation of modern society to a certain intolerant seriousness. The religions of Abrahamic tradition propagated a jealous God. A jealous and exclusive God, when rearticulated in terms of Greek thought, became the God of the Excluded Middle. His intolerance of divine rivals became also the intolerance of simultaneously held contradictory beliefs. Without the impulse to systematise and eliminate incoherence, could it ever have happened? Is this not the crucial clue to the miracle of Cognitive Growth?

The separation of powers between real and symbolic rules does not undermine the political order. A similar separation in the field of thought may end by sapping intellectual curiosity and fastidiousness. Perhaps Chairman Mao was in grave error when he recommended that a hundred flowers be allowed to bloom. (N.B.: the argument here expounded is directed against *logical* tolerance. Social tolerance is another matter and is not impugned.) If we leave the Iron Cage and move to the Rubber Cage, do we not risk losing the former altogether?

As against this, it might be said that the God of the Excluded Middle was merely required as the First Cause of the genuine cognitive growth on which we now all depend. Once that movement has developed, it can be carried on by its own momentum, and no longer depends on the psychic set of men in their daily life. Live your daily life in an incoherent, indulgent, facile Rubber Cage – that is what the propagandists of the Rubber Cage could say, though not in these words – for, you know, the Iron Cage will still be there to deliver the goodies. Fear not.

Which of these two attitudes is correct? Quite obviously, we do not know.

11 Tractatus Sociologico–Philosophicus

1 Men make themselves radically different pictures of reality

The crucial word in this assertion is 'radically'. Its full force is not often appreciated.

But 'picture' also requires some elucidation. The term suggests, like the word 'vision', something relatively static. A 'vision of reality', a style of thought, a culture is in fact a continuing process, and one which contains internal options, alternatives, disagreements. There is no language in which one cannot both affirm and deny. Even, or perhaps especially, a culture which maintains that the big issues have been finally settled within it, can yet conceive of the alternatives which are being denied and eliminated. It must give some reasons, however dogmatic, for selecting that which it does select and for excluding that which it excludes, and thus in a way it concedes that things could be otherwise.

This brings us back to one of the ways, perhaps the most important way, in which visions do differ *radically*. They differ in the criteria, and in particular in the terminal criteria, which they employ for the settling of internal dispute, for judging one option to be superior to its rival or rivals.

Of course, they may also differ radically in other ways. They may differ in the very idiom they employ for the articulation of their view, whether that idiom be linguistic, visual, artistic or whatever. The texture of the tapestry may differ radically; so may its perspective, and so on. Visions will differ in the amount of homogeneity they impose internally; and some may permit great internal discontinuity of texture, style, or perspective.

There is disagreement concerning just how much radical divergence of these kinds there really is in the world. On the one hand, partisans of the fashionable 'incommensurateness' thesis maintain that divergences really are both common and profound, and even conclude that translations from one vision to another are either impossible, or occur only as the result of an accidental, 'fluky' partial overlap between two visions.

On the other hand, anthropologists, who can claim that the noting and documenting of such differences-in-vision is part of their professional task, are not always convinced that the differences really are so profound or pervasive.[1] They may insist that the oddity or eccentricity of a 'vision' is more in the mode of utterance than in what is actually meant; and that the incommensurateness is consequently in the eye or pen of the translator, who translates literally and does not allow for the shorthand, the ellipsis which he takes for granted in his own language or 'vision'. On these lines, it can be claimed that the documentation of 'odd', radically different (from our viewpoint) visions relies too much on solemn, ritual, ceremonial statements and disregards their more humdrum, day-to-day companions in the culture in question, and that the interpretation does not allow sufficiently for what may be called Ritual Licence.

As against this, it can be urged that the comforting view that 'basically all conceptual systems are similar in their basic traits' may itself be an artefact of rules of translation, a projection of conceptual charity, a determination to 'make sense' of alien utterance or conduct, come what may.

The issue is open, and no doubt the questions which make it up could be refined further. But for present purposes, this question need not be settled. There is no doubt whatever about the existence of rival decision-procedures, of terminal courts of appeal, in various styles of thought. In this sense, visions do differ radically.

Once this is admitted, it follows that there is and can be no formal solution of the problem of relativism. If there are two rival visions A and B, and each contains as part of itself the claim that the final court of appeal for cognitive disputes is a' and b', and the application of procedure a' endorses most of A and damns most of B, and vice versa, then there is no *logical* way of converting an adherent of A to B, or vice versa. The situation so described is not a bad model for some intellectual oppositions which actually occur in the real world. This is all that the argument requires.

---

[1] Cf. for instance the celebrated work of the late Sir Edward Evans-Pritchard on *Nuer Religion*, Oxford, 1956, or C. Lévi-Strauss's *La Pensée Sauvage*, Paris, 1962, or, more recently, the arguments of Dr Maurice Bloch, in his Malinowski Memorial lecture, *Man* (N.S.), 12, 1977, 278–92.

2 The important carriers of rival visions are collectivities, and these are neither stable nor discrete

The situation recorded in the above statement is easily confirmed by the straightforward observation of simple matters of fact, the commonplaces of history. Diverse visions are carried by various communities and subcommunities; these change, split and fuse, and their visions are transformed with them.

Perhaps radically distinct visions are also on occasion carried by single individuals, or even by temporary or partial moods of single individuals. Perhaps this is so; the present argument does not require that this possibility be either established or excluded. Recently, an argument was fashionable which purported to show that a 'private language', a system of notions in the exclusive possession of a single individual, was impossible. One point of the argument was that, if valid, it overcame and refuted solipsism, or any form of relativism pushed to the point of insisting on the incommensurateness – and hence incommunicability – of individual visions of single persons. If language or concepts were essentially public, parts of a shared linguistic or conceptual community, then individuals were prevented from the very start from imposing solitary conceptual confinement on themselves. The very act of speaking or thinking forced gregariousness on to them. Man was doomed to be a political animal from sheer conceptual need, as it were – a modification of the Aristotelian view which had already been anticipated by Durkheim. The details of this argument, found in the later work of L. Wittgenstein, are neither clear nor cogent, but it is not necessary to decide its merits here. It is unnecessary to decide that issue here: if a private vision, distinct from all others, can indeed be carried by an individual, or even by a temporary mood of an individual, then the argument which we shall apply to collectively carried visions can easily be extended to such individuals and moods. What is not in dispute is that communities can carry so to speak collectively private views. Wittgenstein did not deny this: on the contrary, he treated it as the solution of philosophic problems, by making those collectively carried visions 'forms of life', ultimate, self-sufficient, self-authenticating. This is wrong: in a mobile world of overlapping communities, the diversity of communal visions is a problem, not a solution. It is in fact *the* problem under consideration.

It is interesting to note that, on this issue of relativism, two recently fashionable doctrines point in quite opposite directions. The denial of the possibility of private languages and hence of private worlds, which if cogent condemns us all whether we wish it or not to share the public world projected by a public language, bans all conceptual Robinson-ades, and thus (if valid) overcomes relativism: the very act of speech, it would seem, establishes a shared public world with shared criteria of validity. At the same time, the just-as-fashionable doctrine of the incommensurateness of diverse conceptual systems makes relativism not merely respectable but virtually mandatory. If conceptual systems *A* and *B* are incommensurate, and if there is no superior and neutral system *C* in terms of which they could be compared, no rational choice between *A* and *B* is possible. If there is no exchange rate between two currencies and no international currency, gold standard, or what not in terms of which they could both be expressed, then there is no possible rational way of assessing their relative cognitive purchasing power.

Note that the philosophical importance of the erstwhile 'private language' thesis upheld or presupposed by some empiricists, when they made the individual's experience ultimate, was precisely that it endeavoured to provide such an international or interpersonal cognitive gold standard. The philosophical importance and role of a private language, that is, of a code attached directly to the actual experiences of a given individual, was that it was meant to provide an idiom in terms of which the theory and assumption-laden language of ordinary life and of science could be assessed, without prejudice and without circularity.

It is a curious fact that these two doctrines, pulling as they do in different directions, have also of late been found together as parts of one and the same system. The denial of private language, the insistence on the publicity, the externality of meaning, is as it were the first step, for instance in the philosophy of Quine; but once the shared objective world is established, then *within it*, the impossibility of ever conclusively establishing the identity of two meanings (which follows from the impossibility of definitively establishing *any* empirical prediction) is used to prove the indeterminacy of translation (because really reliable, demonstrated translation of course presupposes identity of translated meanings and such an identity will ever remain in doubt); which in turn proves incommensurateness of theories.

What this really shows, however, is the innocuousness and so to speak superficiality of Quine's relativism. It is true that the second stage of the argument showed the incommensurateness of rival theories and idioms, and thus, in a sense, vindicated relativism; but this incommensurateness or relativity only operates within a world whose real limits of variability had been very narrowly circumscribed by the earlier, first stage of the argument. It is an orderly and public world such as sober scientific researchers are used to, in which public events are well-behaved enough to warrant the expectation of finding theories, and in which the adjudication between rival theories is carried out in accordance with orderly and, on the whole, shared and recognised criteria.

The actual incommensurateness found in this world and between its diversified visions is far deeper and more perilous, more *troublant* than this. It involves a non-convergence concerning basic views and ultimate criteria of intellectual systems.

Nevertheless – and that is the central point of this section – in one sense, the deep problem which this generates invariably does find solutions. It necessarily finds them *de facto*; but not generally, and perhaps not ever, *de jure*.

That it finds them *de facto* follows from the indisputable historical truth of proposition 2. The communities which carry these radically diverse visions are neither stable nor insulated. The discrepancies between visions which arise through the fusion of two communities, or through the change or fission within one community, invariably lead – in so far as a conceptual, language-sharing community persists at all – to a new vision, however temporary and however internally conflict-ridden it may turn out to be.

These sociological or historical facts may be obvious to the point of banality. But they have philosophical implications which, though immediate, presumably cannot be obvious, in so far as some recent philosophies have denied them.

First of all, these facts imply that philosophic (conceptual-norm-choosing) issues are very real and not at all artificial. In a changing society, the decision whether a given procedure, person, institution or text is or is not final, as a court of appeal in the evaluation of rival claims, is not trivial. It is deadly serious. The problem cannot conceivably be avoided by seeing 'how language really works' or by 'neutralising' allegedly misleading or over-general models of language. The problem arises from the very reality of the situation, and not from anyone's misunderstanding of the situation. The only 'misleading conceptual model', due for rapid and definitive dissolution, is the idea that misleading conceptual models generate philosophical problems ... The weird doctrine that these issues of deep doubt or basic choice can be solved or 'dissolved', by attending to the actual conceptual custom of a community, was historically bound up with the denial of the possibility of 'private language' (i.e. of a carefully minimal data-recording code, which could then judge rival languages). Whether or not this procedure is viable, the problem remains. But the issue of choice arises because of tensions and options in our 'forms of life', and cannot be solved by returning to our 'form of life' and pretending that it is ultimate or self-sustaining.

In other words, there is no neutral, unproblematical residue, left over as a kind of legatee after 'clarification'. The rivalry, incompatibility and incommensurateness of visions generate the problem, and do not allow of such facile solutions.

In a disappointing sense, solutions always do arise, in so far as conceptual communities do survive; but only in the sense that this is what a community *means*. This trite, left-handed, vacuous guarantee of the availability of solutions (which only means that *if* communities survive, which is *not* guaranteed, then in some way or other and within some limits, they continue to communicate), does not mean that such 'solutions' have any merit. They may have it, or not.

The attempt to endow them with some merit *is* philosophy.

3 There are two main ways of doing this: by Cosmic Exile, or by assessing the moral excellence of the contestants

Cosmic Exile (the phrase is Quine's, and denotes a philosophic aspiration which he denigrates) is a philosophic strategy initiated above all by René Descartes, and brought to a high degree of refinement by the entire epistemological tradition of modern thought, notably – but not exclusively – by the empiricists. The underlying idea is simple, attractive and tempting. It is this: if there exist rival, total, internally coherent (not to say circular and self-maintaining), but externally incompatible visions of the world, as indeed there do, would it not be best to stand outside the world, or rather, outside all these rival available *worlds*, and judge their respective merits from such an extraneous, and hence we hope neutral, uncontaminated, impartial viewpoint? Arbitrators or referees are normally recruited from outside the dispute, from amongst people equally unconnected, or only symmetrically connected with the disputing parties. When it comes to choosing a *world*, should one not do the same?

And how does one attain this Cosmic Exile, how does one stand outside the world, or rather all rival worlds? A much favoured recipe for attaining this is the following: clear your mind of all the conceptions, or rather preconceptions, which your education, culture, background or what-have-you, have instilled in you, and which evidently carry their bias with them. Instead, attend carefully only to that which is inescapably *given*, that which imposes itself on you whether you wish it or not, whether it fits in with your preconceptions or not. This purified residue, independent of your will, wishes, prejudices and training, constitutes the raw data of this world, as they would appear to a newly arrived Visitor from Outside. We were not born yesterday, we are not such new arrivals, but we can simulate such an innocent, conceptually original state of mind; and that which will be or remain before us when we have done so is untainted by prejudice, and can be used to judge the rival, radically distinct and opposed visions. This, in simple terms, is the programme.

Assessment by Moral Excellence is quite a different strategy.

The underlying argument or image is somewhat as follows: the world abounds in rival and incompatible visions, each with its own internal standards of validation, and all of them endorse and fortify their carriers and damn and castigate their rivals. Sometimes, no doubt, there are partial overlaps, which enable the debate or dialogue to go on with a semblance of reason, of appeal to shared ground.

But the chaos, the inward-turned approval and the outward-turned condemnation, are not complete. If we investigate the pattern of rivalry and succession, we do find, precisely, a pattern and an order. For one thing, some of these rival worlds are carried by communities much more attractive than others. By their fruits thou shalt know them: is not the blessedness of the carrier some indication of the soundness of the message carried? Moreover, the overlap in criteria, which enables us on occasion to judge worlds which are neighbours in time or space, by norms which both parties accept in some measure – that overlap itself is part of a series, of a grand pattern, with other such overlaps. To take an oft-invoked example, diverse moral worlds sometimes share the same assessment of a given kind of conduct, and differ only in the range of people to whom the obligation, or prohibition, is to apply. Neighbouring communities may share the same principles, endowing one with the capacity to judge the other.

One criticism of Cosmic Exile does not insist that the exercise cannot be carried out, but contents itself with pointing out that if or when carried out, it will not get us anywhere. Pure data are not a world, and they not merely fail to generate a world, but fail even to eliminate any of the rival worlds. The general 'underdetermination of theories by facts', as the phrase goes, makes sure of that. When the neutral, extraneous arbitrator is brought in, it transpires that he is too feeble to pass any judgement. The exiguous data at his disposal permit neither theoretical nor moral nor any other choices or decisions. He lacks evidence for making any identifying of the litigant with the best case. As a cosmic judge, the Pure Visitor is inadequate and a failure.

The weaknesses of the method of Assessment by Moral Excellence are equally blatant. Where Cosmic Exile presupposed a heroic exercise which may be beyond our powers, this method commends an operation which is perfectly feasible – but alas childishly circular. Of course it is possible to evaluate rival worlds in terms of merit – if you have already granted yourself one world, namely your own, complete with its own values and standards of assessment, in terms of which you can then please yourself and graciously award good conduct marks to the other rival worlds, seen through the prism of your own. If this curious if not comic enterprise ends in your granting the palm to yourself – no wonder! The subtler variant of this argument, which invokes the pattern of differences between various visions, is not less circular, even if the circularity is slightly better camouflaged. If your own value is, for instance, universality or non-discrimination, no doubt you can arrange the historically existing value-systems in terms of the closeness of their approximation to that ideal. You can then pretend, if you wish, that the ideal somehow emanates from the historical or sociological pattern. But the truth is, of course, the other way round: the pattern was generated by measuring societies against the tacitly (or overtly) assumed ideal.

Actual examples of this mode of reasoning are of course more complex. The pattern-of-differences is elicited not merely by proximity to the ideal, but also by the location of the society-carrier in the historical process. If it is part of the theory that there is a force making for righteousness which is interfering in history, and if societies and their visions get better as they get later, then the very dating of a vision also gives us a clue to its excellence. Once again, stated brutally and on its own, the theory seems specially weak, and is notoriously open to the charge of victor-worshipping, of endorsing that 'verdict of history' *whatever* it may say. In practice, theories of this kind derive their plausibility from the intertwining of a number of arguments, and hopping from one to the other according to where the criticism comes from. You say we worship might, and turn might into right? Not at all: history is revered only in so far as it is *rational*, in so far as it embodies Reason. Very well: you possess criteria of rationality which are trans-historical, trans-social? You have access to moral or other information which transcends the bounds of this or that concrete historical vision incarnated in a real society, and which gives you *independent* criteria of rationality? But no, not at all: do you take us for naive utopians, men who think they can divide society into two halves, one of which admonishes and guides the other as some cosmic schoolmaster? No, no; our values emanate from historical reality, they are not imposed on it . . .

And so we go round the mulberry bush.

Before we dismiss both strategies on the grounds of their inadequacy, we must remember that we have no other, and the task they are endeavouring to perform cannot be evaded, so we had better make use of the tools we have, appalling though they are.

4 Each of these two grand strategies casts its shadow, and the shadow, in each case, is a particular style of viewing the world, a philosophy

Strictly speaking, the argument now requires that we distinguish, a little pedantically, between two kinds of social 'vision': so to speak primary, unrefined, crude, raw-material ones, and philosophically distilled, smelted, processed ones. *Any* vision within which a community lives can fall into the former class. The second class is more restrictive, and includes only those which have been not merely systematised, but systematised in the face of doubt, the awareness of the problem of diversity of visions and the need to justify one's choice amongst them. The distinction is not a sharp one, but is an important one. The two visions or styles now under consideration belong to the latter class. They are visions which have passed through the Valley of Doubt and they are identified or classified by the *way* in which they have done it.

To a significant degree, belief-systems in our society fall into the refined class. They have been refined in the light of considerations such as have been sketched out above.

The manner in which they endeavour to fortify themselves, to justify confidence, and to by-pass doubt, in the main involves using one of the two major strategies described. These two strategies in turn have profound effect on the world-views which have passed, so to speak, through their sieve. The visions which prevail, at any rate at the intellectually more sophisticated levels of our society, tend to be impregnated with these two general criteria and with their effects.

These criteria cast their shadow: each of them tends to produce rather distinctive *kinds* of world. Let us use the terms 'positivistic' and 'Hegelian', without prejudice, as shorthand code terms for the two strategies – for the attempt, on the one hand, to evaluate rival visions by matching them against pure data, as recorded by a simulated new arrival to the universe, and, on the other hand, for the attempt to evaluate visions by assessing the merit and historic role of their social carriers.

The positivist strategy generates a world which is granular: where the grains, as in well-cooked rice, are discrete from each other, and easily separable; where they have a quality of givenness or hardness, of simply being there for no general reason and without thought of anything outside themselves. The theories which cover or describe them are indeed but summaries of the patterns of those grains, and have no more intimate or intuitively plausible or compelling connection with them. This gives the data a brutish, self-contained, uncommunicative air; the theories are drawn from a reservoir containing an infinity of such possible patterns, and nothing other than the contingent constellation of facts can select one of them in preference to others. So the game is, ultimately, random, 'meaningless'; over and above their lack of inner necessity, the theories may well be formulated in technical language and be counter-intuitive or unintelligible; they are morally indifferent, conveying no morals, passing no implicit judgement on the conduct of men or societies. They are also so to speak identity-indifferent; holding or rejecting any one of them seldom makes any difference to the identity, to the self-definition, of the person holding them; and, by and large, they find their home in the natural sciences, and in the social sciences only when these deliberately endeavour to emulate the natural sciences.

By contrast, the Hegelian strategy tends to leave one with worlds which are not granular/atomic but, on the contrary, pervasively interdependent, intimately intertwined, suffused with a sense of unity – but also pervaded by 'meaning': the interconnected elements have meaning for each other in that they play roles in each other's fates and in the wider plans of which they are part. Elements in the pattern, such as actions, are what they are in virtue of what they *mean* to the agents who perform them, rather than in virtue of merely external traits. 'Meaning' enters at least twice over, as the significance conferred by participants and that conferred by the observer, and each is legitimate, and moreover connected with each other. The relationship of theory to fact is more personal, intimate: the theory confers life and legitimacy and vigour to the fact, it is not alien to it, and is not merely shorthand for it. It animates the patterns: it does not just abbreviate and codify them. The data revel in the place they occupy in the theoretical pattern – they positively wallow in it. Available theories are not technical or drawn from the same infinite reservoir: they are intelligible to the actors, they are finite in number and figure on the list of dramatis personae, and their confrontations and compromises are an essential part of the plot. They are anything rather than morally neutral, and the attitude which a human character adopts towards them profoundly modifies his identity: the choice of theory is but an aspect of a choice of self and life style. The home territory of this kind of vision is of course history and society.

This, then, is the familiar overall confrontation; a granular, cold, technical and naturalistic world confronts a holistic, meaning-saturated, identity-conferring, social-humanistic one. Occasionally they raid each other's territory and even attempt to occupy large parts of it permanently. Much of the so-called social sciences is a dogged attempt to handle and interpret human affairs in the image of natural science. Conversely, *Naturphilosophie* attempts to do the opposite. There are, of course doctrines which endeavour to combine the appeal of both approaches. Marxism contains both a *Naturphilosophie* and a naturalistic, reductive sociology; *and* it tells a moral global tale which reveals the true identity of all characters, and yet also claims impartial, scientific status. Psycho-analysis owes its appeal to the fact that it is simultaneously, through medicine, a part of science, and yet also maintains, nay reinforces, the importance of the intimately personal and immediate, the significance and meaning for the participant. Its theories/interpretations partake all at once of the technical esotericism of science and of the randy immediacy of one's most personal experience. In short, the ideological vigour and intense appeal of doctrines which live on this particular borderline testify eloquently to the importance of that grand opposition in our intellectual life.

But let us leave the hybrid border population and return to the grand positivist/Hegelian opposition. How is one to assess the rival merits of these two great contestants?

Is the world atomic and icy, or warm and intertwined? Which of these two grand meta-visions is the correct one? At this point I shall refrain, from lack of space perhaps, from making any definitive pronouncements and settling the ultimate nature of reality – whether it satisfies the claims of positivists or of Hegelians. Instead, I wish to stress the following interesting points: the two great visions are not only (perhaps not at all) reports on *how things are*; they are reflections, shadows, echoes of the two strategies initially adopted for choosing from amongst primary, unrefined visions. That initial problem leads us to oppose general methods for coping with it; and the choice of method then produces two so to speak meta-visions, the two general styles of seeing the world which are so characteristic of our age.

The generation of these meta-visions, the casting of these grand shadows, works as follows: if you are determined to judge things by confronting them with pure, unsullied, unprejudiced data, you will naturally try to break up data into their constituent parts, if possible relenting in this effort of 'analysis' only when ultimate constituent atoms are located. The granularity or atomicity of the world is not so much in the data in the world: they are a consequence of your manner of handling it. The separation will be both lateral and qualitative; 'lateral' in space and time, isolating experience into blobs and sounds and instants, and 'qualitative' in separating all features which can be separated in thought. The various atomic metaphysics (with sensory, material or logical 'atoms') are the eventual consequences, the shadows or projections of this kind of operation. The same is true for the other familiar traits of the positivistic vision.

And of course, there are very good reasons for proceeding in this manner. The commonest, most familiar ploy employed by primary visions for imposing their authority on men is to present themselves as an integral package-deal, not available for separate, part-by-part examination. These visions generally insist on being swallowed whole. To dissect them, they say, is to travesty them, to miss the point; and if they can get away with it, they declare any such granular examination to be blasphemous. And indeed, as long as they can only be examined as 'totalities', they are generally safe. Long before they reach the level of refinement indicated earlier, that of being articulated in ways which satisfy the general epistemic doubt and criteria, they easily attain a level of internal complexity which protects them from falsification. A system will postulate a given source of authority, a court of appeal; all minor testimony within the system conspires to confirm the authority of that apex; which in turn confirms the veridicity of those testimonies which feed its authorities and withdraws the seal of authenticity from those which do not. The well of truth is within the ramparts; it feeds those within and is withheld from the enemies outside.

So epistemic atomism, whether or not it is a correct report on the ultimate constitution of things, is a device forced upon the honest inquirer by the most common, and perhaps the most important ploy employed by adherent- and loyalty-seeking belief-systems.

Atomism is a method which corresponds to a customs officer's insistence that a trunk be unpacked: you are not allowed to pass through the Customs Examination with your trunk as a whole, on the grounds that unpacking it is to violate your dignity. Once he adopts atomicism, however – the habit of insisting that cognitive claims submit to examination in isolation, one by one, not in total cohesive groups, the inquirer is, for better or for worse, landed with the rest of what we have described as the positivistic vision. Much of it is a corollary of epistemic atomism.

Belief-systems which only submit to *collective* examination can easily make themselves invulnerable, and if collective examination were the rule, there would probably be no cognitive progress. When a contemporary philosopher/logician, Quine, insists that propositions only submit to the ordeal of confrontation with reality as corporate bodies, such a paradoxical claim can only seem plausible just because a very high degree of atomism is now simply taken for granted. If it is well established that cognitive claims don't cheat too much, it is possible to admit publicly that they all do cheat a little, that the absolute atomicity of the empiricist ideal is ever being sinned against. If piecemeal inspection is simply assumed as natural and self-evident (rather than being seen, as is the case, as historically very specific and indeed idiosyncratic), *then* it is possible to say, as a kind of justified correction to a total and unqualified atomism, that a certain amount of systematic interdependence between otherwise decently and properly granular items of knowledge may or must also be tolerated...

So the positivistic vision is in some measure the shadow of a cognitive strategy; but the same is also true of its great rival. Is the world a unity, suffused with meanings, meanings which form a system with its rivals, such that their interplay clicks into a pattern, like a well-constructed play, in which later scenes illuminate the significance of what has passed before, and where in the end everything fuses so as to point a moral? One may well doubt it: but if the Hegelian-type strategy is to work, if the choice of final resting-vision is to be made without standing outside, but rather by evaluating the characters and their messages within the play – well, if all that's to be possible, then something like this must be the case, and those celebrated categories, or slogans, of totality, mediation and dialectic had better apply to the world ... otherwise, it all simply won't work. There must be reasonably coherent characters; they must interact, and their cumulative interaction must add up to a decent plot.

Thus there are good reasons for seeing the world in both the granular and in the holistic manner. To me, the most persuasive argument for atomism in epistemology is that unless it is forcibly imposed, *any* belief system can, through its internal organisation, make itself invulnerable. A strong argument for holism is that systems such as language, in the sense of the capacity to generate and understand an infinite range of messages, cannot function as a consequence of a mere accumulation of grains, but presuppose an underlying mechanism, for reasons which Chomsky has made familiar. Functioning systems, such as organisms or languages, certainly are not mere assemblages of independent atoms.

If the issue between the two styles of seeing the world is fairly even, and if each style casts its own shadow over the world, so that we cannot easily invoke the world to arbitrate between them, how can we choose?

5 God is not garrulous

This in turn is no trite assertion. It contradicts both the Old Testament and Hegel. The contrary idea – that God *is* garrulous – is plausible, well diffused, and if true, would be an important element in answering the question how do we select a valid vision.

By divine garrulity, I mean here the idea that the true verdict is indicated by historical *repetition*. Repetition, Kierkegaard insisted in a different context, is a religious category. It is certainly a mode of persuasion. If you insist long enough and often enough you finally succeed in persuading. Even more persuasive than simple reiterative repetition is repetition with increasing and culminating emphasis, a kind of crescendo: the idea that later prophets fulfil, augment, and complete the prophecies of earlier ones is a case of such a heightened form of repetition.

The curious thing was that when secularisation, loss of faith and the scientific revolution eroded religion in Western society, there was no need to abandon at the same time the belief in the garrulousness of revelation, in the demonstration of ultimate truth by crescendo and repetition. Though the specific *content* apparently had to change, the garrulous-reiterative, increasing-emphasis *form* could remain. Indeed it could stay not in one, but in two media. Two great intellectual events occurred, one towards the end of the eighteenth century, one in the nineteenth: firstly, the crystallisation of the belief in *progress*, in a continuous story of historical improvement which gave sense to human striving and made up for human misery, thus constituting a new and effective secular theodicy; and secondly, the formulation and acceptance of the idea of biological evolution, which said much the same, but on an even larger, indeed incomparably larger, canvas.

It was not surprising that a society habituated by an old religious tradition to confirm its faith by Cumulative Repetition should leap at historical progress or at biological evolution as new sources of grand garrulous repetition, of confirming a vision and its values by repeating the same lesson with ever greater emphasis. This is what the then fashionable philosophies of progress and/or of evolution really said: the thinker discerns the message – say the movement forward to greater complexity and differentiation, to more freedom, more consciousness, more happiness, or what have you – and reminds us of how insistently history, whether biological or human, has by repeated and increasingly insistent reiteration confirmed its truth for us. It sounded plausible, and the West was certainly ready to accept this message, and to a large extent did accept it, thus retaining Revelation by Repetition even when a new revealed message was substituted for the old one.

Alas, it was all false. What differentiates that modern cognitive style which alone made possible sustained growth of knowledge and a technology of unprecedented power, is not simply one further repeat performance, at most on a somewhat larger scale, of improvements or changes in style already anticipated in the Stone Age or by the amoeba. No: it was a new style altogether. There are philosophers of great distinction – such as Quine or Popper – who still hold this Continuity thesis, who believe that the adaptive devices of nature and the intellectual improvements of science are basically instances of the same process, differing in degree rather than in kind. I believe this to be a profound error, due in part to lack of interest in those extensive parts of human history which manifest no cognitive growth, and, together with this, a profound under-estimation of the diversity of human visions, a tendency to interpret the visions distinct from one's own as being closer to us than in fact they are, as subject to the same rules and criteria, and above all as engaged in the same enterprise. In the case of Popper, his willingness to vindicate scientific method or the critical spirit by insisting that it is a venerable custom of the biological race, dating back to Grandfather/Mother Amoeba and his/her capacity to learn from his/her mistakes (albeit without knowing that he/she was doing this), is particularly curious. It is odd in so far as in other and rather more persuasive parts of his work, he has argued eloquently against historicism, against the attempt to validate anything by an appeal to historical trend. I for one feel disinclined to model my cognitive (or any other) habits on customs established by Grandfather/Mother Amoeba, but in any case the question scarcely arises, in so far as I think that the Popperian premiss here is quite wrong: Amoeba and Einstein singly were not engaged in the same enterprise, nor did they use the same methods, even in the most general sense. The style of articulating and evaluating beliefs characteristic of the scientific/industrial age differs profoundly and qualitatively from that which preceded it: but the *kind* of difference is not simply a repeat performance of all or even most previous transformations. The philosophy of Cosmic Exile expressed this discontinuity well. Cosmic extra-territoriality of knowledge may be a myth; but historic discontinuity is not.

This is a big subject, and though the truth of this seems to be evident, it can hardly be demonstrated to those who do not accept it. What can, however, be done fairly easily is to show the implications on this view – if accepted – for what has generically been called the 'Hegelian' strategy of validation.

By this we meant the assessment of visions through the moral merit of their carriers. This whole approach was so often conflated with what I have called Divine Garrulousness that the intellectual image called forth by the term 'Hegelianism' tends to conjure up *both* these views. Yet they are logically quite separable, and the time has now come when it is essential to separate them. God is *not* garrulous; history does not cumulatively reiterate the same message for the benefit of the faithful; but the other ingredient of 'Hegelianism', the evaluation of vision by the evaluation of its carrier, may still have some life left in it. The principle of Reiteration, and the evaluation of messages by excellence of carrier, are distinct ideas. The latter is still of some use.

6 Positivists are right, for Hegelian reasons

Viewed simply as two self-sustaining visions, or meta-visions, positivism and Hegelianism are, each of them, both attractive and haunted by difficulties: but as each of them confirms itself – each is a fort with its own well, sustaining its garrison and excluding the outsiders – there is no reason to expect a 'logical' resolution of their dispute, i.e. a formal demonstration, from shared and neutral premisses, that one of them is superior to the other.

In fact, the choice is made, and can only be made, in the 'Hegelian' manner, in the sense initially defined in this context – that is, by considering, generically, the merits of the carriers of the two doctrines.

Once again, we are in an area so vast and deep that one can only indicate one's conclusions, rather than hope to establish them. It seems to me fairly obvious that intellectual traditions inspired by the Cartesian-empiricist virtues, aspiring to atomism, to the breaking up of questions, to abstention from intellectual package-deals, to the separation of truth from identity, fact from value, are, by and large, traditions which have not only been markedly more successful in their cognitive endeavours, but have also been associated with social orders more attractive and acceptable than their rivals. Notoriously, they also pay a certain price for their achievements: an atomised, cognitively unstable world, which does not underwrite the identities and values of those who dwell in it, is neither comfortable nor romantic. No purpose is served by pretending that this price does not need to be paid; and no doubt there will be many reluctant to pay it, or at least willing to pretend that they will not pay it (whether or not they would seriously forgo the benefits of industrial-scientific civilisation, or merely encourage others to do so); and there will be others still who believe, mistakenly in my view, that the price need not be paid at all, that one can both have one's romantic cake and scientifically eat it.

The irony of the situation, if my account of it is correct, is manifest: the positivistic atomic/empirical vision is to be preferred, but the reasoning which alone can clinch this choice is characteristically Hegelian: it consists of looking at the total complex, at the rival carriers of the opposed visions, and chooses in terms of their merits as totalities. But this procedure does not receive any additional and comforting reinforcement from being one of a long series of similar choices; God is not garrulous, so it is *not* Hegelian any longer in the sense of being inserted into a global series, the successive pronunciamentos of one garrulous cosmic authority. This was but a *single*, though large and immensely important, parting of the ways, and the assessment is made on the merits of that one pair of alternatives, without benefit of an everlasting and ever-louder chorus. The situation is deeply paradoxical. The atomistic vision is chosen as a totality, holistically: because, as a tradition it erodes all others, and creates a society with cumulative knowledge, increasing technological power, and at least a tendency towards liberty. Atomism is bought as a package-deal.

The double confirmation of our vision which is about to be proposed is philosophically most profoundly inelegant. It is also indispensable. The inelegance flows from the fact that the spirit of the two confirmations is so much in a different style, that their juxtaposition really constitutes a stylistic solecism. The very tone and texture of either one of them is calculated to reduce the effects of the other one to bathos... Yet, nonetheless, this is our ideological fate.

The appeal of the given-atoms picture is precisely the simplicity and terminality of these *given* atoms. A celebrated formulation of this vision, Wittgenstein's *Tractatus*, ended up by declaring itself meaningless not merely for technical logical reasons, but also from a kind of aesthetic pudeur... This vision, the work seemed to say, is so unique and final, so devoid of any possible contrast, that articulation sullies it. It cannot bear to stand alongside ordinary assertions. It constitutes the very limits of the world; but to attempt to put those limits in a frame is the height of vulgarity. Silence alone has dignity.

Wittgenstein's case, oscillating as he did in that early work between telling us of the limits and preaching silence about them, was an extreme one. (In fact, what he thought of as the limits of the world were but the shadows of one variant of the atomistic strategy in philosophy.) But even other, less uncompromisingly puritan propounders of this vision, were awed and attracted by its stark simplicity. Here, at the very end of the world, there is no room for petty haggling and weighing of advantages.

Validation by assessing the merits of the social carriers is also rather grand and imposing, but in quite a different and rather messy way. We are no longer at the very limits of the world, where petty specific historical facts are ignored, and where only the most general, formal features of reality are admitted. We are *inside* the world (hence the notorious circularity of 'Hegelian' assessment procedures). Here we look at the tangled, complex social/historical reality of the last few centuries, and attempt as best we can to extract the basic options. On balance, one option – a society with cognitive growth based on a roughly atomistic strategy – seems to us superior, for various reasons, which are assembled without elegance; this kind of society alone can keep alive the large numbers to which humanity has grown, and thereby avoid a really ferocious struggle for survival amongst us; it alone can keep us at the standard to which we are becoming accustomed; it, more than its predecessors, *probably* favours a liberal and tolerant social organisation (because affluence makes brutal exploitation and suppression unnecessary, and because it requires a wide diffusion of complex skills and occupational mobility which in turn engender a taste for both liberty and equality). This type of society also has many unattractive traits, and its virtues are open to doubt. On balance, and with misgivings, we opt for it; but there is no question of an elegant, clear-cut choice. We are half pressurised by necessity (fear of famine and so on), half persuaded by a promise of liberal affluence (which we do not fully trust). There it is: lacking better reasons, we'll have to make do with these.

And yet, the elegance of Terminal Atomism, so to speak, would not on its own convince us (the rival picture was as good); whilst, without that Atomism (or positivism, or mechanistic empiricism, or whatever you wish to call it), a purely sociological account of industrial-scientific society and its ethos would so to speak hang it in the air. Empiricist-materialist philosophy, with its pretensions to terminality, does make it intellectually a bit more appealing and respectable. The elegance of terminal atomism is tarnished by the haggling style of choosing amongst social options; the realism in choosing concrete life styles is a bit weakened by connecting it with the absurd pretension of seeing the world as from outside. Yet, the two validations also strengthen each other. Atomistic, empiricist, mechanistic philosophy gives us some insight into how genuine and cumulative knowledge is possible at all: how the self-serving insular visions to which mankind is prone are broken up, and how whatever genuine order may exist in the data can after all be captured, codified, and extended. The sociology of industrial society, on the other hand, helps explain how a genuine scientific tradition can be socially sustained.

This incongruous double-indication does not amount to an altogether comfortable and satisfying situation, but no better one is available. I didn't invent this situation, I simply tell it like what it is.

7 **He who understands me need not disavow the assertions by which he has reached this perception, but may and should continue to use the ladder by which he has ascended**

Sources

Chapter 1, from *The Times Literary Supplement*, no. 4001, 23 November 1979, 23; chapter 2, from *Proceedings of the British Academy*, 58, 1983, 165–87; chapter 3, from *Man*, 20, no. 1, 1985, 142–55, and also in John Hall (ed.), *Rediscoveries*, Oxford, 1986; chapter 4, not previously published; chapter 5, as 'Accounting for the Horror' in *The Times Literary Supplement*, no. 4140, 6 August 1982, 843–5; chapter 6 from *Dialectics and Humanism*, 6, 1979, no. 4, 27–43 and in G. Andersson (ed.), *Rationality in Science and Politics*, Boston, pp. 111–30; chapter 7 from *Government and Opposition*, 15, 1980, 376–88; chapter 8 from *The Times Higher Education Supplement*, no. 433, 20 February 1981, 10–11; chapter 9 as 'Inside Khomeini's Mind' in *The New Republic*, 18 June 1984, 27–33; chapter 10 not previously published; chapter 11 from S. C. Brown (ed.), *Objectivity and Cultural Divergence*, Cambridge, 1984, pp. 247–59 and in Erik Cohen, Moshe Lissek and Uri Almagar (eds.), *Essays in Honour of S. M. Eisenstadt*, Boulder and London, 1985, pp. 374–85, and in Italian in M. Piatelli Palmerini (ed.), *Livelli di realita*, Milan, 1984, pp. 487–505. The author thanks the editors and publishers for their permission to reprint.

Bibliography of Ernest Gellner (IV): 1983–5

Compiled by I. C. Jarvie

This bibliography supplements those to be found in *The Devil in Modern Philosophy* (London 1974), *Spectacles and Predicaments* (Cambridge 1980), and *Relativism and the Social Sciences* (Cambridge 1985). The numbering continues that used there.
****** indicates reprinted in this volume.

1984

(a) 'Along the Historical Highway', review of Eero Loone, *Sovremennaia Filosofia Istorii*, *The Times Literary Supplement*, no. 4224, 16 March, 279–80.

(b) 'The Gospel According to Saint Ludwig', review of Saul Kripke, *Wittgenstein on Rules and Private Language*, *American Scholar*, Spring, 243–63. Reprinted as 'Concepts and community' in 1985(d).

(c) 'Inside Khomeini's Mind', review of *Islam and Revolution: Writings and Declarations of Imam Khomeini*, *New Republic*, no. 3622, 18 June, 27–33.******

(d) *Slowa i Rzeczy* (Polish translation of 1959(d), Warsaw.

(e) Reprint of 1972(f) in Akbar S. Ahmed and David M. Hart (eds.), *Islam in Tribal Society: From the Atlas to the Indies*, London, pp. 21–38.

(f) Introduction to A. M. Khazanov, *Nomads and the Outside World*, Cambridge, pp. ix-xxv.

(g) 'Tractatus Sociologico-Philosophicus', in S. C. Brown (ed.), *Objectivity and Cultural Divergence*, Cambridge, pp. 247–59; also in Erik Cohen, Moshe Lissek and Uri Almagar (eds.), *Essays in Honour of S. M. Eisenstadt*, Boulder and London, 1985, pp. 374–85; in Italian in Massimo Piatelli Palmerini (ed.), *Livelli di realita*, trans. Gianni Mancassole, Milan, pp. 487–505.******

(h) 'Soviets Against Wittfogel, or the Anthropological Preconditions of Marxism', in Jean-Claude Galey (ed.), *Differences, valeurs, hierarchie:textes offerts à Louis Dumont*, Paris: Éditions de l'École des Hautes Études en Sciences Sociales, pp. 183–211.

(i) Introduction to Mahesh Regmi, *The State and Economic Surplus*, Varanasi: North Publishing.

(*j*)   Foreword to Eva Schmidt-Hartmann, *Thomas G. Masaryk's Realism: Origins of a Czech Political Concept*, Munich, pp. 7–8.

(*k*)   (under the pseudonym 'Philip Peters'), 'The State of Poland', *The Times Literary Supplement*, no. 4246, 17 August, 916.

(*l*)   Foreword to Said Amir Arjomand (ed.), *From Nationalism to Revolutionary Islam*, London: Macmillan in association with St Anthony's College, Oxford, pp. vii–xi.

(*m*)   'Epistemology of Social Science', *International Social Science Journal*, 36, no. 4, 567–86; also in French and Spanish (full version in 1985(*d*)).

1985

(*a*)   Review of *The Engineer of Human Souls*, by Josef Škvorecký, *The Times Literary Supplement*, no. 4275, 8 March, 256.

(*b*)   'The Roots of Cohesion', review article on Émile Masqueray, *Formation des cités chez les populations sedentaires d'Algerie, Man*, 20, no. 1, March, 142–55.******

(*c*)   *Nazioni e Nazionalismo*, Rome. (Italian translation of 1983(*e*).)

(*d*)   *Relativism and the Social Sciences*, Cambridge. Pp. x + 200. Contains: 1985(*e*), 1985(*f*), 1981(*f*), 1984(*m*), 1981(*g*), 1982(*i*), 1984(*b*).

(*e*)   'Positivism against Hegelianism', in 1985(*d*), pp. 4–67.

(*f*)   'The Gaffe-Avoiding Animal or A Bundle of Hypotheses', in 1985(*d*), pp. 68–2.

(*g*)   *The Psychoanalytic Movement*, London. Pp. xii + 241.

(*h*)   'Malinowski and the Dialectic of Past and Present', *The Times Literary Supplement*, no. 4288, 7 June, 645–6.

(*i*)   'Positively a Romanticist', review of A. J. Ayer, *Wittgenstein*, the *Guardian*, 13 June, 22.

(*j*)   Review of Bryan S. Turner, *Capitalism and Class in the Middle East*, *British Journal of Sociology*, 36, no. 2, June, 289.

(*k*)   'A Climate and an Ethic', *The Times Higher Education Supplement*, no. 660, 28 June, 14–15.

(*l*)   Edited *Islamic Dilemmas: Reformers, Nationalists and Industrialization*, The Southern Shore of the Mediterranean, Berlin. Pp. viii + 319.

(*m*)   Introduction to 1985(*l*), pp. 1–9.

(*n*)   'The Bourgeois Marx', review of R. P. Wolff, *Understanding Marx*, A. W. Gouldner, *Against Fragmentation* and Jon Elster, 'Making Sense of Marx', *The New Republic*, 193, no. 3685, 2 September, 32–6.

(*o*)   'Malinowski Go Home: Reflections on the Malinowski Centenary Conference', *Anthropology Today*, 1, no. 5, October, 5.

(*p*)   *Leben im Islam*, Stuttgart. 387pp. (German translation of 1981(*c*).)

(*q*)   'Reason, Rationality and Rationalism', in Adam and Jessica Kuper (eds.), *The Social Science Encyclopedia*, London, pp. 687–90.

Index of names